HANDBOOK OF INVESTMENT ADMINISTRATION

The Securities & Investment Institute

Mission Statement:

To set standards of professional excellence and integrity for the investment and securities industry, providing qualifications and promoting the highest level of competence to our members, other individuals and firms.

The Securities and Investment Institute is the UK's leading professional and membership body for practitioners in the securities and investment industry, with more than 16,000 members with an increasing number working outside the UK. It is also the major examining body for the industry, with a full range of qualifications aimed at people entering and working in it. More than 30,000 examinations are taken annually in more than 30 countries.

You can contact us through our website *www.sii.org.uk*

Our membership believes that keeping up to date is central to professional development. We are delighted to endorse the Wiley/SII publishing partnership and recommend this series of books to our members and all those who work in the industry.

As part of the SII CPD Scheme, reading relevant financial publications earns members of the Securities & Investment Institute the appropriate number of CPD hours under the Self-Directed learning category. For further information, please visit *www.sii.org.uk/cpdscheme*

Ruth Martin
Managing Director

HANDBOOK OF INVESTMENT ADMINISTRATION

....

Kevin Rothwell

John Wiley & Sons, Ltd

Other Wiley Editorial Offices

John Wiley & Sons Inc., 111 River Street, Hoboken, NJ 07030, USA

Jossey-Bass, 989 Market Street, San Francisco, CA 94103-1741, USA

Wiley-VCH Verlag GmbH, Boschstr. 12, D-69469 Weinheim, Germany

John Wiley & Sons Australia Ltd, 42 McDougall Street, Milton, Queensland 4064, Australia

John Wiley & Sons (Asia) Pte Ltd, 2 Clementi Loop #02-01, Jin Xing Distripark, Singapore 129809

John Wiley & Sons Canada Ltd, 6045 Freemont Blvd, Mississauga, ONT, L5R 4J3, Canada

Wiley also publishes its books in a variety of electronic formats. Some content that appears in
print may not be available in electronic books.

Anniversary Logo Design: Richard J. Pacifico

British Library Cataloguing in Publication Data

A catalogue record for this book is available from the British Library

ISBN   978-0-470-03362-3 (PB)

Typeset in 12/16pt Trump Medieval by Aptara, New Delhi, India

CONTENTS

· ·

ABOUT THE
AUTHOR

. . . .

Kevin Rothwell has spent the whole of his working life within the financial services industry and his hands-on experience has given him a detailed knowledge of such areas as private client investment management, investment administration and dealing, settlement and custody.

He has held senior posts in both front-office and back-office positions and has undertaken a varied portfolio of investment projects.

More recently Kevin has set up his own company which excels in providing specialised and bespoke consultancy and training for a number of large financial institutions both at home and abroad.

Already a Fellow of the Securities and Investment Institute (SII), he was delighted to have been made a senior technical advisor for them. As well as teaching towards the SII's postgraduate Diploma in Investment Operations, Kevin is also the author of *International Certificate in Financial Advice Workbook*, which is published by the SII.

INTRODUCTION

· ·

Having spent many years working in investment management, it came as a surprise when moving into investment administration to discover there were very few textbooks available. To obtain any detailed material meant that a significant amount of research was needed from an array of differing books, articles and websites.

I came to realise that what was needed was one comprehensive publication that covered the main processes that are encountered in retail investment administration. It needed to provide the background on why processes are undertaken and enough detail to form a day-to-day reference book with pointers to where to find more detailed explanations. Such a book would, I believe, be a useful tool in any office where investment administration is undertaken.

Investment administration has a key role to play in the many and varied investment products and services that are available in the retail investment market and so the book starts with an overview of wealth management. This provides vital background information on the industry. It then goes on to look at the main activities that are undertaken but also considers ancillary areas as diverse as trusts and powers of attorney.

The book follows a pattern of a short introduction to each chapter which aims to provide some essential and interesting background to the area and is followed by a detailed review of the activities and processes that are undertaken.

Each chapter has been written so that it can be read sequentially to build up a picture of the diverse activities and areas that are involved in investment administration. It is also designed so that the reader or researcher can retrieve just the information they require. The contents of each chapter are clearly noted so that it is possible to dip in and out for the specific information that is required.

The book also contains a suggested reading list so that further information can be readily sought where it is needed. There is also a glossary which includes not only terms used in the book but also serves as a useful reference for many financial service functions.

The book is intended as a useful day-to-day reference book for staff working in investment administration. It should be particularly useful for managers and supervisors but will also be helpful background reading for anyone undertaking the SII IAQ exams.

The audience for the book is not restricted to investment administration staff alone. It has been written so that it should be understandable to managers and staff working in other functions, such as finance, product management, training, IT and HR who would benefit from gaining a broader understanding of this wide and varied area.

Part

I

....

INTRODUCTORY ELEMENTS

Chapter

1

. . . .

WEALTH MANAGEMENT

1.1 INTRODUCTION

The activities undertaken by staff working in investment administration are essential to the successful delivery of investment services and products.

None of these products can deliver what the client expects if dividends do not arrive on time, trades are not placed correctly, purchases and sales do not settle on time, corporate actions are misinterpreted or shares are not correctly transferred when a new account is opened.

There are a myriad of activities that need to be undertaken for an investment account to function smoothly and it does not matter whether this is for a customer who only has a few holdings in his stocks and shares ISA or it is for a wealthy client with a discretionary managed investment account.

For these to run smoothly requires an efficient investment administration function staffed by a team of knowledgeable investment professionals.

Before we can begin to understand the many and varied functions involved in investment administration, we need to appreciate the range of investment products and services that are offered within the wealth management industry that it supports.

This chapter on wealth management provides an overview of the wealth management market and looks at the key role that investment administration plays in enabling these functions to operate effectively.

1.2 WEALTH MANAGEMENT MARKET

Before we look at some key data about the market for retail investment services, we need to undertake a brief review of the role of the financial services industry in order to set the context for products and services that are available.

It is generally accepted that the financial services industry fulfils three core functions within an economy, namely bringing savers and borrowers together through the investment chain, allowing risks to be managed and providing payment systems.

The investment chain links individual savers to firms seeking funds for investment and opportunities for savers to manage their finances. This is achieved through the financial services industry whose function in this chain is the design, manufacture and sale of financial products including such items as:

- banking accounts;
- National Savings investments;
- cash ISAs (Individual Savings Accounts);
- guaranteed growth bonds;
- guaranteed income bonds;
- choice of 2000+ unit trusts
- mortgages;
- life assurance bonds;
- term assurance;
- protection policies.

As well as products, the financial services industry also aids this function by the delivery of investment services to effectively manage an individual's assets and financial affairs, including:

- financial planning;
- fund supermarkets;
- investment wrappers;
- internet stockbroking;
- execution only share dealing;
- self-select ISAs;
- advisory share dealing;
- discretionary investment management;
- Self-Invested Personal Pensions (SIPPs);
- trusts.

The investment services provided to the retail investment market are usually split according to wealth and can be broken down into three elements, namely mass market, self-directed and wealth management.

The mass market is typically where one-off sales of investment products take place. Beyond straightforward product sales, is the market for investment services. The self-directed element of that refers to the situation where an investor takes control of his own investment affairs either with or without taking specialist advice.

Then there is the market for wealth management services, which are usually classified as mass affluent and high net worth. What constitutes either mass affluent or high net worth is usually based on the value of investable assets that a client has available. The wealth management market is usually broken down into four categories based on the US dollar value of assets the client has available to invest:

- mass affluent with assets over $100,000;
- high net worth with over $1 million of assets;
- very high new worth with over $5 million of assets;
- ultra high net worth with over $30 million of investable assets.

1.3 TYPES OF BUSINESS

The market for wealth management services is huge and is of sufficient size to allow a number of firms to specialise in different sectors, from internet stockbroking to full-service private banking.

In this next section, we will look at some of the types of services that are on offer and the delivery channels.

Financial planning

Unless the investor self-selects suitable investments, financial planning is at the heart of selecting which investment products and services a client should use.

Financial planning is the methodology that is used to match appropriate investment solutions to client needs. It is about designing a diversified portfolio of assets that will deliver medium to long-term investment performance which matches the timeframe and level of risk assumed by the investor.

Financial advice can be divided into five distinct stages:

- Determining the client's requirements.
- Formulating the strategy to meet the client's objectives.
- Implementing the strategy by selecting suitable products.
- Revisiting the recommended investments to ensure they continue to meet the client's needs.
- Periodically revisiting the client's objectives and revising the strategy and products held, if needed.

The investment services and products that are selected will clearly depend upon the funds available to invest, the client's objectives and attitude to risk.

Delivery channels

There is a range of ways in which investors can access financial services, including handling the arrangements themselves directly with the provider, taking advice from a financial adviser and using the services of wealth management firms.

Figure 1.1 provides a stylised view of the range of products and services that are available and the potential delivery routes. It gives an indication of the types of investment products and services that are available and

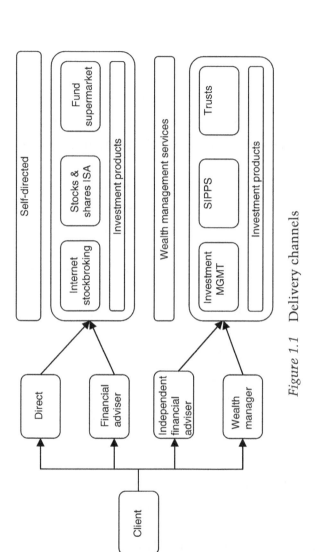

Figure 1.1 Delivery channels

whether these are likely to be sourced directly or via a financial adviser or wealth management firm.

There is a range of investment-related products and services where investors can self-select the investments they wish to buy and sell, such as internet stockbroking accounts, stocks and shares ISAs and fund supermarkets. They can go direct to the product providers to access these services or do so through a financial adviser.

Although Figure 1.1 shows different routes, in practice there is no reason why an investor might use a wealth manager for one service and self-select another.

Indeed, clients can source financial services either themselves or via an intermediary and the market infrastructure recognises that most clients want an option in this regard. The decision on whether to make your own decisions or to take advice can sensibly be based on the complexity of the arrangements to be entered into. Some services, however, are only available through firms due to either the cost of delivery or the complexities involved in the product.

Wealth management services are targeted at the wealthier and can comprise a wide range of services and products. Typically, investment services such as discretionary investment management, SIPPs and trusts require far larger sums to be invested to either qualify for the service or to make it a viable option. As a result, they tend to be offered by firms in conjunction with their financial planning and other services.

The providers of wealth management services range from independent financial advisers, to stockbrokers, private client investment managers and private banks. It is one of the fastest growing and most dynamic sectors of financial services and is known by various names including private clients, wealth management and private banking.

What characterises the services it offers is the investment management of liquid funds for its clients. The common feature of each of these services, therefore, is that they are investment vehicles and so each has a need for investment administration of the underlying assets.

1.4 INVESTMENT SERVICES AND PRODUCTS

There is a range of wealth management services available and in this section we will look at the key features of some of the main ones, obviously focusing on the ones where investment administration forms an underlying core activity.

Figure 1.2 shows the potential range of services that a client might need with the wealth management ones highlighted; although that is not to say that a client will not require the other products as well.

The need for each of these varies depending upon client's stage in life and their wealth. Some are ongoing, whilst others are required only occasionally. Some can be done

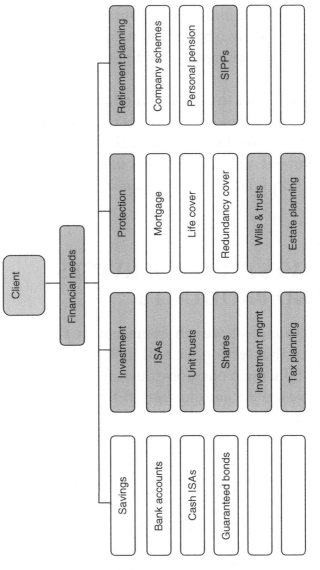

Figure 1.2 Range of services

by the client themselves, whilst others require professional advice. Equally, some are generally available and
others only to a firm's clients.

Stocks and shares ISA

An Individual Savings Account (ISA) is an investment
wrapper that can be used for cash and for stocks and
shares. It can be offered as a standalone product but can
also be offered alongside a stockbroking account and as
an integral part of discretionary and advisory investment
management.

A stocks and shares ISA carries tax advantages and as a
result the rules surrounding ISAs are made by HM Revenue & Customs. Any gains made on the investments
held in a stocks and shares ISA are free of capital gains
tax, making them an attractive vehicle to build up capital in a tax-free environment.

Due to their tax advantages, there are limits on the
amount that can be subscribed each year and on what
type of investments can be held.

Collective investment schemes

There is a bewildering range of collective investment
schemes – that is unit trusts, OEICs (Open Ended Investment Companies) and investment trusts – available to

investors. This makes the selection of the right fund difficult for investors and there are both self-select and managed services available to help investors make the right choices.

Fund supermarkets are designed to make dealing in investment funds easier and cheaper. They are generally internet-based platforms that give investors access to performance data on a range of different types of funds and which then provide an electronic method of buying, holding and selling funds.

To make their services attractive to investors they will usually discount the initial charge that a fund group would otherwise charge. From an investor's viewpoint, they offer the attractive combination of discounted initial fees and ease of dealing and administration.

The alternative is a managed portfolio of unit trusts. This is where a firm uses its expertise to select and manage a diversified portfolio of investment funds. It will do this on a discretionary basis and make changes to the composition of the underlying funds as its view on markets and prospects changes.

The initial investment for this type of service will vary but is usually in the range of £30,000 to £150,000. The firm will apply an annual charge for its management of the portfolio but as this is in addition to the charges for the underlying funds, they will usually negotiate heavy discounts for both initial and annual charges.

Share dealing

Stockbrokers have for years provided a service whereby ordinary investors can trade in bonds and equities. This is the traditional role of a stockbroker, that is acting as an agent for an investor, whether they are buying or selling and involves them taking the order from the client and finding a counterparty offering the best price.

This core service is often referred to as execution-only stockbroking in order to differentiate it from the discretionary and advisory investment management services that a stockbroker will also offer.

In recent years, most stockbrokers have moved on to offering this execution-only service through an internet-based platform. This allows the firm to gain efficiencies by offering automated services and allows the client to gain access to speedier execution.

An internet stockbroking account will involve a client entering into a formal agreement with the provider and the service offered will target those investors who undertake only occasional trades as well as frequent traders. The service will also usually enable any investments purchased to be held in dematerialised form to enable clients to view their portfolio online and trade electronically via the internet.

The charges made will usually depend upon the volume of trading activity that takes place but intense competition between the main providers has driven these down.

Although described as execution only, many firms provide additional services as well and will often give access to research material to its clients in order to aid them in identifying suitable investment opportunities.

Investment management

Provided an investor has sufficient funds, they can use the services of an investment firm to construct and manage a portfolio of stocks and shares to suit their investment objectives.

The portfolio will usually be linked to one or more of the firm's investment models with elements of the construction customised around the investor's attitude to risk, tax position and objectives. This allows the firm to manage a portfolio at an omnibus level and so ensure performance objectives are met, whilst still allowing for client-level adjustments to be made.

The service offered can be either discretionary or advisory. With a discretionary managed portfolio, the firm constructs an initial portfolio to meet the client's objectives, which will often be agreed with the client. Subsequently, it will make changes as and when it believes appropriate and report back to the client periodically on how the portfolio is performing. With an advisory portfolio, the same investment management takes place but any change to the portfolio will require the client's prior approval.

The entry level for discretionary investment management services will vary from firm to firm depending upon which part of the market it is targeting but will usually be in the range of £150,000 to £250,000. There is significant competition for this type of business and as a result, the fees charges are competitive and often in the range of 0.75% to 1.25%.

The minimum investment level for advisory portfolios and the costs may well be higher in recognition of the increased cost that is involved in managing an advisory portfolio.

Self-Invested Personal Pensions

A SIPP or Self-Invested Personal Pension scheme is as its name suggests a pension fund where the investor can direct how the funds are invested instead of having to invest in one of the range of funds available from an insurance company.

Many firms offering SIPPs are stockbrokers and they will construct their product offering in such a way that the administration of the pension element of the plan is out-sourced to a specialist pension provider. This can then leave the investor able to choose to manage the underlying portfolio using an internet stockbroking facility.

Although the title refers to self-invested, it does not mean that investors have to undertake the investment management themselves. They can appoint an investment management firm to undertake discretionary or advisory management of the portfolio.

As with ISAs, a SIPP offers tax advantages and as a result, HM Revenue & Customs also sets maximum contribution levels and defines permissible investments.

As there is a pension plan element to be administered as well as the underlying investment portfolio, costs will typically be higher than other investment management portfolios. There are also usually set-up fees involved and as a result, the usual recommendation is that the level of fees means that the minimum investment fund needs to be around £150,000 for this route to be economic.

Trusts

A trust is a legal arrangement where one person holds assets for another. It can be used in variety of scenarios – for example to hold funds for young or disabled children; for charitable gifts; and in order to minimise tax liabilities

Trusts are subject to a wide range of complex rules and are used for a variety of purposes. Each may therefore vary considerably but within most trusts is an underlying investment portfolio.

Tax and estate planning

It is virtually impossible to undertake wealth management without giving due consideration to an individual's tax position.

As a result, most wealth management firms will also offer tax and estate planning services. The objective of these services is to organise the client's affairs in such a way as to minimise their liability to tax.

The tax services provided can satisfy needs ranging from constructing portfolios to maximising tax allowances to managing capital gains tax on substantial holdings. The services can also be one-off or ongoing and the charges depend on complexity of the client's affairs.

Estate planning is designed to ensure assets go to those intended on death with the amount of tax payable minimised. It can take many forms from drafting tax-efficient wills, making inter vivos gifts, creating trusts, to administering the estate of the client once they die.

1.5 INVESTMENT FIRMS

There is a variety of investment firms that operate in the wealth management market from small privately owned firms to subsidiaries of major international banks.

Firms can be classified generally under the following headings:

- execution-only stockbrokers;
- full-service stockbrokers;
- private-client firms;
- private banks;
- international private banks.

Each will offer a range of investment services from arranging deals, managing investment portfolios to full wealth management. Private banks will typically service fewer but wealthier customers, whilst the others will look to target the mass affluent market.

One of the biggest differentiators between them is the extent to which they use bespoke services to fit individual clients. So at one end of the range, private banks will offer a greater range of personalised services compared to the standardised services offered to execution-only stockbroking customers.

There is also a wide variation in minimum investment levels for investment management services. The sort of minimums levels that might apply are:

- stockbrokers   £100,000
- private clients   £150,000–£200,000
- UK private banks   £1 million
- international private banks   £5 million

Execution-only stockbrokers

An execution-only stockbroker is a firm that arranges to buy and sell stock-market securities on behalf of investors. In doing so, it does not offer advice on what stocks to buy or sell.

Its role is to act as agent for the investor and under the Financial Services Authority (FSA) rules it is required to obtain the best price for the trade. To do this, it will use trading platforms provided by the London Stock Exchange and may either deal electronically with a market counterparty or place a telephone trade.

As far as the counterparty is concerned, it has traded with the broker. It will look to the broker to settle the trade and will be uninterested who the broker's client is. There will therefore effectively be two trades to settle, one between the broker and the market counterparty and one between the broker and the client.

The broker may also trade as principal, which means that instead of seeking a market counterparty to trade with, it deals for its own account. If a client is selling, then the broker will buy the stock from the client and add the stock to its book. It may use that stock to meet other client orders or sell it on into the market. Either way, the broker has an obligation to ensure that its client receives the best execution on their trade and to ensure it discloses to its client that it has traded as principal rather than agent.

Other brokers may be part of a larger organisation and have their own internal market maker and may 'internalise' all of their orders. This is the same as when a broker trades as principal, but where they systematically internalise all of their trades. In order to ensure that their clients get the best execution, they will use a price improvement algorithm that identifies the best price that they could have dealt for the client externally and then add an improvement onto the actual price the client deals at.

Execution-only stockbrokers offer a range of dealing services. They will offer a certificated service where investors place the order with them and sends in their share certificate and stock transfer form for the trade. They will also offer dealing services where they hold the investor's stock in one of their nominee accounts and administer the portfolio, leaving clients free to concentrate on the dealing they wish to undertake.

There tends to be no entry level for these dealing services. Execution-only stockbrokers make their money by charging for trading and so will have a tariff of charges that usually is higher for certificated dealing than dematerialised. Where stock is held in nominee accounts, there will usually be a quarterly administration fee which may be waived where the number of deals exceeds a required level.

Many of these dealing services are offered via the internet. When they first started to be offered, the services were quite basic but they now feature real-time pricing, market reports, graphs and access to research material.

Many execution-only stockbrokers have also expanded to offer discounted unit trust dealing. They are able to use the same systems platforms to administer the unit trusts or OEICs that a client holds and this has enabled them to widen the scope of the instruments their clients can trade.

To make it attractive for their clients and to attract new customers, they usually negotiate discounts on the initial charge that a unit trust makes. Initial charges can easily be 3.75% and these are often discounted to 1.5% making it a very attractive proposition for investors.

Full-service stockbrokers

A full-service stockbroker will offer a range of investment services from unit trust managed accounts to full discretionary management, as well as arranging deals for their clients. I have used the term full-service stockbroker to differentiate from ones who offer execution-only dealing services.

There is a large number of stockbroking firms around the country who have traditionally been the first choice for an investor seeking to have an investment portfolio managed, either on a discretionary or advisory basis. Stockbrokers vary from large to small firms and many differentiate on local service so they are often regionally located.

Stockbrokers will often have more flexible entry levels than private-client firms, which tend to be subsidiaries of larger organisations. They can also tailor their services to the needs of the geographic area in which they concentrate rather than having to offer a nationwide service.

The entry level will usually be a managed unit trust service which can have minimum investment levels as low as £7000. These are designed for clients who are looking to grow their assets and the funds will be invested in a range of well-diversified funds.

Where clients have more substantial funds they will be offered managed portfolio services. The entry level for these may be as low as £100,000 and would involve the firm constructing a portfolio of bonds, equities and investment funds around the specific needs and objectives of the client.

They are also likely to offer other types of accounts that utilise other investment managers. These may be called wrap accounts or manager of manager funds. These are designed to give access to institutional fund managers that would not otherwise be accessible to a private investor.

A stockbroking firm will also offer financial advice and other investment products to its clients. The products will include ISAs to hold some of their investments but will often extend beyond that to offering trading in contracts for difference. The range of products and services might also include child trust funds, SIPPs and tax and trustee services.

Private-client firms

A private-client firm will usually be a subsidiary or division of a larger firm, such as an investment bank.

The services they offer to clients will also include managed investment accounts and a range of financial services and products. They tend to target investors with larger funds to invest and this is reflected in the minimum investment they will accept that can be any-where in the range of £250,000 upwards.

They will generally operate a series of investment mod-els that can be used to meet most client objectives. This allows them to focus on managing the top-level model against a series of benchmarks so that invest-ment performance can be delivered. Changes to the mod-els will then be fed down to the client level where some flexibility in implementation can take place to allow for client-level sensitivities, such as investment restrictions, risk tolerance and capital gains tax. The use of ISAs and Personal Equity Plans (PEPs) will usu-ally be integral to the management of the investment portfolio.

The investment service offered will usually be fully in-tegrated with its financial planning and wealth man-agement services. They will therefore usually offer a wide range of services beyond just investment manage-ment which might include estate planning, tax planning and pension planning. The range of products available will also be wide and might include SIPPs, small self-administered pension schemes and uniquely negotiated investment bonds.

Although the services offered by private-client firms and stockbrokers may sound similar and the bound-aries between what they offer are blurred, it is impor-tant to remember that it is a large market and there is plenty of room for different competitors and different offerings.

Private banks

Private banks will target the wealthier end of the investment market and will look to offer both personalised services and a wider range of services and products designed to meet the needs of their wealthier clients.

The entry level for private banking services is usually at the level of £1 million of investable assets. At this level, clients demand extra service and private banks will focus on the quality not just of its wealth management capabilities but on the quality of its relationship management as well.

As well as investment management, they will also offer a suite of tailored banking services to meet the needs of their clients. They will also offer portfolio borrowing to allow their clients to borrow against their existing portfolio for investment in other assets to create leverage.

They will usually have tailored services that can meet the needs of wealthy investors and which will focus on wealth preservation. By definition, this will make effective estate and tax planning an essential and integral component of the service offered.

International private banks

International private banks offer services that are designed to be the preserve of the ultra-wealthy. It is a huge market that is dominated by the Swiss banks and the major US global banks that are able to leverage their international stance to service the wealthiest.

They are able to offer individual specialist services because of the size of the investable funds and minimum entry levels can be a staggering US$35 million.

Beyond investment management, their services can extend to art, other collectible assets and buying properties overseas. The will also have tax experts that allow them to advise and construct solutions that take account of the many issues that can arise across different tax jurisdictions.

1.6 INVESTMENT ADMINISTRATION

Having looked briefly at the range of investment services and products available, together with the firms who provide these services, we can now turn to see what part investment administration plays.

Investment administration is the core process that underlies many of the wealth management products and services described above and is essential to their effective delivery.

The way in which any of the above firms are organised will obviously vary but they would generally be organised

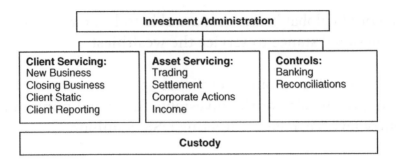

Figure 1.3 Organisational model for investment administration

around the common themes of:

- client relationship management;
- investment management;
- investment administration.

And a firm would typically organise its investment administration area around the core functions that take place as described in Figure 1.3.

The groupings bring together similar functions relating to client or asset servicing, with the control functions separated out.

The client servicing area will deal with new and closing business, which involves all of the activities needed to open or close an account. This encompasses money laundering checks, validating stock, transferring holdings and setting up a myriad of client and asset records so that a portfolio can function effectively. It requires a broad knowledge of financial planning, products and industry processes. It will also deal with issuing detailed investment and transaction reports to the client.

The asset servicing area will handle all transactions that affect a client's holdings. It will deal with the placing of stock-market trades and their settlement. The corporate actions area will deal with events such as takeovers, rights issues, mergers, dividends and interest payments. A controls area will deal with the banking arrangements necessary for the effective running of a portfolio so that payments can be made and received, trades can be settled and dividends collected. This area will also undertake the essential process of ensuring that its record of client investments can be reconciled at all times with its custodian. All three areas are complex and rapidly changing and require staff with specialist knowledge.

We will look at many of these individual processes in detail as we progress through this book.

Part

II

....

INVESTMENT
ADMINISTRATION

Chapter

2

. . . .

NEW AND CLOSING BUSINESS

2.1 INTRODUCTION

The process of handling new and closing business is one of those that on the face of it appears straightforward and yet, can be amazingly complex.

What can be a simple process of opening an investment account and transferring assets can become complicated where the records of a private client are incomplete or simply disorganised. Investors are likely to have acquired their investments over many years and with trading and multiple corporate actions, keeping detailed records can be a time-consuming endeavour. They are unlikely to be complete or comprehensive enough and where they hold their own share certificates, there is every possibility that some are missing.

This can make the process of taking on new clients both very time consuming and expensive. Indeed, many firms recognise the complexities that are involved by allocating some of their most experienced staff to this process.

In this chapter, we will consider some of the detailed processes that take place during the set up of a new investment account and explore what makes it so complex. We will then look at some of the issues surrounding closing accounts and particularly at some of the complex procedures required when a client dies.

2.2 NEW BUSINESS

We will start with a look at the overall end-to-end process that takes place for new business and will then consider some of the areas mentioned in more detail in subsequent sections.

The high-level process steps that take place for the establishment of new business are shown in Figure 2.1.

The process clearly starts with a client wishing to use the investment services of a firm and could range from stockbroking to private banking. A number of key steps need to be completed at this early stage, including:

- classifying what type of investor the client is, so that the appropriate regulatory considerations are applied;
- establishing full details about the client as part of the 'know your customer' (KYC) process; and
- determining the investment objectives and attitude to risk of the client so that an appropriate investment policy can be agreed.

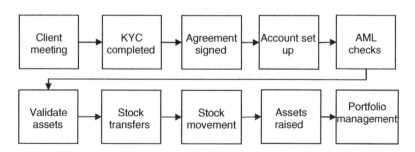

Figure 2.1   Take on of new business

Once they can be determined and agreed, it will usually be necessary for an agreement to be entered into that will detail the terms and conditions of the services that are to be provided.

Details of the client and the assets that they hold will then be passed to the new business department for the set up of the new account. As with any account, data about the client needs to be recorded on a firm's system as this will drive everything from how any investments are managed, to how dividends are processed and how and when reporting to the client will take place.

At this early stage of the account set-up process, anti-money laundering (AML) checks will be completed. If a client meeting has taken place then evidence of the client's identity and address will have been sought as part of that and if not, then they will have to be completed before progressing further. The source of the funds to be invested will need to be validated and further checks may also be required depending upon the type of client and business being opened and the financial crime risk it poses.

The assets of the client will then need to be validated. The amount of effort needed here will depend upon whether they are held by another firm and are simply being transferred or whether they were in the client's possession. If they are held with another firm, then it is a matter of contacting the area dealing with closing accounts and obtaining details of the investments held that are to be transferred.

If they were held by the client, the new business department is likely to receive a bundle of share certificates and other records. They will need to examine these to establish exactly what the client holds, whether all of the share certificates have been received, whether any are missing and whether each looks valid. To appreciate what is involved here can be seen by considering an investor who has a holding of an FTSE100 company which they have held for many years and on which they have taken scrip dividends. It is quite feasible that they may have 20 or more share certificates for just one holding.

Once the assets are validated, it is necessary to prepare stock transfer forms to transfer the holding out of the client's name and into the firm's nominee account. At the same time, other forms may also be required such as indemnities for any lost share certificates.

These will then need to be sent to the client for signature and once returned, sent along with the share certificates to the firm's custodian for lodging into the firm's nominee account.

The client's investments will need to be raised on the firm's systems at the same time. This involves not only raising the number of shares held in each company but considering the value at which they will be raised. If the investments are to be discretionary managed it will be necessary to value the assets at the start of the agreement so that there is a reference point to report subsequent investment performance.

It may also be necessary to establish the base cost for capital gains tax (CGT) purposes so that CGT considerations can be incorporated into the subsequent portfolio management. This can involve trying to recreate share histories for the investments held by the client and can be both time consuming and complex.

Finally, the account will be opened, the investments transferred and the management of the client's portfolio can now commence. As can be appreciated from the number of steps involved, to get to this stage requires quite some time and it is vital that it is undertaken both swiftly and accurately as, until it is completed, the service that the client has signed up for cannot be effectively started.

In the following sections, we will consider some of these processes in more detail.

2.3 CLIENT TYPES

At an early stage in dealing with a new client it is essential to establish how the client will be classified for regulatory purposes.

Compliance regulations are designed to provide the greatest level of protection to those private investors who are in greatest need of it. For more sophisticated investors and market counterparties, fewer rules apply. It is therefore important to understand this at the beginning of the relationships so that the appropriate regulations can be followed and the necessary agreements and risk warnings issued.

The FSA Conduct of Business sourcebook contains the detailed requirements to be followed for client classification. It requires that before conducting investment business, a firm must determine whether the client is:

- a private customer;
- an intermediate customer; or
- a market counterparty.

To understand which type of client falls into which category, it is easiest to start with the market counterparties. From there we can consider who can be classified as intermediate customers and then anyone who does not fall into either category is by definition a private customer and entitled to the highest level of protection under FSA rules.

Market counterparties are, as you would expect, other investment firms but the classification also includes governments, central banks, supranational agencies and state investment bodies. In essence they are firms or organisations where it is reasonable to expect that they should have the highest level of knowledge in their market dealings and therefore require the least protection.

An intermediate customer is simply one who is expected to require more protection than market counterparties. They can reasonably be expected to have greater knowledge of the arrangements they are entering into than a private customer and not require the same degree of protection.

Examples of intermediate customers include large businesses such as local or public authorities, listed companies or other corporate bodies with net assets of at least $5 million. The designation can also apply to another firm that is acting for an underlying customer and to unregulated collective investment schemes.

The rules recognise that some private investors will have the knowledge and experience to be able to dispense with the protection and restrictions that the rules impose. These investors are known as expert private customers and they can be reclassified as intermediate customers. FSA rules require that before a client can be classified as such, they must have received appropriate warnings and have consented to be treated as such, after having been given sufficient time to consider the implications.

This leaves the category of private customer, which covers clients who are private individuals and small firms. Firms dealing with retail-type investors are therefore most likely to be dealing with clients who will be classified as private customers or maybe intermediate customers.

These classifications are due to change as a result of the Markets in Financial Instruments Directive (MiFID), which is intended to be effective from November 2007.

MiFID will introduce a single set of conduct of business rules across the EU. As with the current rules the greatest protection will be accorded to those who need it most, namely private investors. The classifications will, however, change and there will be three categories of client under MiFID:

- eligible counterparties;
- professional clients; and
- retail clients.

There will be two types of eligible counterparty, ones who are automatically treated as such and others who can agree to be treated the same. The ones who are automatically treated that way are the type of firms that you would expect, such as investment firms, investment funds, pension funds and national governments. The ones who may opt to be treated as eligible counterparties include large firms and professional clients.

The classification of professional clients includes any of the above plus a handful of others, such as institutional investors. Importantly, both professional clients and eligible counterparties may choose to opt down to a more protective client classification.

MiFID classifies investment managers as eligible counterparties. However, it is likely that many will request opt downs, in particular to avoid a mismatch between duties they will owe to their clients and the duties they are owed by firms they deal with.

This leaves retail clients who are private individuals. They may be treated as professionals on request but the requirements are more onerous and require the firm to assess the client's expertise, knowledge and understanding of risks.

As well as changing how clients are classified, MiFID will also bring about changes in the way that a firm is required to make sure that the services it provides to a client are both suitable and appropriate.

The existing obligation to ensure that advice and services are suitable for a client will be extended to professional clients. There will also be a new requirement to ensure that the services provided to a client are appropriate. A firm will need to request information from the client regarding his knowledge and experience to enable the firm to assess whether the service or product is appropriate for the client.

2.4 KNOW YOUR CUSTOMER

Having dealt with the regulatory requirement to classify clients so that they can have appropriate protection, we can move on to look at the information that needs to be established about the client before an investment account is opened.

The amount of information that needs to be obtained will depend upon whether financial advice is being given or not. In the following paragraphs we will consider the information that is needed where an investment management service is being entered into. If a client is opening a self-select ISA or an execution-only stockbroking account, then the amount of information that the firm will need to obtain will be more limited.

A fundamental part of the new business process is to undertake a fact find to establish all pertinent data about a potential client before recommendations can be made. Know your customer (KYC) refers to this fact-find process. A KYC is also the document that is used to record data about the client.

When making investments and considering their needs, individuals have varying objectives and expectations. Before appropriate advice can be given it is essential to establish full details about the client, their assets and liabilities and the life assurance or protection products or arrangements that they may have in place. Their family circumstances, health and future plans and expectations are equally important.

The information that will have to be established will therefore need to include among other things:

- personal details;
- health status;
- details of family and dependants;
- details of occupation, earnings and other income sources;
- estimates of present and anticipated outgoings;
- assets and liabilities;

- any pension arrangements;
- potential inheritances and any estate planning arrangements, such as a will.

When it comes to looking at potential investment recommendations, another set of factors need to be established, including the following:

- investment objectives;
- attitude to risk;
- liquidity requirements and time horizon;
- tax status;
- investment preferences.

The client's investment objectives will drive the eventual investment policy that is agreed and implemented. Typical investment objectives include maximising future growth, protecting the real value of capital, generating an essential level of income and protecting against future events.

Establishing the client's attitude to risk is essential especially for investment-related products which will be exposed to stock-market movements. To meet the client's investment objectives will involve an exposure to risk and the client's risk tolerance will determine the asset allocation and instruments used within an investment account.

It also needs to be remembered that the client is also likely to have more than one investment objective, such as funding a child's education as well as maximising future growth and their attitude to risk may change from one objective to another.

Having established the client's investment objectives, it is necessary to understand their liquidity requirements and the timescale for achieving their objectives.

Where the liquidity requirements are low and the timescale is long, there will be a greater choice of assets available to meet the client's investment objective. By contrast, the need for high liquidity allied to a short timescale demands that the client should invest in lower risk assets such as cash and short-dated bonds, which offer a potentially lower return than equities.

Whatever their requirements, it is important, however, that the client maintains sufficient liquidity to meet both known commitments and possible contingencies. This may require setting aside a cash fund to meet immediate liquidity requirements and ensuring there are assets within the portfolio that will mature to meet known liabilities or can be readily encashed without incurring excessive cost or losses.

As well as the above, it is also necessary to establish the client's tax position so that their investments can be organised in such a way that the returns attract the least tax possible.

Finally, any investment preferences the client has need to be understood. Clients may have investment restrictions they wish to place which will exclude certain areas of the investment spectrum from their portfolios or require a concentration on a particular investment theme, such as ethical investment.

There is no simple way of establishing all of this information quickly. It usually requires a detailed and lengthy interview with the client and is usually collected by completion of a KYC questionnaire.

This latter document will provide the data that a new business department will need to set up the client account and associated static data records.

2.5 AGREEMENTS

FSA rules require a firm to pay due regard to the information needs of its clients, and communicate information to them in a way which is clear, fair and not misleading.

It is a requirement that customers have all of the information they need about a firm, the services they intend to use, their charges and the basis on which the firm will be doing business with them before a firm acts for a client. Typically, this will be achieved by the firm providing its customers with a 'terms of business' letter.

A terms of business letter must be provided to a private customer before any investment business is conducted and within a reasonable period after beginning to conduct investment business for an intermediate customer.

Like a terms of business letter, a client agreement sets out the basis on which investment business will be done and the major difference is that it requires the customer's acceptance, namely his signature indicating his acceptance of the terms.

A client agreement must be used when a private customer is agreeing to complex services being provided including:

- managing investments on a discretionary basis;
- doing business in contingent liability investments, such as futures;
- stock lending;
- underwriting.

2.6 ACCOUNT OPENING

Once the client has agreed to open an investment account, copies of the agreement, KYC questionnaire and share certificates will normally be handed to the new business department for the account to be opened.

When a new account is opened on a firm's system it will be necessary to populate static data fields with information about the client that will drive the subsequent investment management, investment processing and client reporting that will take place.

The data will come from the information established during the fact find and the new business department will extract what it needs from the KYC and any other internal forms that a firm requires to be completed.

The data that will need to be set up will include such items as:

- Client name and address – this will drive all internal processing, reports and be used for investment reporting to the client.
- Business type – this will include the type of investment account such as a personal account, an ISA or PEP, a SIPP, a charity or a trust.
- Investment objectives – this will record the investment objectives and will be used for managing the investment portfolio.
- Investment model – this will drive comparisons of the client's actual portfolio to the firm's preferred model for that type of client and provide suggested trades.
- Investment powers – this will show whether the account is to be managed on a discretionary or advisory basis and any investment restrictions that have been imposed.
- Investment reporting – this will record any benchmarks that are to be used to measure performance against and the dates on which investment valuations, periodic statements and performance reports are to be issued.
- Diary dates – these will be used to trigger processing events such as regular payments of income to clients.
- Fees – this will generate charges based on a scale of fees agreed with the client.

2.7 MONEY LAUNDERING

Anti-money laundering checks will need to be under-taken as part of the account opening process.

The regulations relating to money laundering derive from the Proceeds of Crime Act 2002 (POCA) and the Money Laundering Regulations 2003. The act makes money laundering a criminal offence and the regulations contain the requirements for systems and training to prevent money laundering and the requirements to check the identity of new customers which have been introduced as a result of EU Directives.

Detailed guidance on how to comply with money laundering requirements is provided by the guidance notes issued by the Joint Money Laundering Steering Group (JMLSG), the latest of which were issued in 2006.

The core anti-money laundering (AML) activities require checks to be made on the identity of the client, verification of their address and checks on the source of funds being used. Guidance on the extent to which these and any other checks are to be carried out for different sectors of the industry is provided in the JMLSG guidance notes.

The JMLSG guidance notes divide the core checks that a firm should carry out into two main areas:

- Identification of the client – usually referred to as ID & VA or identification and verification of address.

- Obtaining additional information about the client where appropriate, including the source of funds and the purpose of specific transactions.

The occasions where a firm will obtain additional information will depend upon the level of money laundering risk that an individual or type of customer presents.

ID & VA relates to determining exactly who the customer is and then verifying that by obtaining proof.

There will be occasions where verification of identity is not required and these are mainly where a one-off transaction for less than € 15,000 is involved. In all other cases, a business relationship is regarded as having been established and the firm must undertake verification procedures.

For a private individual, this involves obtaining their full name, address and date of birth. To verify this, an official document with a photograph will prove the name, for example, a passport or international driving licence, whilst a utilities bill, which includes their name and address, will prove the address supplied is valid. Many firms will use agencies who can electronically verify the address of a customer.

For a corporate entity, it is necessary to obtain the full name of the company, its registered number, its registered office and its business address. Proof of identity and existence would be drawn from the constitutional documents, namely, the Articles and Memorandum of Association and sets of accounts.

For private companies it will also be necessary to prove the identity of the directors and any shareholders holding more than 25% of the company.

The guidance for other types of business include:

- Pension schemes – identification can be confirmed by checking they are approved by HM Revenue & Customs. The identities of the scheme's signatories need only be identified if the firm's risk assessment requires it but the identity of the principal employer should be verified and the source of funding recorded to ensure that a complete audit trail exists if the employer is wound up.
- Charities – details of all registered charities can be confirmed from the Charity Commission website and the Commission will confirm the registered number of the charity and the name and address of their principal contact.
- Trusts and foundations – details of the full name of the trust, its nature and purpose, the country of establishment and the names of the trustees or protector should be obtained. The identity of the trustees should be verified and further checks made depending upon the assessment of the financial crime risk it poses.
- Unregistered charities and church bodies – the same procedure as for private companies or trusts should be followed.

There will be occasions where one firm introduces a client to another firm. These will arise, for example, where a firm transfers a holding back into a client's name, where a financial adviser introduces a client to a stockbroker and where one part of a group introduces a client to its investment management or private banking arm. In those scenarios, the introducer can provide confirmation of the identity of the client.

For certain clients or certain types of business, a firm may decide that additional information is required. This additional information may take the form of identifying the source of the funds being invested but may also go much further and require establishing the source of the client's wealth and any relationship with any beneficial owners of the funds.

The JMLSG guidance notes are intended as guidance and it is up to each firm to assess the level of risk it faces and put in place appropriate risk mitigation processes.

The FSA view compliance with the guidance as a key factor in assessing a firm's compliance with the money laundering regulations.

2.8 VALIDATING THE ASSETS

The next main phase of activity to take place is to validate the assets that the client is introducing into the investment portfolio.

Where the existing investments are held by another firm, then an up-to-date schedule of the investments will be readily obtainable.

Where the client held the share certificates representing their investments, this will be more complex. Each certificate will need to be checked for validity and the extent of the total holding of each investment will need to be clarified and verified.

There is a variety of reasons why the certificates that the client provides may not be representative of their current portfolio. The client may hold share certificates for companies that were taken over years ago, are in liquidation or are wound up. Equally the investigations may throw up that there are some missing or lost certificates.

This makes it essential to validate the holdings the client has. A good starting point is the last dividends paid which will show the nominal holding on the tax voucher and immediately identify any discrepancy. If they are not available or there are incomplete records, then checks should be made with the company registrars.

The checks may identify that there are missing certificates and if so, an indemnity form will need to be requested from the company registrars. This is used to obtain a replacement share certificate and Figure 2.2 gives an indication of what a standard indemnity form would look like.

INDEMNITY FOR LOST CERTIFICATE

To the Directors of ....

The original certificates of title relating to the under mentioned securities of the above
named company has or have been lost or destroyed.

Neither the securities, nor the certificates of title there to have been transferred, charged, lent or
deposited or dealt with in any manner affecting the absolute title there to and the persons named in the
said certificates is or are the persons entitled to be on the register in respect of such securities.

We request you to cancel the certificates of title for such securities and, in consideration of your doing
so, undertake jointly and severally to indemnify you and the company against all claims and demands,
and any expenses thereof, which may be made against you or the company in consequence of your
complying with this request and of the company permitting at any time hereafter a transfer of the said
securities, or any part thereof, without the production of the said original certificates.

We undertake to deliver to the company for cancellation the said original certificates should the same
ever be recovered.

Particulars of lost certificates

Certificate Numbers	Amount and Class of Securities	Name and Address of Shareholders

Dated this .... day of 2007

Shareholder's Signature

....

We hereby join in the above indemnity and undertaking

....

UK Bank, Insurance Company or Guarantee Society

Figure 2.2   Example of an indemnity for a lost share certificate

An indemnity form has to be signed by the shareholder
and records as much detail about the missing certificate
as can be ascertained. The registrar will use this to replace the certificate and as there is a risk that the original might turn up and be legitimately used leaving them

exposed, they will require that appropriate insurance is taken out.

This is achieved by requesting a bank, insurance company or guarantee society to join in on the indemnity in exchange for payment of a fee. Alternatively, registrars will undertake this and make a charge in addition to the administration fee that will be charged for the lost certificate.

2.9 TRANSFERRING ASSETS

The next process when opening a new account is to transfer the assets to the investment account.

There are three potential processing scenarios to consider, namely:

- the client is only introducing cash;
- the assets are already held in dematerialised form by another firm and require transfer; or
- the client held the assets themselves in certificated form.

The first clearly represents the simplest scenario to deal with as all that is required is a straightforward funds transfer from the client's bankers. Details will need to be provided of the firm's bank account so that the client can give instructions for the funds to be transferred. Once received, the funds will be credited to the client's account and when cleared the investment of the funds can be undertaken.

If existing investments are to be transferred from another firm, then they will be held in dematerialised form and a transfer between Crest accounts will be required. Crest is the electronic settlement system through which the London Stock Exchange settles bargains.

The firm will need the client's written instruction to authorise the transfer and once it has this, it can contact the other provider and make arrangements for the transfer. Details of their Crest account or that of their custodian will be needed along with details of the Crest account that is to be credited. A date for the transfer can be agreed and the custodian can then be instructed to accept a free of payment delivery. The stock will then move into the account with the custodian and the assets can be raised in the client's investment portfolio.

Where the client holds the certificates representing their holding, then Crest transfer forms will need to be completed and the client's signature obtained. These are standard forms and require details of the holding and number of shares to be completed. The full name and address of the registered holder as shown on the share certificate is entered and the form will usually be precompleted with details of the firm's nominee account and the custodian's Crest ID.

Where the client is introducing holdings in unit trusts or OEICs, a standard stock transfer form will need to be used instead.

Once the client's signature is obtained, the transfer forms and the certificates are sent to the custodian for lodging into Crest. At the same time, the asset can be raised in the client's account.

2.10 RAISING ASSETS

Raising the assets on the client's investment account involves passing ledger entries to record the holding and the number of shares or stock held. It also involves applying a value to each asset.

The value that is used will depend upon the type of investment account that is being opened.

If no investment management is involved, then clients will often be asked what the acquisition cost of the holding is, so that can be used. This has a practical benefit from the client's perspective in that the value appearing on statements represents the base cost of the investment and so an easy indication of whether the holding is showing a profit or loss can be seen. If the client does not provide a value, then the asset will be valued at the date of lodgement and that value used instead.

Where investment management services are being provided, then there are a number of FSA requirements that have to be met. The investments that are introduced into the portfolio need to be valued as at the date of the agreement and this initial value is then used to record the subsequent investment performance.

A firm is required to issue a six-monthly periodic statement to the client that records the starting value of the portfolio, any additions and withdrawals, the closing value and the change in value over the period. This is intended to give a clear picture to the client of the change in value of the portfolio and the initial valuation therefore plays a critical role in commencing this process.

The other value that may need to be recorded at this stage is the acquisition cost of the holding for capital gains tax (CGT) purposes. CGT can be a major consideration when managing a private client's portfolio, whether it is maximising the use of the annual CGT allowance or reducing a large holding of a particular stock over a period of time.

Establishing this can, however, be a complex process and can involve recreating the capital history of the holding. The client's investment records or those of their tax adviser will need to be examined to see the extent to which full details are available. If they are not available, it is possible to reconstruct the history by obtaining details from the company registrar. This is, however, a time-consuming and expensive business and most firms would only undertake this where absolutely essential.

There are a number of CGT packages available on the market that can be used to set up CGT records and which can assist with the recreation of capital histories. These can provide extremely valuable information for the subsequent investment management of the portfolio and the optimisation of CGT allowances.

2.11 CLOSING BUSINESS AND TRANSFERS

An investment account will close for a number of reasons, including where the client has decided to dispense with the services of a firm or when the client dies.

Equally, transfers out of the account may be needed as a result of spitting a joint account into sole name accounts, because of a divorce settlement, where a new trust is being created or where the assets are being transferred to another as a result of a gift.

Whatever the reason for the transfer, the process is the reverse of transferring stock into a new investment account.

Where differences may arise is where transfers outside of Crest are required and when a client dies. We will look at transfers outside of Crest and consider some of the complex issues that arise when a client dies in the following section.

Transfers outside of Crest

Apart from transferring assets when new business is taken on, other occasions will arise when transfers may need to be made. These may take place outside of Crest and we need to look at how the transfer process operates and then look at stock transfer forms and the information required when completing them.

First, it needs to be noted that a shareholder has the right to transfer their shares in a company, subject to certain legal restrictions and any restrictions on transfer provided in the articles of association of the company.

When a transfer is to be made, company law and the Stock Transfer Act 1963 require that a stock transfer form is used to transfer ownership. The stock transfer form should also:

- be executed by the transferor;
- specify the amount of the consideration;
- provide a description and the number or amount of securities;
- state the name and address of the transferor;
- identify the person to whom a transfer is made and provide their full name and address.

Once a transfer has been completed, stamp duty must be dealt with. This requires completion of the reverse of the stock transfer form and if necessary, payment of stamp duty which will be evidenced by HM Revenue & Customs stamping the document.

After stamping, the transfer is delivered to the company registrar along with the old share certificate, who will undertake certain checks to ensure that the transfer is valid and can be accepted. A new certificate will then be prepared by the registrar and must be issued within two months from the date on which the transfer was lodged.

Stock transfer forms

We can now turn to look at the information that is needed when completing a stock transfer form. Figure 2.3 provides an abbreviated example of the standard layout of a stock transfer form.

Stock transfer form	(Above this Line for Registrar's Use Only)

Consideration £...	Certificate lodged with Registrar (For completion by Registrar/Stock Exchange)
Name of Undertaking	
Description of Security	
Number or amount of Shares, Stock or other security	Words / Figures (units of)
Name(s) of registered holder(s)	In the name(s) of

I/we hereby transfer the above security out of the name(s) aforesaid into the person(s) named below.
Signature(s) of Transferor(s)

Please Sign Here

1 ....

2 ....

3 ....

4 ....

Bodies corporate should execute under their common seal

Stamp of Selling Broker(s)

Date ....

Full name(s) and full postal address(es) of the person(s) to whom the security is transferred

I/We request that such entries be made in the register as are necessary to give effect to this transfer

Stamp of Buying Broker (if any)

Stamp or name and address of person lodging this form (if other than the Buying Broker)

Figure 2.3   Example of a stock transfer form

The form requires the usual details to be entered for a transfer. Details of the company in which the investor is a shareholder need to be entered into the box headed Name of Undertaking. The type of shares held are entered in the box headed Description of Security and the number of shares held in the boxes headed Words and Figures.

The name and address of the registered holder should include the full details of how the existing holding is registered, which will be either the full designation used by the firm or if the stock is in the client's name, their full name and address including middle names and postcodes. If the client's name has changed, say because of marriage, then the client's new name should be entered and a copy of the marriage or other certificate will need to be lodged along with the transfer.

Details of the name and address of the person to whom the holding is being transferred need to be entered. This should show their full names including middle names and titles and their full address and postcode.

Holdings can be registered jointly and up to four names are allowed. Designations can also be added to differentiate this investment from other holdings the transferee may have.

A shareholding can only be registered in the name of a legal person. As a result, that means a registrar will not accept a transfer into the name of 'The treasurer of ...'

or 'The trustees of ... '. This is because they are not legal entities and instead the holding should be registered as John and Fred Smith as trustees of Smith Trust. In this way, it is the trustees as individuals who are registered and the designation that follows will differentiate the holding from any other they may have.

Equally an organisation cannot be registered that is not a corporate body, such as a club or a society.

The other area that should be noted is the Consideration box which is used to determine whether stamp duty is payable. There are three main scenarios that might arise, namely where a gift is being made, where a transfer is taking place and where a payment is being made for the shares.

If the shares are being transferred to another person as a gift, for example, a transfer between husband and wife or a gift from a grandparent to a child or grandchild, then the word 'Gift' should be entered.

A transfer of shares may take place when an estate is being wound up or where there has been a change of trustees. In these cases, the word 'Nil' should be entered into the Consideration box.

The other occasion, although rare, is where the shares are being transferred to someone else in exchange for a payment, in which case the amount being paid should be entered.

Transfers and stamp duty

When shares are purchased they incur a charge to stamp duty that is added to the cost of the purchase and is shown separately on the contract note. The other term that is often seen is SDRT which stands for stamp duty reserve tax.

The essential difference between the two is that stamp duty is, in fact, the charge that is made on documents that transfer securities whilst SDRT is the tax that is charged on purchases of dematerialised shares.

Registrars are under a legal duty to ensure that transfers are properly completed, which includes ensuring that they are properly stamped or that an exemption certificate has been completed. Under the stamp duty regulations, certain types of transfer are exempt from stamp duty provided that the certificate on the reverse of the stock transfer form is completed.

The reverse of the stock transfer form is divided into two sections:

- a certificate that declares the transfer is exempt from stamp duty; and
- a certificate where the transfer is not exempt and is liable to stamp duty.

There may be other rare occasions where stamp duty is payable because the transfer is taking place in exchange for a payment. In those cases, the two exemption certificates are not relevant and stamp duty will be payable. This requires the transfer to be submitted to the Stamp Taxes Office for adjudication. Once the tax is agreed and paid, the transfer can be stamped and then submitted to the registrar.

In most scenarios, the transfer that is taking place is likely to be exempt from stamp duty and it is necessary to determine which of the exemptions are being claimed so that the form can be correctly completed and executed.

The form of certificate provides for 11 categories which can qualify as being exempt from stamp duty. It is necessary to select which category applies and state the letter assigned to it in the declaration.

The descriptions are technically worded and it can sometimes be difficult to determine which the correct one to select is. It is better therefore to view these as a series of groupings as follows:

- trusts and estates;
- gifts;
- divorce settlement;
- company liquidation;
- specialist property scenarios.

There is a range of categories available that can be grouped under the heading of trusts and estates. There is only one that specifically deals with a change of trustees and the remainder can apply to both trusts and estates. See Table 2.1.

Table 2.1 Stamp duty certificate – change of trustees

Code	Description	Use where
A	The vesting of property subject to a trust in the trustees of the trust on the appointment of a new trustee, or in the continuing trustees on the retirement of a trust	Any change to the named trustee
B	The conveyance or transfer of property the subject of a specific devise or legacy to the beneficiary named in the will (or his nominee)	A transfer arising from a specific instruction in a will
C	The conveyance or transfer of property which forms part of an intestate's estate to the person entitled on intestacy (or his nominee)	A transfer to the person entitled where someone has died without leaving a will
D	The appropriation of property within section 84(4) of the Finance Act 1985 (death: appropriation in satisfaction of a general legacy of money) or section 84(5) or (7) of the Act (death: appropriation in satisfaction of any interest of surviving spouse and in Scotland also of any interest of issue)	A transfer representing a sum of money left specifically to a beneficiary
E	The conveyance or transfer of property which forms part of the residuary estate of a testator to a beneficiary (or his nominee) entitled solely by virtue of his entitlement under the will	A transfer of the remaining assets in an estate after payment of debts, expenses and legacies
F	The conveyance or transfer of property out of a settlement in or towards satisfaction of a beneficiary's interest, not being an interest acquired for money or money's worth, being conveyance or transfer constituting a distribution of property in accordance with the provisions of the settlement	A transfer from a trust to a beneficiary where the trust was set up under a will
M	The conveyance or transfer of property by an instrument within section 84(1) of the Finance Act 1985 (death: varying disposition)	A transfer arising where a will has been changed

Table 2.2   Stamp duty certificate – gifts

Code	Description	Use where
G	The conveyance or transfer of property on and in consideration only of marriage to a party to the marriage (or his nominee) or to trustees to be held on the terms of a settlement made in consideration only of the marriage	Used for gifts made on marriage but is only exempt if marriage actually takes place
L	The conveyance or transfer of property operating as a voluntary disposition inter vivos for no consideration in money or money's worth nor any consideration referred to in section 57 of the Stamp Act 1891 (conveyance in consideration of a debt etc.)	Used where there is a gift without any payment being received in return

There are two categories that relate to gifts. The most common one that will be used is category L which is used when gifts are made out of investment accounts. See Table 2.2.

There is one category – H – that is used only for transfers in connection with a divorce. The remaining categories deal with company liquidations and specialist property transactions that are unlikely to be encountered.

2.12 DEATH OF A CLIENT

The other significant occasion when an account will close will be on the death of a client.

When a client dies, it often presents difficulties due to the lengthy processes involved in obtaining probate and so this section provides an overview of what needs to take place to obtain a grant of probate and deal with an investment account.

Process overview

An investment firm will be involved in a number of activities and processes when a client dies and has an investment account.

These can be conveniently grouped into a number of phases that represent the occasions when a firm will potentially become involved. They are:

- advice of death;
- valuation of assets;
- probate application;
- registering the grant;
- distribution instructions.

We will consider what takes place at each stage and the implications that may have for the investment administration of the late client's account.

Advice of death

When a client opens an investment account they enter into an agreement with the firm to manage or administer their investments. As part of the account opening process they will identify the client and therefore the firm will be able to confirm that any instructions that are received are legitimately from the client.

When the client dies that authority ceases and the firm will need to know that any subsequent person that they deal with is legally authorised to give them instructions. All financial institutions need to have some certainty that they are able to take an instruction from someone else; otherwise they are open to the risk of being liable if they were to pay the funds to the wrong person. This is the purpose behind obtaining a grant of probate.

A grant of probate is a court document that confirms the appointment of an executor or administrator. Any financial institution is therefore able to accept the instructions of the executor or administrator to deal with the deceased's assets.

An executor is an individual who is named in the will and given authority to administer the estate in accordance with the instructions that the will contains. An administrator is the person who is appointed to administer the estate when someone dies without leaving a valid will. This is known as dying intestate.

There will be occasions where an executor is appointed by a will and for whatever reason is unable or unwilling to act. The person who will be appointed in that scenario is also known as the administrator.

The process starts when an advice of death is received. A copy of the death certificate should be requested and be held with the client records.

If the account was held in joint names, such as an investment account in the name of a husband and wife, then the action that is needed is straightforward as the assets will pass automatically to the survivor.

The firm can therefore take instructions from the survivor as to what they wish to do with the investment account and action them appropriately. If the survivor decides to retain the investment account, then the account can be switched into a single name. The firm should, however, consider revaluing the assets as the base cost for capital gains tax purposes will need to be amended to reflect the half share that was acquired at the date of death.

In any other case, the firm's systems will need to be amended to record the death and to cancel any standing instructions they have to make payments or issue reports. The firm will also need to ascertain who is to act as the executor or administrator.

The firm will need to acknowledge receipt of the death certificate and confirm that they will need to have sight of the grant of probate before they can accept any instructions.

It is important to note that at this stage the authority of the firm to take action under any agreement has ended. This does not mean, however, that they cannot do anything as they have a fiduciary duty to take appropriate action to protect the assets.

In practice, this means the firm should continue to administer the portfolio but not pay away any funds as they have no authorisation. Corporate actions may arise and they will need to consult with the executors or administrators on the action to be taken. In the event that they cannot receive any instructions, then they should take the action that is most consistent with protecting the asset.

A firm may decide to go further but if it does so, it should assess the risk it poses. If it has a longstanding relationship with the late client and family, then it may well be very appropriate to do so.

Valuation of assets

At this stage, the firm will also need to provide details of the assets they hold to the executors.

The executors are required to establish what the assets and liabilities of the estate are. This is so that they can take control of the assets and take action if necessary to protect them until they can obtain probate. They are also required to value the assets and liabilities of the estate so that they can disclose these as part of the application for a grant of probate.

The firm will therefore need to provide details of the following assets and liabilities as at the date of death:

- details of all investment held;
- the capital cash held;

- any income that has been received and not paid over;
- the amount of charges that have accrued to the date of death but have not yet been debited.

The firm is therefore providing a comprehensive balance sheet to the executors of the value of all assets and accrued liabilities as at the date of death.

When the firm provides details of the quoted investments it holds, it is likely to do so by providing a valuation. The prices that are used for a valuation will normally be mid-market prices, but for probate purposes, however, the investments need to be valued at quarter up.

To arrive at a quarter-up valuation involves taking the closing bid and offer prices at the close of business on the day the investor died and adding one-quarter of the difference between the two to the bid price, that is the lower of the two prices. To the value of each holding needs to be added the value of any accrued interest on any bonds and the mount of any prospective dividend for any shares quoted ex-dividend.

The executors will need to obtain what is known as a probate valuation of the quoted investments to be able to apply for probate. They may obtain this from the firm if they have the systems functionality to produce it or from a specialist provider.

Probate application

Once the executors have been able to gather sufficient information about the assets and liabilities of the estate, they will be in a position to apply for a grant of probate.

The application for probate involves two key elements. It is an application to the court to obtain the grant which is the legal document that confirms the authority of the executor to proceed to deal with the assets, settle the liabilities and expenses and then distribute the estate. It must also be accompanied by a submission to HM Revenue & Customs of the value of the estate and a payment of at least a proportion of any inheritance tax due.

The probate submission is required to include an inheritance tax (IHT) return that sets out the value of the estate along with a calculation of the total amount of inheritance tax that is due. A proportion of this has to be paid at the time of the application otherwise the grant will not be forthcoming.

This can place the executors in a quandary. They need funds to be able to pay the IHT that is due when they apply for the grant, yet they cannot give instructions to realise assets and raise the funds until they have the grant.

The executors are therefore likely to have to arrange an overdraft to fund the payment. This can be expensive and the firm may be approached to raise funds and make them available instead. Whether they will do so, is a matter for each firm but where a firm has a close relationship with the family, it is not unusual for it to raise funds and provide the executors with a cheque payable to HM Revenue & Customs.

Registering the grant

The whole process of gathering sufficient information to apply for a grant and then waiting for the grant to be issued is both lengthy and time consuming. The timescales are impossible to estimate as it depends upon the range of assets held by the deceased and the efficiency with which the executor can obtain and deal with the information. It is possible to obtain a grant within six weeks but it can equally take months.

When the grant is issued, it will be either a grant of probate if the executor has applied or a grant of letters of administration. Both are court-sealed documents authorising the executor or administrator to act. As well as the original grant, the court will issue court-sealed copies that can be used to send to financial institutions to speed up the process.

The executors should lodge a copy of the grant with the firm. Once it receives it, a copy should be taken for its records and the firm is then able to accept instructions on what to do with the assets.

Distribution instructions

It will be up to the executors to determine what action they wish to take with the assets held in the investment account.

Their obligation is to collect the assets, settle debts and expenses, pay legacies and then account for the remainder to the residuary beneficiaries. They will therefore need to raise cash to fund this, but it may also need to arrange for certain investments to be transferred if they have been left as a specific bequest under the will. Once all debts, expenses and legacies have been settled it is normal to consult the residuary beneficiaries about whether they wish to have their share of any remaining investments transferred to them or sold.

A firm may therefore receive a combination of instructions that it will need to action ranging from selling an investment to transferring it to multiple beneficiaries.

Chapter

3

....

TRADING

3.1 INTRODUCTION

The concept of a stock market has been around for hundreds of years and there are examples of their early development across Europe, including the trading of government debt by brokers in twelfth-century France.

The first official stock exchange is, however, recognised as being the Amsterdam Stock Exchange which was established in 1602. At the time, the Dutch government needed to reorganise its economy and came up with the novel idea of allowing shares to be issued to the public. The first stocks traded were shares in the Dutch East India Company which enabled the company to raise finance from the general public and become perhaps the first multinational.

By the early 1700s there were fully operational stock exchanges in France and England. The London Stock Exchange can trace its history back to the coffee houses of seventeenth-century London, from which the Exchange quickly grew to become the City's most important financial institution and the driver of the British industrial revolution.

The concept of publicly held equity spread across Europe and into the US where the forerunner of the New York Stock Exchange was established in 1792.

Stock exchanges are now regarded as an essential feature of modern economic systems and they operate in virtually every country around the world.

3.2 STOCK MARKET DEVELOPMENTS

The last 10 years have seen major activity in the industry with consolidation of trading and post-trading infrastructures taking place at an increasing pace. Examples of this include the merger of the French, Belgian and Portuguese exchanges to form Euronext and the merger of Archipelago and the New York Stock Exchange.

The rationale for this consolidation is to increase liquidity as trading naturally flows to those exchanges that have the most liquidity.

Whilst historically consolidation has taken place at a national level, a number of significant mergers and alliances have also taken place at a pan-European level. At the time of writing, this process is developing to a trans-continental level as can be seen with the New York Stock Exchange's plans to merge with Euronext, whilst at the same time creating an alliance with the Tokyo Stock Exchange.

A number of factors are driving both changes and the integration of capital markets in Europe:

- The scale of the demand for capital has exceeded the capability of national markets to service this, leading investment banks to become increasingly international in their activities.
- IT developments have removed the need for any physical trading floor and trading platforms are increasingly being accessed cross-border.

- Recognition of the impact of trading costs on portfolio performance is creating the demand to reduce trading costs which tends to increase and concentrate liquidity into a smaller number of venues.
- EU plans to create a single market in financial services and directives such as the Markets in Financial Instruments Directive (MiFID) are creating the opportunity for both change and further consolidation.

How European markets will develop is still uncertain but it is clear that further structural changes are likely. It remains to be seen whether the current trend will lead to the consolidation of trading into one or two major exchanges that are pan-European.

Whilst consolidation of exchanges should produce deeper pools of liquidity, it does not necessarily follow that this will reduce the implicit costs of trading. Reduced competition among providers can lead to exchanges using their monopoly position to increase their margins rather than reducing trading costs.

This has led a number of leading investment banks to use the opportunity MiFID provides for alternative trading systems, to look at the development of a user-owned trading platform as is proposed under the banner of Project Turquoise.

It is impossible to forecast what the European market infrastructure will look like in a few years' time, other than to be certain that a period of major change is underway.

3.3 EQUITY TRADING

Introduction

There is a variety of venues where an investor can execute a trade including traditional stock exchanges and alternative trading systems. In this section, we look at the features of the main types of trading and at how trade takes place in both order-driven and quote-driven markets.

Methods of trading

There are a range of methods that can be used to trade equities and which method is used will depend on the firm undertaking the trading or the stocks involved.

The main types of trading are:

- Trading using the dealing platforms of traditional regulated exchanges, such as the London Stock Exchange's SETS system.
- Using an alternative trading system or electronic communications networks (ECN) such as virt-x.
- Over-the-counter trading (OTC), where the trade is negotiated directly between two counterparties.
- Internalising orders where an investment bank will take its customer orders and trade these on its own book rather than with an external counterparty.

Each of these is considered more fully in the following sections.

Exchange trading

A stock exchange is the traditional route by which most transactions have been carried out.

Until the development of modern communications methods, buyers and sellers needed to congregate in one place to be able to trade. The role of the exchange was to bring them together and provide an infrastructure of rules and regulations to ensure that trades were executed fairly and settled without delay.

The stock exchanges themselves would have historically been responsible for setting their own rules and regulating the activity of their members to ensure appropriate standards of market behaviour were observed. In most markets now, however, this is usually done under the scrutiny of an external authority such as the Financial Services Authority (FSA) in the UK or the Securities and Exchange Commission (SEC) in the US.

Apart from the listing of new shares, the main business activity of an exchange is the secondary trading of listed shares. Exchanges generate their trading income by charging firms for being a member, for connecting to their dealing systems and for orders executed.

An exchange will create a market in shares and there are two main types known as order-driven markets and quote-driven markets. They can exist in physical form such as with the New York Stock Exchange but more usually these days, the market is a virtual one where its participants are connected electronically to a dealing platform.

Order-driven markets

An order-driven market is also known as an auction market. This method of operation used to require market participants who wished to buy and sell to congregate in one place where they could agree the prices at which they were willing to execute their trades.

Traditionally, this took place at a single physical location within the stock exchange, the floor of the exchange. Buy and sell orders were matched by intermediaries within the exchange giving rise to a series of competitive prices for the shares listed on the exchange.

This way of trading is the style that is still in use at the New York Stock Exchange and which has been featured in many TV programmes and films. Each stock that is listed on the exchange is traded from a specific location on the exchange floor. Exchange members who are interested in buying and selling a particular stock on behalf of investors will gather around the appropriate post where the stock is traded. A specialist broker then acts as an auctioneer and so facilitates bringing buyers and sellers together. As part of its merger with Euronext, the New York Stock Exchange intends to move away from trading this way and utilise Euronext's electronic dealing platform.

Few order-driven markets now meet physically in one place, however, and instead they are generally managed electronically. Many stock exchanges use a call auction at the opening of a day's trading and then use an electronic limit order book to execute trades. The computer system controlling the electronic order book matches buy and sell orders and executes them immediately where possible or holds them until a suitable matching order is entered.

The London Stock Exchange SETS system is an example of an order-driven market and electronic order books also operate at Euronext and the Tokyo Stock Exchange.

Quote-driven markets

In a quote-driven market, firms will specialise in making a market in certain securities, that is they will buy and sell securities in response to demand from investors. The firms that undertake this type of trading are known in the UK as market makers and as dealers elsewhere.

Under this method of trading, the market maker is required to quote two-way prices for the securities it is making a market in. The price charged to buyers is known as the ask price, while the price offered to sellers is known as the bid price.

Market makers are required to make two-way prices at all times and be prepared to deal at that price for all trades up to a certain amount of stock, known as normal market size or NMS. In this way market makers provide liquidity by being willing to buy and sell securities for their own account at all times.

The market maker makes its profit from the difference between what it buys at and what it sells at, that is from managing its investment book.

The advantage of this method of dealing is that the investor is not required to wait for a seller of that security to come along before a transaction can occur. Instead, the trade is executed immediately with the market maker. There will also usually be more than one market maker in any one stock, in order to ensure that competitive prices are quoted.

The NASDAQ stock exchange is perhaps the best known example of a quote-driven market.

Alternative trading systems

The alternative to traditional exchanges is electronic communication networks (ECNs), which are computer systems that enable the trading of securities outside of a regular exchange.

A subscriber to an ECN will enter limit orders and the system will display these orders for other subscribers to view and then attempt to match them. Generally, the buyer and seller are anonymous, with the trade execution reports listing the ECN as the counterparty.

ECNs originated in the US and were created as a result of a class-action lawsuit that alleged that market makers at NASDAQ set and maintained wide spreads as part of an industry-wide conspiracy. The litigation was eventually settled for $1 billion, which was the largest antitrust settlement at that time.

Since then they have flourished to the point that by May 2004 over half of the trading on NASDAQ was handled by ECNs. The increased competition they have brought about has resulted in lower transaction costs.

ECNs have flourished where the main method of dealing is quote driven as these are relatively less efficient than order-driven markets. The growth of these in Europe has been much slower as European exchanges moved earlier to order-driven trading systems which drove trading costs down and improved their efficiency.

The major ECNs have since been acquired by either NASDAQ or the New York Stock Exchange. Another example of an ECN, however, is Bloomberg's TradeBook.

OTC trading

Over- the-counter (OTC) trading refers to a trade that is executed privately between two parties rather than through the dealing platform of a recognised stock exchange.

It would typically involve two dealers trading directly between themselves using either the telephone or electronic messaging. Its use tends to be limited to trades that are too large to be traded without materially affecting the share price and where the price and quantity need to be negotiated between the parties.

Internalising orders

The last type of trading method is internalisation.

This is where a firm will match the orders of two of its clients using its internal network rather than trading these through an exchange's trading platform. It also refers to the scenario where a firm will take its customer orders and execute them against its own trading book.

Where a firm internalises orders in this way, it will ensure that it has price improvement algorithms built into its trading systems so that its clients can obtain best execution.

Mechanics of trading

Having looked at the main methods of trading, we can now turn to how trades take place in practice in order-driven and quote-driven markets.

An investor who wishes to place an order to buy or sell a stock will typically place that order through a broker, who will then execute the trades on their behalf. To do that, the broker will seek another trader who is willing to buy or sell as appropriate and be the counterparty to the trade. In most cases, there will be more than one trader willing to trade in that line of stock and the broker will seek the one with the most advantageous price for its client.

How the trade is executed in practice will depend upon whether the broker undertakes the trade in an order-driven or quote-driven market.

Quote-driven trading

In a quote-driven market, the broker will approach the market makers who specialise in making a market in the shares that the client wishes to either buy or sell.

Figure 3.1 shows an example of how a client order to buy shares might operate in a quote-driven market.

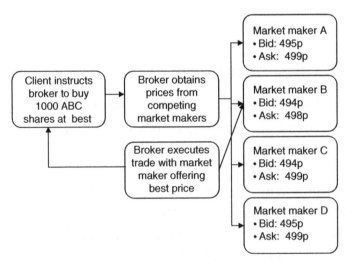

Figure 3.1   Trade in a quote-driven market

Let's assume that the client has given his broker an order to buy 1000 ABC Co Ltd shares at best; that is at the best price available in the market at the time the broker executes the trade.

The broker will identify the market makers who make a market in that stock and obtain quotes from them. The quotes will be in the form of a spread where the bid price is the one that the market maker will buy shares and the ask price, the one where they will sell shares.

The prices the market makers quote will be driven by competition between each of the market makers so the difference between their price quotes will be small and on many occasions, their prices will be identical. What will make their prices different is the view they take on the stock, the demand they anticipate and the position of their book, that is whether they wish to add to their existing holding or reduce it.

The broker is acting as agent for the client and is obliged to seek the best price for the client. As the order is to buy shares for the client, then the broker will trade with market maker B as they have the most competitive price at 498p. Having executed the trade, the broker will then issue a confirmation or contract note to the client.

Figure 3.1 can also be used to look at what would happen if the client had wished to sell instead of buy. In this scenario, the broker would be looking at the bid prices offered by each market maker. Market makers B and C are both offering the best quote at 494p and the broker could trade with one or the other. From the client's point of view it would be immaterial who the broker traded with and make no difference to achieving best execution.

To obtain the quotes and execute trades with the market maker, the broker could contact each directly but is more likely to use a stock-market dealing platform that supports quote-driven trading. An example is the London Stock Exchange's SEAQ system which shows each market maker's quote and which has a yellow strip that displays the best prices and the market makers offering them.

Order book trading

In an order-driven market, the mechanics of trading will differ as the client's order will be entered into an order book and traded against other orders that have been posted there.

Figure 3.2 shows an example of how the same type of client order to buy shares might operate in an order-driven market.

Again, let's assume that the client has given his broker an order to buy 1000 ABC Co Ltd shares and that this time the client instructs that it is a market order. A market order is one that is to be executed immediately against the best price that the market has to offer.

Let's also assume that the broker chooses to use the London Stock Exchange's electronic trading platform SETS

ABC Co Ltd		ABC			P Close	496	GBX
NMS	100,000		Segment	FT10		ISIN	GB012345678
						TVol	5.5m
Last	495½	AT		at 10.00	Vol	2500	
Prev	495½	495AT		495	495	495	
Trade Hi	496	Open		496	Current	495½	−0.01%
Trade Lo	494	VWAP		495	Current Hi	495½	−0.01%
Total Vol	1.75m	SETS Vol		1.25m	Current Lo	495	−0.02%
	TVol	189,000	Base		495	TVol	
BUY	MOVol					MOVol	SELL
1		5,000		495 - 496		5,000	2
495	5,000	5,000	495	496	5,000	5,000	496
494.8	15,000	10,000	494.75	496.25	10,000	15,000	496.2
494.7	25,000	10,000	494.50	496.50	10,000	25,000	496.3
494.5	50,000	25,000	494.25	496.75	25,000	50,000	496.5
494.2	100,000	50,000	494	497	50,000	100,000	496.8

Figure 3.2 SETS order book *Source:* London Stock Exchange

to execute the trade. SETS stands for Stock Exchange Trading System and is an electronic order book where trades are input and then automatically executed against other corresponding orders.

The process this time does not involve the broker approaching other market counterparties or market makers direct. Instead the broker will input the trade into SETS.

Before the broker inputs the trade, the SETS order book looks as shown in Figure 3.2.

A SETS display contains a lot of data to enable trading decisions to be made. To understand how a trade using an electronic order book operates, we need to be aware of just some of the data that is shown.

The highlighted strip in the middle of the screen shows the number of buy and sell orders at the best price. It is showing that the best buy order is someone who is prepared to pay 495p for 5000 shares and that the two sale orders with the best price are from parties who are prepared to sell 5000 shares at 496p. The spread is also shown on the highlighted strip at 495–496. These are limit orders as are the trades listed below them.

When a broker inputs a market order it will execute immediately against the best-priced limit orders outstanding on the order book on the opposite side of the market. So a buy market order will execute against the limit orders with the lowest ask prices, and a sell market order will execute against the limit orders with the highest bid prices.

So, staying with our example, if the broker now inputs a market order to buy 1000 ABC Co Ltd shares, it will immediately execute against the best available price, that is the limit order to sell 5000 shares at 496p. The remaining 4000 shares will remain on the order book for possible execution against later orders.

The prices used in both examples are meant for illustration only and do not necessarily indicate that trading via an electronic order book is necessarily better than through a quote-driven system. Which one will generate the best result will depend upon the volume of trading in a stock and the number of potential counterparties.

According to the London Stock Exchange, however, the introduction of SETS and electronic order book trading has resulted in a narrowing of spreads. This is an experience that has been seen in other markets, hence the popularity of electronic order books.

Types of order

In the previous example, we referred to the order being at best, that is at the best price available in the market at the time the broker executes the trade.

Unsurprisingly, this is not the only type of order that can be given and investors can choose from a range of order types depending upon what they are trying to achieve.

The most common types of order are detailed below.

- *Market order* – This is a simple buy or sell order to be executed immediately at any price the market will offer. Market orders execute immediately against the best-priced limit orders outstanding on the order book on the opposite side of the market: a buy market order will execute against the limit orders with the lowest ask prices, and a sell market order will execute against the limit orders with the highest bid prices.
- *Limit order* – A limit order involves an investor specifying the prices at which he is willing to buy or sell a security. The trade is then executed when the market price falls to the limit price on a limit-buy order, and conversely when it rises to the limit price on a limit-sell order. Even limit orders that are relatively far from the current market price can add liquidity to the market.

- *Stop-sell order* – This is a limit order designed to prevent losses and requires that the stock is sold when its price falls below the stipulated level.
- *At-best order* – These are orders with specified size but no prices quoted, and are to be traded at the best possible price.
- *Iceberg order* – These are large limit orders where the order is divided into several tranches, each of which enters the central order book once the previous tranche has been executed. These are also called hidden orders, since the overall size of the order is not visible to other market participants.
- *Fill-and-kill order* – These are also called execute and eliminate orders. The size and limit price are specified. They are meant to be executed fully or partially but immediately, the remaining unexecuted part is then discarded. They are essentially limit orders with limited time validity.
- *Fill-or-kill order* – This is an order with a specified size; price is optional. It is to be executed fully or rejected.

3.4 BOND TRADING

Introduction

Trading in bond markets differs from what is seen in the equity markets. The value of the trades undertaken in any day can be significantly larger than the trading that takes place in equities but the volume tends to be much lower.

This reflects the fact that the main investors in bonds are institutional investors who will often be long-term holders, hence the relative lower volume of trading that takes place.

UK government bond trading

The gilt market also operates and is organised differently than the equity markets.

Responsibility for issuing new gilts lies with the Debt Management Office (DMO). The DMO is an executive agency of the Treasury which is responsible for organising the issue of all new UK government securities and maintaining an oversight of subsequent trading to ensure that the secondary market operates effectively.

Gilts are traded on the London Stock Exchange by what is known as a primary dealing system. The primary dealers are known as gilt edged market makers (GEMMs), who have to be both authorised by the DMO and be a member of the London Stock Exchange.

There are 16 firms recognised as GEMMs, who in return for certain privileges when gilts are issued, are required to make a market in gilts. This requires them to quote effective two-way prices to customers on demand and in all market conditions so that market liquidity is provided for customers wishing to trade.

There are also gilt inter-dealer brokers whose role is solely to act as an agent between market makers. When one market maker trades with another market maker, it can use an inter-dealer broker to keep the trade anonymous so that it does not have to reveal its trading position. They will act as an agent for the market maker, but settle the transaction as if it were a principal, in order to preserve the anonymity of the market maker. They are not allowed to take principal positions, and are only allowed to act as a broker between GEMMs.

Other London Stock Exchange members are also permitted to buy and sell gilts and can do so either as a principal or as a broker or agent. Where they act as a broker, they are bound by the best execution rules.

Trading in the gilt market is undertaken by a combination of OTC trading and electronic platforms. The main electronic platforms are TradeWeb and Bloomberg's BBT system, while retail trades are often executed through Bondscape. Trade reporting is undertaken on the London Stock Exchange.

Corporate bond trading

Unsurprisingly perhaps, there is a significant difference in how corporate bonds are traded compared to other instruments, primarily due to the frequency of trading in individual bonds.

Corporate bonds tend to attract a specific type of investor, namely pension funds and insurance companies who wish to hold bonds to meet long-term liabilities.

They are typically therefore buy and hold investors, which severely limits secondary market trading in many bonds.

This is borne out by recent research undertaken by the Centre for Economic Policy Research. It showed that the average number of trades per bond is slightly above three per day for euro-denominated bonds and just two per day for sterling-denominated bonds.

The market in corporate bonds is an over-the-counter market with trades negotiated individually between the parties.

It operates by the investor contacting a dealer directly or a broker who will direct them to interested counterparties. So, for example, an institutional investor who wishes to trade would contact one or several dealers and give details of the bond and quantity he wishes to trade. The dealers will make price offers for the whole trade and the institutional investor will trade with the best offer.

The dealer does not charge commission for the trade and instead this is factored into their pricing. After trading, the dealer often unwinds at least part of his inventory on the inter-dealer market.

Dealers will also contact investors and advise them of trading opportunities to see if they are interested in trading. As a result, there is regular contact between investors and dealers who will have good information about which bonds are easier to trade at a given point and who is interested in trading them. It is these relationships which are key to the efficient operation of the market.

The traditional method of dealing in the bond market has been by telephone which has helped to facilitate and foster relationships between dealers and investors.

Electronic communication now complements this with brokers, dealers and investors able to communicate through electronic messaging and through Bloomberg.

The dominant electronic trading platform for corporate bonds is MarketAxess. It is used by large institutional investors and has around 20 dealers providing quotes. The system is similar to the telephone method described above, in that it involves investors entering the amount and quantity of the bond they wish to buy or sell who then receive quotes from dealers. The quotes remain firm for about three minutes and the investor can accept a quote by clicking on it.

There are alternative systems as well, such as the fixed income trading capability offered by Bloomberg and Reuters.

Retail bond trading

Individual retail investors in the UK do not often hold bonds directly; instead they are more likely to hold these through a collective investment scheme such as a bond fund or a pension fund. This is in contrast to some countries in Europe, such as Italy and Germany, where individual direct holdings of bonds can be quite high.

Where an individual investor does hold bonds directly, they will usually trade these through a broker who will deal direct with a market maker specialising in retail bond trading.

Some market makers specialize in supplying liquidity at the retail end of the market and aim to keep a balanced position. If they accumulate a large position in a bond, once it has reached a standard market size they unwind it by selling to other market makers. The process therefore looks as shown in Figure 3.3.

From an individual investor's viewpoint, trading in bonds is therefore little different to trading equities on a quote-driven market.

Electronic trading platforms have been developed for retail bond trades. The most notable is Bondscape which

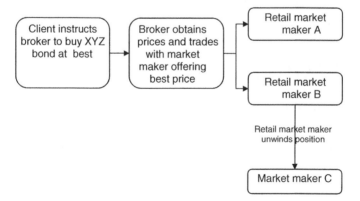

Figure 3.3 Retail bond trade

was developed as a joint venture between Barclays Capital and Winterfloods and was launched in 2001.

It is a screen-based dealing system that is available to brokers and wealth managers and which specialises in providing dealing facilities in retail size deals in UK government stock and a selection of corporate bonds.

Bondscape provides access to more than 400 instruments from UK gilts and European government bonds, to sterling, euro and dollar credit bonds as well as retail notes. The instruments quoted include AAA rated bonds from the World Bank and European Investment Bank and corporate bonds from entities ranging from the main UK clearing banks to Coca-Cola and General Electric.

It is an attractive platform for retail size deals as the minimum trading size is simply the minimum deliverable amount for each instrument and the maximum is 250,000 nominal for core instruments and 100,000 nominal for all others. It offers competitive pricing from Barclays Capital, Winterfloods and HSBC with a yellow strip on-screen indicating the most competitive price.

3.5 REGULATION

When a broker takes an order from a client they have a duty to obtain the best price possible for the deal taking into account its size and where it can be dealt.

The obligation to obtain the best price for the client is known as best execution and it arises from the fiduciary duty that the broker owes to its client. It is fundamental to the relationship between the broker and the client and so is, unsurprisingly, the subject matter of regulation by the FSA.

MiFID and changes to best execution

The rules surrounding best execution are due to change as a result of the Markets in Financial Instruments Directive (MiFID).

The directive aims to bring about a single conduct of business rulebook across Europe and one of the areas where it seeks to have a common approach is the subject of what constitutes best execution.

The new rules are significantly different than UK investment firms have been used to in the past and will become effective from November 2007.

Best execution under MiFID

The directive contains an express article setting out the obligation on firms to execute orders on terms that are most favourable to the client.

It requires firms to act honestly, fairly and professionally when dealing for clients, in other words to act in their best interests. Specifically it requires investment firms when executing a client order to take all reasonable steps to obtain the best possible result for the client. The factors that a firm are required to take into consideration include:

- price;
- costs of dealing;
- speed of execution;
- certainty of settlement;
- size and nature of the order.

The change that MiFID brings about is to move from the existing rules where best execution can be shown to have been achieved by comparing only the price that the trade was dealt at with comparable trades taking place at the same time.

In its place, it brings a much broader requirement to consider a range of other factors. For example, it requires firms to consider other areas such as whether settlement will take place on the intended settlement date, which might incur additional costs or prevent the client being able to trade again as early as they would wish.

Execution policy

As well as setting out the considerations that a firm must take into account when executing an order for a client, MiFID also requires firms to have an order execution policy.

This policy has to cover all of the instrument types under MiFID and requires a firm to take a three-step approach to designing and implementing its execution policy:

- It needs to assess the factors that will affect achieving best execution for the customers it deals with.
- It then needs to determine what venues are available to execute the trade and achieve the best result for the client.
- Client orders should then be routed to the appropriate venue taking into account the factors it assessed as important in achieving best execution.

This is not a one-off requirement, however. MiFID requires that firms must also regularly consider other execution venues and if a new one is identified it must consider including it. Unless it can show a sound reason such as the cost would be unreasonable for the firm, then the firm has a duty to use the execution venue.

This requirement applies to all firms with a best execution responsibility to their clients, no matter where they are placed in the execution chain.

Firms also have a requirement to disclose their approach to clients.

Application to different instruments

The instruments to which MiFID applies include the following:

- transferable securities;
- money market instruments;

- UCITS funds (a unit trust or OEIC that meets certain requirements);
- options, futures and other derivative contracts relating to securities, currencies, interest rates or yields;
- options, futures and other derivative contracts relating to commodities;
- credit derivatives;
- contracts for differences;
- options, futures, and other derivative contracts relating to underlyings such as climatic variables.

Best execution criteria

The obligation to achieve best execution will depend upon the type of client that the firm is executing the trade for.

As we saw earlier, MiFID will bring about new definitions of the types of client a firm will deal with. There will be three categories of client under MiFID:

- eligible counterparties;
- professional clients; and
- retail clients.

Where a firm is executing a trade for an eligible counterparty, there is no requirement on the firm to follow the new rules as the investors for whom they are trading will be experienced firms who do not require the same level of protections as less knowledgeable investors.

There will be two types of eligible counterparty, ones who are automatically treated as such and others who can agree to be treated the same. The ones who are automatically treated that way are the type of firms that you would expect, such as investment firms, investment funds, pension funds and national governments. The ones who may opt to be treated as eligible counterparties include large firms and professional clients.

The classification of professional clients includes any of the above plus a handful of others, such as institutional investors. Importantly, both professional clients and eligible counterparties may choose to opt down to a more protective client classification.

MiFID classifies investment managers as eligible counterparties. However, it is likely that many will request opt downs, in particular to avoid a mismatch between duties they will owe to their clients and the duties they are owed by firms they deal with, especially as regard best execution.

The achievement of best execution for a professional client will need to take into account the factors mentioned earlier, namely price, costs, speed, likelihood of execution and settlement, and the size and nature of the order.

For retail clients there is a slightly different approach. Retail clients are said to have achieved best execution when they have received the best price net of expenses. This recognises that the order size for a retail client will mean that the net price should usually be the most important factor. The other factors can still play a role but in a limited manner.

In practice, the result of these requirements will force firms to reconsider where and how they place their orders. Where a firm normally trades on its own account when dealing for clients but has access to a better price from a third party, then it will be obliged to trade with that third party.

If a firm normally subcontracts its dealing to a third party, it will be faced with the issue that it must assess all execution venues not just the third party, making it very difficult to continue with that policy.

And if a firm normally executes retail orders internally using a price improvement algorithm, it will need access to multiple price sources and the ability to consolidate those prices to achieve and manage best execution.

Chapter

4

....

SETTLEMENT

4.1 INTRODUCTION

Trading of securities involves the transfer of ownership from the seller to the buyer and the exchange of cash to pay for the purchase. Clearing and settlement are the processes that allow these transfers to take place efficiently and safely.

In this chapter, we start by looking at the fundamentals of settlement and then see how these fit in with the settlement process before moving on to how the settlement process operates in the UK and internationally.

4.2 FUNDAMENTALS OF SETTLEMENT

Introduction

Settlement refers to the process that takes place following execution of a trade whereby there is an exchange of securities for cash, the latter representing the cost of purchase of the securities.

For settlement to take place, the necessary legal formalities for the transfer of the securities needs to be undertaken. Traditionally that would have required completion of a stock transfer form and the physical delivery of the transfer form and the certificates to the purchaser. They would then arrange for these documents to be deposited with the company registrar in order that the purchaser's name could be recorded on the company share register. At some point during this process, a transfer of cash would take place using the banking system.

Most modern settlement systems have removed what was a long-winded and paper-intensive process and have replaced it with electronic transfer of title accompanied with a simultaneous exchange of cash.

Before looking at how settlement takes place in the UK and elsewhere, we will look in this section at the underlying rules for the transfer of title, consider the background to the development of modern settlement systems and then look at their key features.

Transfer of title

Share registers

Among the many records that a company has to maintain, company legislation requires it to maintain a register of its members or shareholders.

In the UK, this requirement is set out in Section 352, Companies Act 1985 which requires a company to keep a register, enter details of its members and maintain the share register. The company secretary has a duty to ensure compliance with legal requirements and that the register contains the following:

- shareholders' names;
- addresses;

- date of registration;
- date of cessation of membership;
- type, class and number of shares held;
- amount paid;
- amount and class of stock held;
- class to which the member belongs if no share capital but classes of membership.

The key point to note from this is that an investor only becomes a member of a company – a shareholder – when their name is entered on the register of members of that company.

Having become a shareholder, an investor has the right to transfer shares in a company when and to whoever they choose, subject only to any legal restrictions and any restrictions on transfer that might be contained in the articles of association of the company.

On the sale or transfer of shares, legal title to the shares will only pass when the company enters the transferee in its register of members.

Development of modern settlement systems

Settlement systems have developed considerably over the last 15 years driven initially by the impact of significant delays in settlement and later by the need to remove the risk that settlement failure would have both on individual firms and the market as a whole.

Traditional settlement

Before the introduction of electronic settlement systems, the settlement of a stock-market transaction would have involved the physical movement of paper.

An entry on the share register of a company was essential to establish legal ownership of a share. When a stock market trade took place, a stock broker would issue a contract note to its client along with a stock transfer form. The transfer form would be completed with the name and address of the client as recorded on the share certificate and the client would be asked to sign this and return it along with the share certificates representing the holding.

On settlement, the client's broker would pass this to the buying broker in exchange for payment of the cost of the purchase. The broker would then enter the name and address of the purchaser on the stock transfer form and lodge it with the company registrar.

The company registrar would inspect the stock transfer form to ensure that all legal formalities had been complied with. If they had, the transfer would go through a further process at the end of which, the purchaser would be recorded on the share register and a new share certificate issued.

The whole process could take six weeks or even longer before the legal title to the holding was recorded in the purchaser's name.

The lengthy delays that were in-built into the system were not the only problems. As the whole process involved paper instruments there were the attendant risks of lost certificates and fraud, as well as the processing delays that could arise in times of heavy trading volumes.

The United States, as the world's largest stock market, was the first to experience the impact that this physical settlement process could cause. In the 1970s the markets experienced what became known as 'the paper crunch' as settlement delays threatened to disrupt the operations of the securities markets.

At that time, the New York Stock Exchange was handling around 10 to 12 million trades daily and brokers were buried in paperwork. The crisis was so severe that, in order to help reduce the backlog, the exchanges closed every Wednesday and shortened trading hours on other days.

This led to the formation of the Depositary Trust Company where all physical share certificates were held or immobilised and where changes of ownership took place by entries in their accounting records or book entry.

Big Bang and the stock-market crash of 1987

In the UK, it was not until the 1980s that the weakness of paper-based settlement was exposed.

The 1980s saw two major developments, a programme of privatisation of nationalised industries and the Big Bang changes to the stock market, which combined, led to an explosion in the volume of trades. Bearing in mind the long-winded and inefficient settlement process that was in place, it was, perhaps unsurprisingly, accompanied by a level of settlement delays that became significant.

What then compounded the problem even further was the stock-market crash of 1987. That was the largest one-day stock-market crash in recent history which saw the Dow Jones Industrial Average fall by 22.6% wiping US$500 billion from share values. Markets in every country followed suit and collapsed in a similar fashion.

When individual investors heard that a massive stock-market crash was in effect, many tried to limit their losses by selling their holdings but found that the inherent weaknesses in the settlement process either prevented them from selling or left them exposed to a real risk of loss due to the potential bankruptcy of market participants.

In the wake of the crash, markets around the world were put on restricted trading to try and find time to sort out the backlog of orders that required settlement. The central banks had to pump liquidity into the system to prevent further falls and the systemic risk that failure of one market counterparty could have created a domino effect.

The shock of the crash and the recognition of the systemic risks it posed became the catalyst for the development of today's electronic settlement systems.

G30 recommendations

The Group of Thirty (G30) is a global industry working group which has representatives from financial services companies, regulators, central banks, academics and a range of other industry bodies.

In order to provide guidance on the development of settlement systems, they issued recommendations in 1989 on the principles and standards that markets should look to adopt.

One of their principal recommendations was that stock exchanges and regulators should work with issuers and market participants to phase out physical certificates without delay.

Some of their key recommendations were:

- Eliminate paper and automate communication, data capture and enrichment.
- Harmonise messaging standards and communication protocols.
- Develop and implement reference data standards.
- Synchronise timing between different clearing and settlement systems and associated payment and foreign-exchange systems.

- Automate and standardise institutional trade matching.
- Expand the use of central counterparties.
- Permit securities lending and borrowing to expedite settlement.
- Automate and standardise asset servicing processes, including corporate actions, tax relief arrangements and restrictions on foreign ownerships.

These recommendations and ones they have subsequently issued have set the standards by which settlement systems have been developed and are responsible for the significant reduction in risk that has taken place.

Key features of settlement systems

Introduction

Phasing out the use of physical share certificates was a key step in reducing the risks of traditional settlement systems and required a move to electronic record keeping and transfer of ownership.

In the following sections, we will look at some of the key features of modern settlement systems.

Central Securities Depositary

A robust settlement system requires a single entity to be responsible for maintaining shareholder records and for effecting transfers. This organisation is known as a Central Securities Depositary or CSD.

A CSD is responsible for holding securities in either certificated or uncertificated form and for arranging transfers of stock. The largest CSD in the world is the Depositary Trust & Clearing Corporation which is the CSD for the US market. It has custody of over US$25 trillion of bonds and shares and settles trades worth more than US$1000 billion every year.

International Central Securities Depositaries (ICSD) settle trades in international securities. Two of the best known are Clearstream and EuroClear, which are responsible for clearing and settling cross-border trades in bonds, equities and investment funds.

Book-entry transfers

Using electronic systems to record share ownership and transfers involves making entries in accounting records and so is known as book-entry transfer. This transition from physical to book entry has commonly taken place in two phases.

First, the physical share certificates are deposited at a CSD so that they no longer need to be delivered from the seller to the buyer. The securities are then known as immobilised as they remain in the vaults of the CSD and transactions are settled by the security being debited from the account of the seller and credited to the account of the buyer.

In the second phase, the security ceases to exist in paper form, with the certificate being replaced by computer records. This transition from physical to electronic format is known as dematerialisation.

The move to an environment in which securities have been dematerialised has addressed some of the inefficiencies and risks that were seen in the crash of 1987, by:

- improving efficiency by allowing the increasing automation of trading, clearance and settlement processes; and
- improving security by reducing the risk that share certificates may be lost or stolen.

Settlement timescales

One of the key recommendations of the G30 was also to reduce the time that it took for settlement to take place.

The reason behind that recommendation was that the longer the period from trade execution to settlement, the greater the risk was that one of the parties may become insolvent. Longer periods also mean that there is a larger number of trades awaiting settlement. Both of these increased the risk that prices would move significantly away from the traded price and increase the potential loss that might be incurred if the need to replace the unsettled contracts arose.

Its original recommendation was that final settlement of transactions should occur on T+3, that is three business days after the trade date. Most countries have now adopted rolling settlement under which trades settle a specified number of business days after the trade date but the actual settlement period varies from market to market and between bonds and equities.

This has undoubtedly contributed to risk reduction but there is still the risk that settlement will be delayed, either because of lack of stock or cash on the part of the buyer or seller.

This has led custodians to offer guaranteed settlement to some of their clients so that they have greater certainty over their cash flows and can utilise either stock or cash sooner. This is known as contractual settlement date accounting which involves, subject to certain conditions, funds being credited or debited on settlement date even if the trade is not yet finalised.

Settlement finality

Automating settlement was a major step in reducing the inherent risk in settlement but also required development of standards to minimise the risks of default by either counterparty.

This required development of settlement procedures that only allow securities to be delivered to the buyer in exchange for a simultaneous and irrevocable payment of cash. This allows the parties to safely use the shares and cash without risk that the trade might fail and need to be unwound.

To achieve this requires rules that specify the moment when finality of transfer takes place and is known as settlement finality.

Next we will look at the principle of delivery versus payment and the payment systems that play an important role in ensuring settlement finality and in limiting systemic risk.

Delivery versus payment

Delivery versus payment (DvP) refers to the exchange of securities for a simultaneous and irrevocable payment of cash. This process is fundamental to all settlement systems and requires that the exchange happens at the same time and that there is no chance of one side of the transaction failing.

It is a fundamental concept that is used throughout the securities industry worldwide to manage the risk of default.

To operate effectively, it requires linked systems for the securities and cash sides of the transaction. The CSD will handle the securities side of the transaction and it will usually generate the guaranteed movement of cash within the banking system.

In the UK this is undertaken by Crest. At settlement, full legal title is transferred to the purchaser in the Crest system. It is accompanied by a simultaneous payment from the buyer's settlement bank to the seller's settlement bank across the books of the Bank of England. Using central bank money provides further certainty that payment will always take place.

Payment systems

Using central bank money to settle transactions involves payment systems known as RTGS or real-time gross settlement.

RTGS is an online system for settling transactions between financial institutions. These payment systems are normally maintained or controlled by the central bank and involve the central bank making adjustments to the accounts of the banks making or receiving payments rather than any physical exchange of money.

The RTGS system is suited for low-volume, high-value transactions. In an RTGS system, transactions are settled across accounts held at a central bank on a continuous gross basis. Settlement is immediate, final and irrevocable.

There is a range of domestic and international payments systems that offer finality of payment in central bank money.

The UK has the clearing house automated payments system (CHAPS), which is one of the largest RTGS systems in the world. It provides RTGS payments functionality in sterling and euros, as well as providing access into the European Central Bank's TARGET cross-border RTGS system for the euro.

TARGET consists of the national RTGS systems of the 12 euro area countries and, in addition, the national euro RTGS systems of Denmark, Sweden and the UK are also connected to TARGET. These 16 systems are all interlinked in order to provide a uniform platform for the processing of euro payments.

In the US, the bulk of large dollar transfers are conducted through the clearing house interbank payments system (CHIPS), a private sector funds transfer network specialising in international payments, and through the Federal Reserve Bank's Fedwire funds transfer service.

Netting

RTGS systems have an important role to play in ensuring real-time settlement finality and in limiting systemic risk. However, trade-for-trade settlement can place substantial demands on liquidity, requiring that cash and securities obligations are met in full for each trade. This can create problems when delivery of funds or securities does not move sufficiently quickly to release the liquidity needed to allow subsequent trades to settle.

The alternative method of settling transactions is known as netting. This happens when trading partners agree to offset their transactions and by doing so, they reduce a large number of individual transactions to a smaller number, and it is on this netted position that the two trading partners settle their outstanding obligations to transfer cash or securities. Besides reducing transaction costs and communication expenses, netting is important because it reduces credit and liquidity risks.

Netting can be bilateral, that is between two counterparties only, or multilateral, that is involving many counterparties. The latter requires the use of a central clearance system, such as a central counterparty.

Central counterparty

A central counterparty (CCP) interposes itself between the counterparties to a trade, becoming the buyer to every seller and the seller to every buyer. As a result, buyer and seller interact with the CCP and remain anonymous to each other. This process is known as novation.

Each market participant communicates only with the CCP, which will net each participant's respective sales and purchases into a single transfer of securities and a single transfer of cash. The CCP is obliged to settle the transactions and thus reduces the risk of any one institution going into default.

4.3 SETTLEMENT PROCESS

Now that we have looked at the key features of modern settlement systems, we can turn to look at where they fit within the settlement process.

Clearing and settlement

Trading involves not only the execution of a trade but also the transfer of ownership and exchange of cash. Clearing and settlement are the processes that allow these transfers to be made in a controlled manner.

The processes involved in settling a trade can be broken down into four main activities:

- Confirmation – agreement of the terms of the trade.
- Clearance – establishing the respective obligations of the buyer and the seller.
- Delivery – transfer of securities from the seller to the buyer.
- Payment – transfer of the funds from the buyer to the seller.

Clearing refers to the first two of those processes and settlement the latter two. They are essential features of a smoothly operating securities market.

Clearing

Clearing relates to the following two processes or activities:

- Provision of trade matching and confirmation of the terms of a trade that have been agreed between the buyer and the seller.
- Provision CCP services and particularly netting and novation.

Clearing is therefore the whole process whereby each of the counterparties establishes what is expected to be received when the trade is settled and what actions need to be taken to deliver the security and the cash.

Trade matching and confirmation

The first step in settling a trade is to ensure that buyer and seller agree on the terms of the trade.

This involves the issue and capture of details of the trade and matching of these to the original instruction to ensure that the trade has been carried out correctly and as intended. This is a vital process and errors need to be identified at an early stage otherwise the trade may need to be reversed and create a loss or cash may not be available to settle the trade or not be utilised effectively. The process is known as trade confirmation and the following items would normally be included in the confirmation:

- Title, quantity and identification number of the security traded.
- The date of the trade, whether it was a purchase or sale, the price, whether it was ex-dividend and any accrued interest.
- The name and account number of the counterparty, the intended settlement date and settlement method.

There is a range of trade confirmation systems that allow this to take place electronically and so are known as ETC or electronic trade confirmation systems.

An example of this is Swift which has a suite of standardised ETC messages that have allowed firms to automate their processing. This has enabled firms to reduce errors and therefore trade failures and at its most sophisticated allows, for example, straightforward trades in UK equities to be captured, matched and settled completely electronically and without any human intervention.

Clearance

Once the terms of a trade have been confirmed, the respective obligations of the buyer and seller are established and agreed. The next step is for each party to the transaction to submit trade instructions to a clearing house.

A clearing house is usually a specialist clearing organisation, a CSD or an ICSD. In the UK, for example, Crest is a recognised clearing house.

The clearing house will gather and match settlement instructions from the counterparties and report the results to the participants.

Clearance can be carried out on a gross or net basis. When clearance is carried out on a gross basis, the obligations of the buyer and seller are calculated individually on a trade-by-trade basis. The alternative is netting where a number of trades between the buyer and seller are set off against each other leaving a single obligation to be settled.

Market participants may also choose to use the facilities of a CCP, which is an entity that interposes itself between the buyer and seller. As a result, each party to the trade settles its part of the transaction with the CCP thus reducing its credit risk exposure.

Settlement

Once the trade has been confirmed and matched, the clearing house will hold the settlement instructions until the intended settlement date.

The activities undertaken will vary both in the number of steps and the location depending upon where the security is held and will range from straightforward transactions, such as the settlement of a simple UK equity trade, to quite complex ones, such as the settlement of a cross-border transaction.

Before settlement can take place, trade positioning takes place. This involves the buyer ensuring that there is sufficient cash to pay for the purchase and the seller ensuring that sufficient stock is available to deliver.

Delivery of securities is typically carried out at the CSD or ICSD, and as the vast majority of securities are immobilised or dematerialised, the security can be transferred by book entry.

Payment for the purchase of the security can be effected using the settlement system but more usually it is via a banking payment system.

Post settlement

As well as looking at clearing and settling, we need to consider what takes place post settlement, particularly at the actions needed to correct trade failures.

Settlement failure may be caused for a number of reasons but they will essentially revolve around one of three scenarios, namely: the nonmatching of settlement instructions; that there are insufficient securities to settle the trade; or the purchaser has insufficient cash to pay for the securities.

If a trade fails to settle on time, the other party is likely to be disadvantaged and will either seek recompense by charging an interest penalty or seek remedial action by initiating a buy-in of securities to settle the trade.

Interest claims

If a trade fails to settle on time, the seller is disadvantaged as they cannot invest the proceeds and earn interest. As a result, the seller can make an interest claim for the loss of interest on the net amount they would have received had settlement happened on time.

There are market standards for making claims issued by the International Securities Association for Institutional Trade Communication (ISITC) for equity trades and the International Capital Market Association (ICMA) for fixed income products.

The amount is calculated on the net amount due and at the overdraft rate that is applicable to the seller and excludes any claim for additional administration costs for the time and effort of calculating and chasing the claims.

Buy-in procedures

Markets have remedial processes to deal with scenarios where a trade fails to settle known as either a buy-in or sell-out.

If the seller fails to deliver securities in time, the buyer may initiate a buy-in to allow settlement to be completed. This involves the buyer or the exchange issuing a notification to the seller that it will take place following a specified deadline. If the seller fails to deliver, a third party is then charged with buying the securities at the current market price and delivering these to the purchaser and charging any costs to the seller.

If the trade has failed the other way round and the seller is ready to deliver the securities but the buyer is unable to deliver the cash, a sell-out can take place. This is simply the reverse of a buy-in, so a third party will sell the securities and pay the proceeds to the seller. If there is any shortfall, it will be raised from the market and the costs will be passed on to the purchaser.

Settlement fines

As well as the above, most markets have other tools they can deploy in order to ensure that settlement discipline is maintained.

The most commonly used is settlement fines which involves a firm being fined if it fails to match or settle a trade within a defined period or if its performance over a period of time does not meet required standards.

As a result, firms will often borrow stock, known as stock borrowing or lending, as a means to cover any shortfall of securities.

4.4 UK SETTLEMENT

Introduction

In the UK, the main settlement system is Crest, which is a computer-based system for the electronic transfer and settlement of shares and other securities in uncertificated form.

However, there is still the traditional paper-based system whereby title to shares is evidenced by share certificate and transferred by a stock transfer form and as a result, two sets of rules also exist. One set of rules relating to Crest transactions and another set of rules derived from the provisions of the Companies Act which are relevant to companies whose shares are not traded in Crest or for transfers of certificated shares outside of the Crest system.

The majority of trades in the UK are settled using Crest and so the next sections provide an overview of the operation of Crest, explains its legal status and describes the processes that take place in settlement of trades. It then looks at how trades that take place in certificated form are handled.

Overview of the Crest system

Crest is the CSD for the UK market. Unusually for a CSD, it also operates across legal jurisdictions and is the CSD for Irish equities as well as for those of Jersey, Guernsey and the Isle of Man.

It is a computer-based system operated by CrestCo Limited which provides electronic holding and settlement of equities, bonds and government stocks. It started operating on 15 July 1996 replacing the Talisman system operated by the Stock Exchange and merged with Euroclear in September 2002.

Securities held in Crest are recorded electronically only and no physical share certificates are issued. Transfers take place by way of electronic instructions and ownership is recorded in the name of the Crest member rather than Crest itself. For UK securities, the electronic records in Crest represent the share register and so legal title passes at the time of transfer within the system.

The system undertakes matching and settlement of transactions in multiple currencies and processing of a range of corporate actions including dividend distributions and rights issues. Trades are settled by the electronic movement of stock and are accompanied by an irrevocable instruction for the guaranteed exchange of cash by designated settlement banks.

As well as settling uncertificated trades, Crest also supports settlement of trades where one party is a Crest member and the other holds their stock in certificated or physical form.

Legal status

Holding and transferring securities in electronic form has required most countries to make changes to their legal system.

In the UK, this required amendments to the Companies Act 1985 which set out the legal requirements governing the transfer of shares and which required the issue of share certificates and the use of stock transfer forms to transfer holdings.

This was achieved through the Companies Act 1989 which conferred powers on the Treasury to make regulations to enable title to securities to be evidenced and transferred without the need for a written instrument.

This was implemented by the Uncertified Securities Regulations 1995 which established the generic legal framework for dispensing with share certificates and the electronic transfer of securities.

CrestCo and the Crest settlement system were then recognised as the operator and relevant system, respectively, the following year. Its operation is supervised by the Financial Services Authority.

These regulations have since been amended to take account of the progressive enhancement of the Crest system. This included the transfer of responsibility for settlement of UK gilts from the Central Gilts Office to Crest in 2000.

The Uncertificated Securities Regulations 2001 brought in a major change by eliminating the interval between settlement in Crest and transfer of legal title by entry on the register of members. This established the Crest records as the register of title for UK securities held in uncertificated form and thus introduced transfer of legal title at the point of electronic settlement known as ETT – electronic transfer of title.

Share registers and transfers of title

As mentioned earlier, the 2001 Regulations established that the Crest records constituted the share register for uncertificated securities in order for electronic transfer of title at the time of settlement to take place.

This did not, however, replace the traditional register and the regulations therefore introduced a differentiation between the register operated by Crest and the issuer.

The regulations require the register to consist of two parts, the operator register and the issuer register as described in the Figure 4.1.

In practice, the registrar for the company needs to have a complete record of all shareholders as it is responsible for issuing company reports, paying dividends and notifying shareholders of corporate actions. As a result, the registrar acting for the company or issuer maintains a copy of the uncertificated register and is notified of any changes to it by Crest.

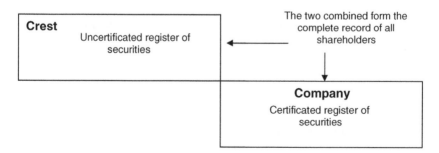

Figure 4.1   Components of the UK share register

The key elements of this structure are:

- Crest maintains the uncertificated part of the register – the operator register of securities.
- The relevant issuer maintains the certificated part of the register – the issuer register of securities.
- The issuer also maintains a record of securities held in the operator register.
- When any transfer of title occurs in Crest, the system will generate a register update request requiring the issuer to amend the relevant record of uncertificated shares.

Structure of Crest

To hold a securities account in Crest, investors need to be either a full member or a sponsored member.

A full member is typically an investment firm that has the ability to connect and interact with the Crest system, while a sponsored member will use the services of a firm who is a member of Crest. Both full and sponsored members have their own name on the share register.

Alternatively, an investor may use a custodian or a nominee and it is that firm's name which appears on the register.

Each Crest member has a participant ID and one or more member accounts which allow it to have designated holdings on the share register.

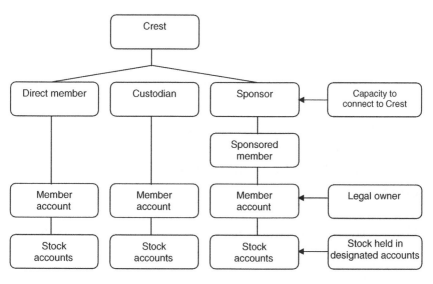

Figure 4.2   Crest account structure

Shares of different companies are held within separate stock accounts which represent their total holding of a security on the share register. The stock accounts distinguish amounts that are available to settle outstanding transactions, amounts that are in escrow and amounts that are in deposit which are used to facilitate transfers of certificated shares.

This structure can be seen in the Figure 4.2.

System messages

Securities held in Crest may only be transferred by secure electronic instructions and members effect settlement by sending an electronic instruction to Crest to make or receive a delivery of securities.

Crest users input their instructions and receive information via one of the three electronic networks operated by Syntegra, SWIFT and the London Stock Exchange. Users are only able to communicate with Crest through the network, and do not communicate directly with one another.

Under the Uncertified Securities Regulations, participants are able to rely upon messages sent and received through the Crest system and assume that the instruction is correct, is sent by the person from whom it appears to have been sent and is made with authority.

Settlement banks and cash memorandum accounts

When settlement takes place, the electronic transfer of stock takes place within Crest which at the same time generates an irrevocable payment instruction for the exchange of cash by designated settlement banks.

As a result, Crest members are required to appoint a Crest settlement bank to receive and pay out moneys in respect of settlements in Crest. Settlement banks control the credit they are extending to their customers by a system of debit caps and Crest checks that the debit cap would not be breached before settling the trade.

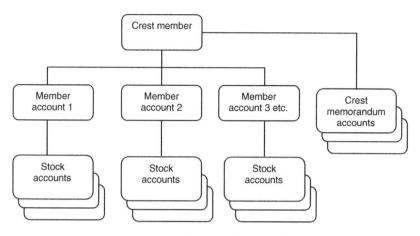

Figure 4.3 Crest account structure *Source:* CrestCo

Settlement is instantaneous and payments are made between settlement banks on the central accounts at the Bank of England on a gross basis as they occur.

In order for the settlement process to operate effectively, Crest maintains one or more cash memorandum accounts for each member. This is effectively a cash ledger which shows the net balance of payments made and received at any time during the course of the settlement day. Separate accounts will be held for different currencies.

The structure of member accounts, stock accounts and cash memorandum accounts can be seen in Figure 4.3.

Settlement process

The process of settlement begins with either members or an exchange communicating trades to Crest.

Once Crest has received a settlement instruction it will look to match it with another instruction by searching for key features such as the identity of the counterparty, the security, the number of shares, the amount of consideration and the intended settlement date.

Once a trade has been matched the two sides of the trade are locked and the system takes no further action until the specified settlement date.

On settlement day, Crest checks that there is sufficient stock in the seller's stock account and sufficient headroom in the buyer's cash memorandum account to settle the cost of the trade. It will also check that the buyer's settlement bank has sufficient credit at the Bank of England for the transaction to settle. Once these tests are satisfied, settlement of the trade will take place.

A trade will only be settled when there is sufficient stock and cash for it to settle. Where there is not, the system will continue to check until settlement can take place.

Finally, once settlement takes place Crest creates an electronic notification to the issuer registrar to update their register. Figure 4.4 illustrates how a sale is input, matched and settled in Crest.

Stage 1 – Trade matching

- The buying and selling members input instructions in Crest detailing the terms of the agreed trade.

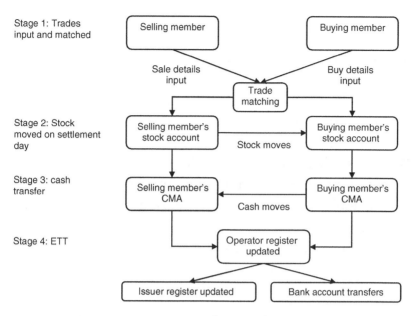

Figure 4.4 Crest matching and settlement

- Crest authenticates these instructions to check that they conform to the authentication procedures stipulated by Crest. If the inputted data from both members is identical, Crest creates a matching transaction.

Stage 2 – Stock settlement

- On the intended settlement date, Crest checks that the buying member has sufficient funds or credit facilities in its cash memorandum account (CMA), the selling member has sufficient stock in its stock account, and the buyer's Crest settlement bank has sufficient liquidity at the Bank of England to proceed to settlement of the transaction.
- If so, Crest moves the stock from the selling member's account to the buying member's account.

Stage 3 – Cash settlement

- Crest also credits the CMA of the selling member and debits the CMA of the buying member which simultaneously generates a settlement bank payment obligation of the buying member's settlement bank in favour of the Bank of England.
- The selling member's settlement bank receives that payment (in Bank of England funds) immediately upon the debit of the purchase price to the buying member's CMA.
- Therefore, as between the Crest members, a 'Crest payment' is made and completed at the moment of debit and credit to the relevant CMAs.

Stage 4 – Register update

- Crest then automatically updates its operator register of securities to effect the transfer of shares to the buying member.
- Legal title to the shares passes at this point – 'electronic transfer of title'.
- This prompts the simultaneous generation by the Crest system of an RUR (register update request) message requiring the issuer to amend its record of uncertificated shares.

In practice, stages 2, 3 and 4 occur instantaneously.

Settlement through custodians

Many investment firms will not be direct members of Crest but will instead use the services of a global custodian.

The custodian will have safekeeping of the assets and will be a Crest member. The securities will generally be kept in a designated account in the name of the custodian's nominee company which means that the custodian will need to be a party to the trade and be instructed to settle the trade.

When an investment firm trades, it will need to advise the broker it uses that the trade should be alleged against its custodian and provide details of the Crest participant ID and the designated account for the trade.

The trade will then be broken into two legs, the market side and the client side. The market side represents settlement of the trade against whichever counterparty the broker dealt with and the client side represents settlement of the trade between the broker and the custodian.

This process can be seen in Figure 4.5.

Residual settlement

The use of Crest is voluntary and so trades can and are undertaken involving physical share certificates.

All professional firms have dematerialised their holdings and are either Crest members or use the services of a custodian. Private investors, however, are likely to still hold physical share certificates. When they wish to trade, their broker will use functionality within the Crest system to dematerialise the shares so that the trade can settle in Crest and rematerialise share certificates for purchases.

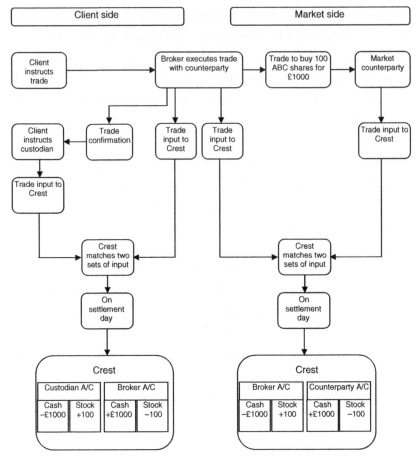

Figure 4.5   Settlement through custodians

Figure 4.6 shows the process that takes place and is described below.

If a member of Crest sells securities in certificated form, the member or his broker will deposit a Crest transfer form and the relevant share certificate at one of four regional Crest counters and input an electronic Crest record.

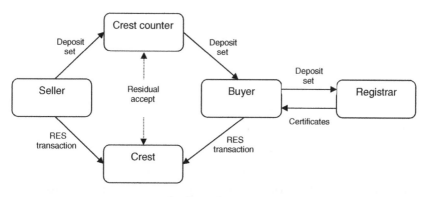

Figure 4.6   Residual settlement*Source:* CrestCo

The transfer form and certificate are processed and transferred to the appropriate registrar. The registrar will
check the documents and delete securities registered in
the name of the transferor from the register and ensure
that the securities are credited to the Crest membership
of the buyer as specified in the transfer form. The buyer
thereby obtains title to the securities in electronic form.

Similarly, if a member purchases and receives securities
in electronic form but wishes to hold them in certificated
form, when the seller receives the purchase funds he will
instruct Crest to remove the securities from his register
and instruct the registrar through Crest to register the
securities in the name of the purchaser. The registrar will
then produce a certificate in the purchaser's name.

Dematerialisation of shares

The Institute of Chartered Secretaries and Administrators (ICSA) undertook a public consultation process in

2006 about proposals for the compulsory dematerialisation of the remaining physical share certificates held in the UK.

The consultation paper made the point that dematerialisation has already taken place in many other countries across the globe, such as France, Denmark, Sweden, Italy, India, Australia and New Zealand. Other countries which are in the process of doing this include Ireland, Belgium, Netherlands and Spain and it is being examined as a proposal in the USA.

It also provided some interesting statistics on how shares are held in the UK. There are some 34 million shareholdings which are owned by some 12 million shareholders. Of these about 9 million hold paper certificates but this only represents about 15% of the total value of the share market. The remaining 85% is already traded electronically using Crest and about 10,000 share transfers using paper share certificates as proof of ownership are processed through Crest every day.

The result of the public consultation was published in October 2006 and showed that two-thirds of respondents were in favour of the proposal. The consultation paper contained a model of how the paperless system might operate and is now being revised in light of the responses and will be presented to the Treasury in due course.

To introduce a mandatory dematerialisation will require changes to the legal system. At the time of writing, the latest revisions to company legislation are still progressing through parliament and so action has been taken to ensure that the Act once passed can facilitate the transfer to dematerialisation.

4.5 INTERNATIONAL SETTLEMENT

Introduction

Investment firms dealing with private investors traditionally restricted their trading activities to UK securities but that has now changed and international stocks are found not only in the portfolios of high net worth clients but also are available to clients of execution-only stockbrokers.

Holding international securities and settling trades in them is a complex activity. Global custodians specialise in this type of activity and have networks of agents worldwide that they can use for the safekeeping of securities and to settle trades.

Although settlement activity will generally be undertaken by the custodian, it is important to have an understanding of how the process operates and the differences from settlement of a Crest trade.

The following sections provide an overview of the international settlement process and background on some of the major international CSDs.

Settlement process

Trading in international securities is usually referred to as cross-border trading because settlement of the resulting trade may not only take place outside of the UK, but may also require the movement of the underlying security from one CSD to another.

The fundamental activity that takes place is the same as for domestic settlement in that there needs to be an exchange of cash and securities. It will start therefore with preparations for the transfer of securities and cash and end with the seller's account being debited with the security and credited with the proceeds and vice versa for the buyer. The variations arise in the involvement of more than one CSD and how the cash is transferred.

As more than one CSD is involved, one needs to take the lead in issuing instructions to the other. The one taking the lead is referred to as the instructing CSD and the other as the settling CSD. Which one takes the lead varies but the most common method is for the issuer CSD to act as the settling CSD. An alternative model is possible in the euro zone as both are operating in the same currency where the buying CSD can act as the settling CSD.

The process followed will vary from market to market and possibly trade by trade, but Figure 4.7 describes the process that takes place.

The first step that is undertaken is at the instructing CSD, which carries out what are known as provision checks. If the transaction is a delivery then the securities are blocked in the account of the participant. If the transaction is a receipt, the checks will relate to the cash

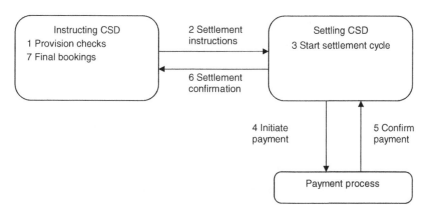

Figure 4.7 International settlement Source: *ECSDA Report on Cross-Border Settlement Links*

side of the transaction and may involve blocking cash or credit lines.

Once the checks are completed, the second step is for the CSD to issue a settlement instruction.

The third step is when the normal settlement cycle takes place at the settling CSD, when the securities will be transferred between the account of the counterparty and the omnibus account of the instructing CSD.

Stages 4 and 5 will depend on whether settlement is DvP or free of payment. If the trade can be settled DvP, the settling CSD will initiate and control payment for the transaction.

The final steps, 6 and 7, take place once the trade has settled where the settling CSD will inform the instructing CSD who will debit the blocked assets and credit counter value in the accounts of the participant.

International central securities depositaries (ICSDs)

An ICSD is an organisation that settles trades in international securities and in various domestic securities usually through links to various local CSDs. Euroclear and Clearstream are the two main ICSDs. They came into being to meet the needs for integrated clearing, settlement and custody services of the eurobond market.

The eurobond market developed in the early 1970s to accommodate the recycling of substantial OPEC US dollar revenues from Middle East oil sales at a time when US financial institutions were subject to a ceiling on the rate of interest that could be paid on dollar deposits.

Since then it has grown exponentially into the world's largest market for longer term capital, as a result of the corresponding growth in world trade and even more significant growth in international capital flows, with most of the activity being concentrated in London.

The services offered by the ICSDs have also grown and they now offer a range of services that overlap with those offered by custodians. The services offered by the three organisations are described below.

Euroclear

The Euroclear system was set up by Morgan Guaranty Trust of New York to meet the needs of itself and its clients in 1968 in Brussels. It is now part of the Euroclear Group.

It is the world's largest ICSD and provides settlement services for international bonds, money market equities and fund instruments. Euroclear offers clients in more than 80 countries a single access point to post-trade services for equities in 25 countries, bonds in 30 countries, as well as international securities.

In addition to its role as an ICSD, it also acts as a local CSD for the Belgian, Dutch, French, Irish and UK securities.

Participants hold a depot account with Euroclear Bank which records the securities they hold and provides a consolidated logical view of the assets held regardless of where they are physically deposited. The reason for this is that the securities are immobilised at one of their networks of depositary banks, including specialist depositaries for bearer securities. Cash is held with Euroclear Bank in up to 30 currencies.

The Euroclear system provides DvP settlement with simultaneous and irrevocable transfer of securities and cash. Communications can be routed through their proprietary system, Euclid or via Swift.

The settlement process goes through a number of stages. Instructions are validated and then matched with a counterparty's instruction or are cycled until they can be matched. Once matched, they are included in an overnight batch for settling against the participants' accounts.

As well as settling trades with other CSDs, Euroclear can settle transactions with Clearstream. This is achieved by an exchange of messages using the bridge system which is an electronic bridge between the two ICSDs.

Clearstream International

Clearstream also has a similar history. It was originally known as Cedel and was created in 1970 in Luxembourg by more than 90 of the world's major financial institutions to provide clearing and settlement services.

It has since been acquired by Deutsche Börse and operates out of offices in Luxembourg, Frankfurt, London, New York, Hong Kong and Dubai. Clearstream provides settlement and custody services for around 2500 customers in over 100 countries and its global network extends across 42 markets. In addition to its role as an ICSD, it also acts as a local CSD for the Luxembourg and German markets.

Its customers communicate with it via its proprietary system, CreationConnect, or via Swift. Its settlement engine, the Creation Platform, provides a central point of access to a wide variety of markets, offering fully automated overnight and daytime processing.

Chapter

5

. . . .

CORPORATE ACTIONS

5.1 INTRODUCTION

Administering corporate actions can be one of the more complicated activities undertaken in any investment firm due to the complexities involved in the processing of an event and the varieties of events that can arise.

This chapter will focus on how corporate actions are managed and processed in an investment management firm and consider the range of issues that arise for private investors.

In order to set the context for a detailed review of the types of corporate action, we will look at the general background to the corporate actions industry. We will then investigate how these are managed and processed in a retail investment firm before considering the main types of event in detail.

5.2 CORPORATE ACTIONS INDUSTRY

Corporate actions take place whenever there is a change to the capital structure of a company or organisation that affects the shares or bonds that it has issued.

A corporate action will impact virtually every security at some point and typical well-known examples include dividend payments, rights issues and takeovers. Indeed, it is estimated that nearly a million corporate actions take place every year worldwide.

Table 5.1 Number of global corporate actions in 2003–4

	Number of corporate actions	% of global total
North America	624,700	66.8
Europe	203,600	21.8
Asia-Pacific	62,000	6.6
Other	44,900	4.8
Total	935,200	

Source: DTCC

The US central depositary, the DTCC, has published data on the number of corporate actions that take place each year. The information that they have provided, which is shown in Table 5.1, is for the year to March 2004 and gives an insight into the number of corporate actions that take place and their global distribution.

Unsurprisingly, the majority of corporate actions affect companies in either the US or Europe, reflecting the size of their respective stock markets.

Equally interesting is that these account for corporate actions only and that there are a further three million interest payments and bond redemptions on top of that. This reinforces the fact, if it was needed, of the critical part that processing corporate actions has globally in the administration of investment portfolios.

The DTCC has also produced data that analyses the types of corporate action that take place worldwide and is shown in Table 5.2. The terminology used for events differs from country to country which means that the

Table 5.2 Most common types of corporate action

Corporate action	% of total
Cash dividend	26.9
Income distribution	16.4
Partial call redemption	14.6
Full call redemption	12.5
Meeting	7.1
Dividend omitted	2.7
Return of capital	2.0
Name change	1.8
Other	16.0

Source: DTCC

information has to be treated with care, but it does provide a useful indication of the types of events that occur.

As you would expect, dividend payments and income distributions are the most common types of corporate action worldwide. The other category includes voluntary corporate actions or mandatory actions with options. Although they represent only about 10–15% of all corporate actions taking place globally, this translates into approximately 90,000–140,000 of such complex actions each year.

5.3 TYPES OF EVENT

There are more than 150 types of corporate action and despite the wide variety that can be seen, it is generally accepted that they can be classified into three main types, which are known as:

- voluntary events;
- mandatory events; and
- mandatory events with options.

As the name implies, voluntary events are ones where there is no obligation on the shareholder or investor to take any action. Generally, these are the most complex types of events such as takeovers and mergers.

In contrast, mandatory events take place regardless of the view of the investor. One of the most straightforward examples is a repayment of a government bond at its final redemption date.

The final category of a mandatory event with options is a variation on the latter where the investor is able to express a preference over some of the detail of an event. So, for example, a company may determine to pay a dividend which can clearly be seen as a mandatory event, but it may also give options to its shareholders to receive the dividend as either cash or additional shares.

Within these broad headings lie a wide range of different types of corporate action event. The European Central Securities Depositories Association (ECSDA) has categorised the events that can arise under four main headings:

- compulsory cash distributions;
- compulsory stock distributions;

- optional stock distributions;
- other types of event.

Table 5.3 shows the types of event that are categorised under each of the headings followed by a brief explanation of each type.

Compulsory cash distributions

- Cash dividends – the regular distribution of cash to shareholders, in proportion to their equity holding which is paid on dates specified at the time the dividend is announced.
- Interest payments – interest paid at specified dates to holders of a stock based on the nominal value of stock held at either a fixed or floating interest rate.
- Capital repayments – part repayment of capital to holders out of a company's cash reserves which reduces its market value but where the number of issued shares or other securities normally remains the same.
- Redemptions at maturity – repayment in full of a stock at its stated maturity date.
- Partial redemptions – repayment of part of a stock before its scheduled final maturity date and where the stock to be repaid may be drawn by lots.

Compulsory stock distributions

- Bonus issues – the issue of further shares to shareholders in proportion to their existing holding without any payment.

Table 5.3 Classification of corporate action types

Compulsory cash distributions	Compulsory stock distributions	Optional stock distributions	Other events
Cash dividends	Bonus issues	Subscriptions	Call payments
Interest payments	Conversions	Conversions	Enhanced scrip dividends
Capital repayments	Consolidations	Redemptions	Optional call payments
Redemptions (at maturity)	Enfranchisements		Mergers
Partial redemptions	Open offers		Schemes of arrangement
	Pari passu		Scrip dividends
	Rights issues		Takeovers
	Subdivisions		Demergers
			Resale
			Other payments
			Early redemptions
			Share capital reduction
			Closed offers
			Minority redemptions
			Euro conversions

Source: ECDSA

- Conversions –where the issuer of a stock compulsorily converts a holding into a different type of stock.
- Consolidations –where the issuer decreases the number of shares in issue by consolidating them into a share with a different nominal value.
- Enfranchisements –where a share class that does not have voting rights is given that right and then merged with existing voting shares.
- Open offers –similar to a rights issue except that the rights are not transferable and are usually issued in proportion to the underlying holding.
- Pari passu –where there are two lines of identical shares but one does not rank for a dividend until a specified time.
- Rights issues – where a company gives existing holders the right to subscribe for further shares at a specified price and within a specified time period.
- Subdivisions –where the number of shares issued is increased by reducing the nominal value of the shares.

Optional stock distributions

- Subscriptions –where the holder of shares, such as warrants, has the right to subscribe for shares of a different class.
- Optional conversions –where the holders of a convertible bond can convert their holding into shares without any payment.
- Optional redemptions –where the holders of a bond have the right to require redemption of a bond before the scheduled maturity date.

Other events

- Compulsory call payments – new shares or stock may be issued in partly paid form and the holders will be required to make further payments on specified dates.
- Scrip dividends and enhanced scrip dividends – where the holder opts to receive further shares instead of the cash dividend.
- Optional call payments – where a holder elects to make a call payment to subscribe to a new issue.
- Mergers –where two companies merge either into one of them or into a new company.
- Schemes of arrangement –often used in a merger where the existing holdings are exchanged for new shares, stock or cash or a combination of them.
- Takeovers –where an offer is made for a company's shares and where combination of new shares, stock or cash is offered.
- Demergers –where a company splits off part of its operations into a new company and issues the shares to existing shareholders.
- Resale –where a selected group of investors are invited to subscribe prior to an open offer with subscription, after which their stock will be transferred to the investors in an open offer.
- Early redemption –either a partial or full redemption of a stock in advance of the schedule's maturity date.
- Share capital reduction –where the nominal value of shares is reduced normally as part of a return of capital to shareholders.

- Closed offer –where a selected group of investors are invited to purchase shares as opposed to all shareholders.
- Minority redemption – occurs on a takeover where the buyer acquires more than a specified limit and the remaining minority shareholders can be compulsorily redeemed.
- Euro conversion –where the share capital and nominal value of stock and shares is converted into the euro.

5.4 PRIVATE CLIENT CORPORATE ACTION PROCESSING

Introduction

For an investment firm that provides services to retail clients, the management of corporate actions is a major undertaking that is complicated by the potentially large number of clients.

The main corporate action processing will take place in firms that provide discretionary investment management, advisory investment management or execution-only stockbroking.

In most cases, these firms will use the services of a global custodian who will broadcast details of the event and provide deadlines by when they require instructions. From the perspective of the global custodian, they are simply requiring an instruction from the client and this market view of the process taking place can be seen in Figure 5.1,

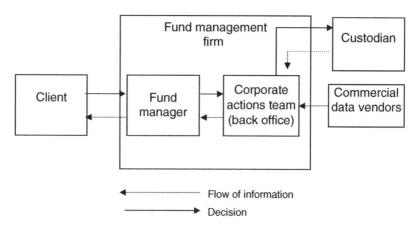

Figure 5.1 Overview of retail corporate action processing *Source:* DTCC Oxera Study

which is based on data in the DTCC Oxera study on corporate action processing.

Overview of private client processing

For a retail investment firm, however, this is the start of an intense period of further activity.

Receipt of a broadcast from a custodian is a key step in the corporate action process for a retail investment firm. This and the other processes it may need to follow are summarised in Figure 5.2.

Establishing the terms of an event

The process obviously starts with the announcement of a corporate action. Although many firms use a custodian who will broadcast details of the event, it is normal

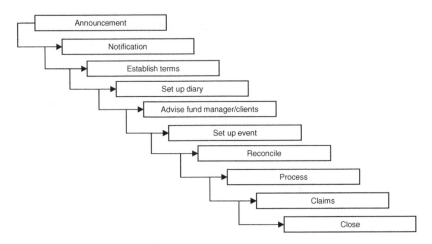

Figure 5.2   Corporate action process flow

practice in most firms to ensure that they have an independent process to capture details of forthcoming corporate actions.

The way in which firms will do this varies from using commercial data vendors, to tasking a member of the corporate actions team to monitor announcements that might affect their firm's holdings and working closely with their investment management team who are likely to be one of the first to identify a forthcoming action that will affect the firm.

A corporate actions team may need to have such alternate sources of information about events for a variety of reasons. One of the main ones will be to get advance notification of an action especially if they have a large number of underlying holders. This will then allow them extra time in which to plan the actions and the resources that are needed to process the event.

Assuming a firm is using a custodian they will receive a broadcast from the custodian providing details of the event, the options available, the timetable and the internal deadlines for instructions to be given back. At around the same time, they will also receive details of their holding with the custodian.

On receipt of the broadcast, a corporate actions team will begin to establish the terms of the action. Although the details of the event will be contained in the broadcast from the custodian, this is usually expressed in such terms so that it can be sent to all of the custodian's clients, rather than being tailored for the needs of one customer or another.

The corporate actions team will need to examine and understand the detailed proposals. The reason for this is that the action that needs to be taken may vary by client type.

From the custodian's perspective, the firm may have one single omnibus holding on which it wants an instruction but the retail investment firm is more likely to have many hundreds or thousands of underlying customers. Additionally, the type of customer may vary. The customer may be a discretionary client where the investment manager can make a decision or an advisory one where the client's approval is needed. The underlying holder could be a private individual or a trust or the holding may be held as an ISA or a SIPP.

A corporate actions team will therefore need to understand who the underlying clients are because different action may be needed and different considerations may apply depending upon what type of account contains the holdings. For example, the investment may be held in an ISA or SIPP, so the firm will need to establish whether the proposed new holding is eligible for inclusion under HMRC rules.

Corporate actions diary

Having understood the detail of the forthcoming event and established the range of client types who are the underlying investors, a corporate actions team will need to set up a diary for all of the key dates associated with it.

Just as the custodian will have set a date by which it must receive instructions for the omnibus holding, the retail corporate actions team will also need to set internal deadline dates by which it must have received instructions from its investment managers or clients. These will usually be set some time in advance of the final date given by the custodian as the corporate actions team will need to analyse the responses and collate these into a combined instruction for the omnibus holding.

This will effectively establish a plan for processing the event. Establishing the terms of an event and converting these into an executable plan is undoubtedly the critical process in a retail client environment.

Get both of these right and it will be possible to process the rest of the event with fewer issues; get the interpretation and planning wrong and the firm will probably end up compensating its clients because it will not process the event either correctly or in a timely manner.

To both control the event and mitigate the inherent risks is the part of the process where most firms will use its more experienced staff and where it will apply rigorous checks and sign-off procedures.

Advising investment managers and clients

The next stage will be to communicate the information it has established to its internal investment managers and to its advisory or execution-only customers.

The action taken will depend upon the client type and what is spelt out in the client agreement or terms and conditions.

If the firm is undertaking discretionary investment management on behalf of clients, it would be normal for the investment manager to make a decision without contacting the client. This decision would be based on the firm's view of the action and the options available. The decision may well vary by client type because what is suitable for a client requiring capital growth may not be appropriate for one requiring income or what is suitable for an adventurous client may not be for a cautious one.

As a result, the investment manager will need to base his decision on both the firm's opinion of the proposals and the investment objectives and risk tolerance of the underlying investors.

If some of the underlying clients are advisory ones, then the investment manager will go through the same process. He will establish a proposed course of action based on a combination of the firm's opinion and the client's investment objectives and attitude to risk. The firm will then need to communicate this to the advisory client and seek their approval to their recommendation.

This builds additional steps into the process and so the timetable set by the corporate actions team needs to build in this time period. The firm will still need to meet the deadline set by the custodian and so if it is a written communication, it will request a response by a given date. It will also usually state that if a response is not received by that date, that the firm will follow a default course of action. This has the benefit of protecting the client's interests in case they are away or out of the country and the authority to act in this way will usually be contained in the client agreement or terms and conditions.

Where the underlying accounts are execution-only clients, then the firm will clearly not provide advice. Instead, the corporate actions team will advise details of the event to the client and request an instruction no later than a given date. Again, they will also usually state that a default action will be taken if a response is not received by the due date.

Investment management decisions

Some of the considerations that the investment manager may need to make are mentioned above, but there are many more.

Figure 5.3 gives an indication of how the process might operate in order to bring out some of the areas that need to be considered in making a decision for a discretionary or client or coming to a recommendation for an advisory one. The headings above the model indicate some of the main phases that will take place.

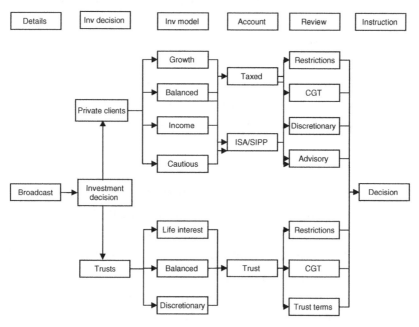

Figure 5.3   Decision model for corporate actions

The process will clearly start with consideration of the terms and will lead to the firm establishing its investment view on the action that should be taken. This will be its general stance on what it believes is the right investment decision to make and from this the firm will drive the actions that it will need to take for different types of client.

For private clients, the decision may well vary between clients with differing investment objectives. An example of this would be, say, on a takeover involving receipt of a new holding.

The investment view may be that they will accept the offer and take the new investment but the firm will need to establish if that new holding is appropriate for inclusion in the client's portfolio given their investment objectives and risk profile. They will also need to look at the overall construction of the portfolio as the new holding may change the percentage representation they have in a sector to an unacceptable level or even introduce representation in a sector which is unsuitable for certain types of client.

As a result, the original decision to accept the offer may change and they may then have different decisions for the different types of investment model they are following. The choices may widen to accept the offer and the new holding, to accept the offer but sell the new holding and reinvest in something more appropriate or sell in the market and make the investment switch immediately.

There are then further considerations that need to be applied depending upon whether the investment is held in the general portfolio or within an ISA or SIPP. If it is held in an ISA or SIPP, checks will need to be made to see whether the new holding is an eligible investment under HMRC rules for inclusion in the account.

Having got past that stage, the firm will also need to check whether there are any client restrictions that would prevent them accepting the new holding, such as where the client has set restrictions barring the purchase of a particular stock or representation in a sector. They will also need to consider the impact of capital gains tax and whether that might change their decision such as by accepting a loan note alternative so that they can defer crystallising the gain until later tax years.

A similar set of considerations will need to be applied for trust portfolios with potentially different investment models for different trust types generating yet further possible option.

At the end of these considerations, investment decisions or recommendations will be made to clients. The results will need to be collated by the corporate actions team to provide a comprehensive instruction to the custodian. All of this, of course, needs to take place within the time-frame set at the beginning of the process.

A question is often asked as to why a decision is not made at the omnibus level holding and applied across all of the underlying clients. The range of possible actions mentioned above is what prevents this and what introduces such complexity in managing and processing corporate actions.

Processing the event

The remaining steps in the process can be summarised under the heading of processing the event.

This includes setting up the event on the firm's systems, reconciling the omnibus holding to the underlying investors, capturing the instructions, instructing the custodian, and concludes with processing the event across the firm's systems and resolving any outstanding claims and queries.

The systems used will clearly vary from firm to firm and depend upon whether the firm uses proprietary software or a specialist corporate actions application and the level of automation it has built into its systems. Whatever system is used, the firm will need to pass accounting records across each client account to record the corporate event and the action taken. The actions that are needed will be common but how each firm achieves the end result will depend upon the systems it deploys.

Processing the event will start with raising the event on the systems used by the firm. There are not only a wide variety of types of corporate action but these are also constantly being developed and changed. The result of this is that it is usually not possible to have an individual template for each type of corporate action. Instead firms will usually develop their systems based on a series of generic templates that can be used for multiple events since, after all, if a new type of event was announced, a firm would not be able to wait for systems development before it processed it.

The firm will then be involved in reconciling the event. This will involve reconciling the position held by the custodian with the underlying records it has for each client. This sounds simple in practice but invariably presents issues as there will usually be transactions in mid-flight as a result of trading and new or closing business which will mean that there are discrepancies between the two positions.

Reconciliations will need to be carried out to identify which clients are entitled in order that an appropriate communication can be issued. Having received instructions from its investment managers and clients, the corporate actions team will then provide a composite instruction to its custodian.

It will then need to process entries across the ledger accounts for the clients who are entitled to the event. This will take place on the record date or when it receives stock or funds for the event depending upon the type of event and how its systems operate.

Finally, there will remain the need to resolve any queries that could not be dealt with during the course of the event, such as claims that need to be settled with brokers where trading took place.

5.5 CORPORATE EVENTS

Introduction

In the following sections we will look in more detail at some of the more common types of corporate action.

Bonus issues and other stock events

In the following section, we will look at bonus issues and some of the other more common stock events.

Bonus issues

A bonus issue involves an issue of further shares to existing shareholders that is made without the existing shareholder making any payment for them. The number of new shares issued to the existing shareholder is in proportion to the number of shares they already hold.

Bonus issues are also referred to as capitalisation issues and scrip issues. The three terms indicate the same type of event and are often used interchangeably.

A bonus issue is usually described by its terms, so for example, if a company decides to issue one new share to existing shareholders for each four shares that they hold it will be referred to as a 1 for 4 bonus issue.

The effect of a bonus issue is to increase the number of shares that a shareholder has and proportionately reduce the share price. This occurs because the company is not receiving any new funds, so it is worth exactly the same after the bonus issue as it was beforehand.

This can be seen in Table 5.4. An investor holds 1000 shares in ABC Holdings which are priced at 100p per share and are therefore valued at £1000. A bonus issue is announced under which the investor will receive one new share for every four held and so he will receive an additional 250 new shares. His total holding is now 1250 shares but it will still be valued at £1000. The revised share price is calculated by dividing the value, £1000, by the new number of shares held, 1250, which means that the share price will reduce to 80p.

On the face of it, a bonus issue does not add any value to either the investor or the company and raises the reasonable question as to why a company should undertake one and why they are so popular.

They are undoubtedly a feature of UK equity markets and their widespread use is usually attributed to the belief that a high share price deters investors and therefore announcing a bonus issue will make the company's share price seem more attractive and therefore more

Table 5.4 Bonus issue

	Shareholding	Price	Value
Before the bonus issue	1000	100p	£1,00
After the bonus issue	1250	80p	£1,00

marketable. In practice, to be in such a position a company will usually be performing well and the attraction of a bonus issue may well be more a reaction to that.

A bonus issue will usually be announced with the results of a company. A record date will be set for the event and the shares will be credited to existing accounts by Crest overnight on that day so that they are available the next business day. Fractions are usually either disregarded or are instead aggregated and sold for the benefit of the company.

From time to time, the new shares may be issued and only qualify for dividends after the next dividend that is due has been paid. In these cases, the new shares will be issued as a new line of stock – a pari passu issue – and later amalgamated with the existing holding into the same class of shares.

Consolidations and Subdivisions

Consolidations and subdivisions are opposite in that one is used to reduce the number of shares in issue and the other is used to increase the number of shares in issue.

A consolidation is where a company reduces the number of shares in issue by consolidating the existing shares into new shares with a higher nominal value. This might, for example, be where a company decides to consolidate four existing ordinary 25p shares into one new ordinary £1 share.

Table 5.5 Consolidation

	Shareholding	Price	Value
Before the consolidation	20,000 ordinary 25p shares	5p	£1000
After the consolidation	5000 ordinary £1 shares	20p	£1200

As with a bonus issue, this does not involve any payment by the shareholder and will have an opposite effect of increasing the share price. A consolidation will often be used where the share price of a company is too low, which makes it unattractive to investors.

In Table 5.5, the share price of the company is in the 'penny share' stakes and by consolidating the shares the company is hoping that the shares may attract other investors. The company announces a consolidation whereby each existing four ordinary 25p shares are consolidated into one new ordinary £1 share, which has the effect of increasing the share price.

By contrast a subdivision is where a company increases the number of shares by reducing the nominal value and proportionately increasing the number of shares held. This would be the reverse of the above example where a company might decide to issue four new ordinary 25p shares in place of an existing ordinary £1 share.

This might be used by a company who wants to reduce itsr share price and make it more attractive to investors. In Table 5.6, it can be seen as having the same effect as a bonus issue except that the nominal value of the shares would change.

Table 5.6 Subdivision

	Shareholding	Price	Value
Before the subdivision	1000 ordinary £1 shares	£10	£10,000
After the subdivision	4000 ordinary 25p shares	250p	£10,000

A bonus issue and a subdivision will have the same effect and be used for similar reasons and which route is chosen will be driven by accounting considerations.

Rights issues

Rights issues and open offers are methods available to a company to raise additional finance from its existing shareholders.

In this section, we will concentrate on rights issues but it should be borne in mind that an open offer is similar to a rights issue except that the right to subscribe for further shares is not transferable.

What is a rights issue?

A rights issue is an offer that is made to existing shareholders of a company to subscribe for additional shares. The offer is made by the company itself and leads to new shares being issued in exchange for additional capital from the shareholders.

It is one of the methods that a company can use to raise additional capital and is generally regarded as an efficient and cost-effective way of raising long-term funds. The rationale behind this is that if the company can make an effective case for use of the additional funds then the existing shareholders as long-term investors in the company are best placed to provide finance at the lowest cost.

Whether a company uses the rights issue route to raise funds will depend upon the cost of funding from other potential sources. A company will clearly look to source any additional funds by the cheapest method possible and will take into account many factors including the cost of long-term borrowing from banks, interest rates on quoted corporate bonds, the level of financial gearing that is appropriate for a company of its type and the tax effectiveness of any selected route.

Terms of a rights issue

A rights issue offers existing shareholders the option to take up additional shares at a set price and as a result, rights issues are usually referred to by their terms.

So, for example, a company might have 10 million shares in issue and wish to raise additional capital of £600 million for expansion. To do so it might announce a rights issue to raise that capital by offering existing shareholders one new share for each five existing shares that they hold at 300p each. Assuming that all of the shareholders took up the offer the company would issue 2 million new shares at £3 each and receive the £600 million capital it required. So the rights issue would be referred to as a 1 for 5 rights @ 300p.

The price of the new shares will obviously be set at a discount to the current price; otherwise the investor would simply buy further stock in the market. The amount of the discount will vary and may be either at a small discount to the current market price or deeply discounted.

A deeply discounted rights issue used to be seen as a sign that a company was in financial distress but its use has steadily increased and is now seen as the norm. The deep discount lowers the underwriting risk and, in volatile markets, allows companies to raise large amounts of equity that would not always be possible under a standard tightly discounted rights issue.

Timetable

When a company announces a rights issue, it must go through certain procedures which start well before the record date, including potentially calling an extraordinary general meeting (EGM) and obtaining approval for any changes to pre-emption rights.

Under UK and European company law, shareholders have what are known as pre-emption rights. Under this, it is obligatory for companies to offer existing shareholders the right to take part in an issue of new shares. Without this protection, companies would be able to issue new shares to other investors, dilute an investor's holding and change the ownership of the company.

The rights are contained either in the Articles of Association or imposed by Section 89 of the Companies Act 1985. These pre-emption rights may be disapplied either by a provision in the Articles of Association or by a special resolution of the company for a particular new issue.

Once any issues associated with pre-emption rights are resolved, the company can proceed to launch the rights issue. The launch will be accompanied by a press release which will be broadcast by the London Stock Exchange via its Regulatory News Service and by issue of a Stock Situations Notice and will then be covered on the main financial websites and newspapers.

The rights to subscribe to the new shares can be traded separately from the main holding and are therefore issued as a new stock line. Rights start of as being referred to as nil paid, that is the cost has yet to be paid. Once the investor decides to take up the rights and pays the cost, they then become known as fully paid and those shares will eventually be added to their existing holding.

Rights issues follow a standard timetable set by Crest that allows a period of approximately three weeks for the event to be managed and processed. The timetable for a rights issue refers to the start of dealings as D and the deadline for action to be taken as D plus the number of business days later, for example, the last date for acceptance and payment in full is D+22.

Some of the main milestones for a rights issue would typically be as shown in Table 5.7.

Table 5.7   Rights issue timetable

Action	Timetable	Description
Record date	D−3	The record date would typically be three days prior to commencement of dealing
Dealing	D	Dealing starts in nil paid rights
Take up	D+22	Final date for acceptance and payment
Certificates	D+37	Shares credited to Crest stock accounts

Options available to the investor

Investors have a number of choices about what action they take over the rights issue. They can:

- take up the rights;
- sell the rights;
- sell sufficient to take up the balance;
- take no action and allow the rights to lapse.

Each of these is considered below.

Take up of rights

As the name suggests, this is where the investor acquires additional shares in exchange for a cash payment.

When the investor subscribes for the new shares, they will be transferred on to a new fully paid stock line. The custodian will advise when the stock is credited to the Crest stock account and the fully paid shares will be transferred to the main stock line and merged with the investor's underlying holding.

Sell the rights

The investor may, however, not wish to invest more money into the company either because they are not convinced about management's investment plans, or they have insufficient funds or for a myriad of other reasons.

In this scenario, one of their options is to sell the shares. Not all investors will want to take up their entitlement and others will want to use the timing of the rights issue to increase their holdings. As a result, there is invariably a ready market in rights.

An investor wishing to sell his rights will normally do so while the rights are still nil paid. During the period of the rights issue, the rights will be traded as a separate stock in its own right. It will usually trade at a premium and its price will depend upon the difference between the market price of the underlying shares and the cost of taking up the new shares.

In practice, however, the price or premium will be determined by supply and demand. Most trading in nil paid rights takes place in the early days of a rights issue and as demand drops off, the price will also often fall away.

Sell sufficient

Alternatively, the investor may want to take up the shares but has insufficient funds to do so or may want to take up only a proportion of their holding.

They may therefore sell sufficient of the rights to raise the funds to take up the remainder.

Allow to lapse

Finally, the investor may choose to take no action and allow the rights to lapse; in other words, they have decided to reject the offer to subscribe for further shares.

This also means that they have chosen not to sell the rights in the open market. The reasons for this will usually be cost related, such as minimum stockbroking charges which may make the transaction not worthwhile or the premium is so low as not to warrant a trade.

In a rights issue, the company will recognise that not all shareholders will take up the rights and they offer an alternative to a direct sale by the investor. Any rights that are not taken up are treated as lapsed and the company's broker will endeavour to sell these in the market. The company will then distribute the proceeds to the lapsed shareholders.

Return of capital to shareholders

Return of capital to shareholders has been a regular type of corporate action for the last few years as companies have used periods of low interest rates to increase their gearing and return the capital raised back to shareholders.

This type of financial engineering usually involves a number of corporate actions including share buy-backs, the issue of B shares and consolidation of the original equity. We will therefore look at each of these types of corporate action as part of an overall scheme.

Share buy-backs

A share buy-back is when a company buys its own shares in the market from other investors and then either cancels the shares or holds them in treasury for reissue later on.

A share buy-back programme will usually be launched when a company has surplus capital and the effect of this will be to reduce the number of shares in issue and increase net assets per share and hopefully earnings per share. The company may also hope that the share price will rise as a result.

Companies need to seek shareholder approval to buy their own shares and constraints will be set on how this can operate. These will usually include a limit on the number of shares that can be bought of 10% of the issued shares, that the minimum price paid is not less than the nominal value and that the maximum price paid does not exceed the mid-market price by 5% for the preceding five business days.

There is a number of ways in which a share buy- back can be implemented. The company can buy shares in the market from other shareholders, it can buy a set proportion from each shareholder or it can invite shareholders to tender.

Once it has bought them, the company can either cancel the shares or hold them in treasury. The latter refers to the company retaining the shares for reissue later on, such as when it issues shares to employees under a share option scheme.

B shares

A company will usually issue B shares as part of a plan to return capital to shareholders as this offers the company both cash flow and tax advantages and at the same time, can maximise the return to individual shareholders.

An issue of B shares is achieved by way of a bonus issue. A bonus issue is also referred to as a capitalisation issue and the issue of B shares is a good example of why that term is used. A company will capitalise funds held in the company's share premium account and apply the funds to paying up in full the B shares that are to be allotted to shareholders.

The terms of the issue will state how many B shares each shareholder will receive for each existing ordinary share held. Typically, the B shares will carry limited voting rights and a stock exchange quote will not be sought.

For capital gains tax purposes, the B shares are treated as having been acquired at the same time as the ordinary shares and the base cost will therefore be apportioned between the two shareholdings based on their respective market values on the first day of dealing. Two sets of transactions will therefore need to be posted to client's accounts, one to reduce the book cost of the ordinary shares and the other to raise the B shares with the apportioned value.

As the purpose of issuing the B shares is to return capital to shareholders, the issue documents will declare a dividend on the shares but provide options to shareholders on how they receive it. There will typically be up to four options:

- receive a cash dividend;
- elect to redeem the B shares;
- elect to redeem some of the B shares at a later date;
- elect to convert the B shares into ordinary shares.

An investor can elect to receive a cash dividend in which case the company will make a dividend payment on the B shares, following which they will be converted into deferred shares of negligible value. The dividend will be treated as with any other dividend as income for tax purposes.

Alternatively, a shareholder can elect to have the B shares redeemed. The amount they will be redeemed at will be the same as the cash dividend. This redemption is treated as a disposal for capital gains tax purposes and provided that the investor does not make gains in excess of the annual allowance, no liability to capital gains tax will arise. For higher rate taxpayers, therefore, this has the effect of providing an enhanced return compared to taking the cash dividend which would suffer additional tax.

The third alternative is to defer some or all of the redemption to a later date. This later date is usually in the next year and the option is included so that investors can phase the realisation of the gains over two tax years, allowing them to potentially manage their CGT liability by utilising two years' worth of annual CGT allowances.

The other alternative that a company might offer is to convert the B shares into additional ordinary shares.

Consolidation

The issue of B shares involves capitalising part of the funds held in the share premium account and distributing this to shareholders. An adjustment to the number of ordinary shares in issue will therefore be required to reflect this and this is usually achieved by way of a consolidation.

The corporate action will therefore replace the existing ordinary shares with new ordinary shares.

Demergers and spin-offs

A demerger or spin-off occurs when a company decides to separate out a division of the firm into a separate company and thenissues the shares in the new company to its existing shareholders.

A company may demerge a subsidiary for a number of reasons but typically this might be because two separate companies would be valued at more than the combined one or it considered that the business of that subsidiary was not a core competence of the company and that it would produce better performance if it focused on its main business.

A demerger will involve the issue of shares in the new company to the existing shareholders. The distribution does not represent a chargeable event for capital gains tax purposes and instead the base cost for the existing holding is apportioned between that holding and the new one.

The base cost is apportioned based on their respective market values on the first day of dealing. Two sets of transactions will therefore need to be posted to clients' accounts, one to reduce the book cost of the ordinary shares of the original company and the other to raise the new company shares with the apportioned value.

Takeovers and mergers

Takeovers involve one company making a formal offer for the shares of another company in exchange for cash, stock or shares or a combination of each. The takeover will usually be contested by the target company as opposed to a merger, which is where two companies mutually agree to the terms.

The process of acquiring another company, either by way of a takeover or by a merger, is supervised by the Panel on Takeovers and Mergers. Its role is to ensure that shareholders are treated fairly and that shareholders of the same class receive equal treatment. Any wider questions of public interest are dealt with by the Competition Commission, the Office of Fair Trading, the Department of Trade and Industry or the European Commission.

Once a bid is announced, both companies become subject to a strict timetable as shown in Table 5.8.

The potential range of options that might be available under a takeover or merger is wide and so no typical offer can be described. As part of the bid, the bidder is quite likely to offer a series of options from cash to shares or bonds or a mixture of all three. What option is selected will vary also depending upon the investment view taken

Table 5.8 Bid timetable

Day	Action
–28	Bid announced
0	Bidder must dispatch its offer document within 28 days of announcing and state the offer price and at what level of acceptance the offer will become unconditional
+14	Within 14 days of the offer document being issued, the board of the target company must advise its shareholders whether it believes the offer to be in the interest of shareholders or not
+21	The offer must remain open for a minimum period of 21 days. If the bidder has received enough acceptances, then the offer becomes unconditional. If it has not received enough acceptances, then the offer can be extended for another 39 days and the offer price increased
+39	This is the last day that the target company can issue a defence document if it continues to reject the offer
+46	This is the last day that the bidder can revise its offer
+60	If the offer has not gone unconditional by day 60, the bid lapses and the bidder cannot make another bid for a further 12 months

on the bidding company and the tax position of the investor.

If the investor chooses to accept a single option, such as cash or shares, the processing of the event is straightforward. Where the cash offer is accepted, the old holding will be written off the client's account, recording that the offer was accepted and the cash amount posted to the client's capital account. If shares were taken, then the old holding will be written off and the new holding will be raised using the same book cost. If a mix of options is taken, it will be necessary to apportion the book cost between them to ensure that the correct book cost is applied to each.

Once a decision is made and if it is to accept the offer, a corporate actions team will need to instruct its custodian accordingly. As part of its Crest stock accounts, a custodian will also have an escrow account. Once the offer is accepted, the shares are moved into this account until the offer is unconditional and the proceeds are paid.

ISAs and SIPPs

Processing a corporate event for an investment held in an individual savings account (ISA) or self-invested personal pension plan (SIPP) is no different than processing the event in the client's taxed account.

Additional considerations do, however, need to be applied by a corporate actions team when processing any of the events mentioned above. These arise because HMRC set rules on what are permissible investments that can be held within either account.

Checks should be made when an investment is purchased to ensure that it is an eligible investment for inclusion within an ISA or SIPP. As long as that check has been undertaken, the only time when the nature of the asset should change is on a corporate action.

Where the nature of the underlying investment is changing or an alternative investment is being received as a result of a corporate action, checks should be undertaken to validate that the new asset is a permissible one.

The rules for both are similar but not identical and so it is necessary to check both sets of rules to ensure that they are being followed.

5.6 INCOME EVENTS

In the next sections, we will look at the processing of income events and some of the differences that are seen with collective investment funds and investments held within ISAs.

Interest payments

A standard feature of bonds, whether they are issued by governments, supranational agencies or corporate bodies, is that they pay regular interest payments.

The amount of interest payable is agreed at the issue of a bond and is expressed as a coupon that is payable on the nominal value of the bond.

This can be seen by looking at an example of a government bond, such as Treasury $4^3/_4$% Stock 2015. At the time of writing, the stock is priced at £99.44; that is each £100 nominal of stock will cost £99.44. If an investor were to purchase £10,000 nominal of stock it would cost him £9,944 excluding costs. The investor will receive interest on the nominal amount of £10,000 not on what it has cost to purchase. The investor will receive $4^3/_4$% interest on the £10,000 nominal of stock or £475 gross per annum.

Most bonds have similar characteristics that enable straightforward processing of interest payments. Any differences they have usually revolve around when interest will be paid and whether the interest rate is fixed, floating or index linked.

Interest from UK government and corporate bonds is generally payable half yearly, so in the case of the example above, interest on Treasury $4^3/_4$ Stock 2015 is payable on 7 March and September. The interest can be paid either gross or net of tax. Interest on eurobonds, by contrast, is paid annually and is paid gross.

The majority of bonds have fixed coupons as in the example above. The coupon may, however, be floating or index linked. With floating-rate bonds, the rate of interest will vary during its term and the rate payable will usually be set by reference to a benchmark index, such as LIBOR, the London inter bank offered rate. The UK government has issued index-linked bonds where the rate of interest paid is uplifted to allow for the effect of inflation. In both cases, there is a time lag between the calculation and the time of payment to allow for the rate to be disseminated by vendor price feeds and the new rate used for interest processing.

Most bonds can be paid either gross or net of tax. The subsequent tax treatment will depend upon the tax position of the investor and Table 5.9 shows the tax treatment of interest when it is received gross and net.

Gilt strips and zero coupon bonds

Gilt strips and zero coupon bonds differ from standard bonds in that neither pays any interest. Instead, the bond is priced in such way that the amount that will be repaid at maturity is enhanced to allow for lost interest.

A zero coupon bond is, as the name implies, a bond that does not have a coupon and does not pay any interest during its life. Instead the bond will be priced in such a way that the amount payable at maturity provides the investor with a similar return to what they would have received from a conventional bond.

A gilt strip is a type of zero coupon bond. Stip stands for separate trading of registered interest and principal. If an investor purchases a conventional gilt, they will receive

Table 5.9 Treatment of interest

Tax band	Tax rate	Gross interest	Net interest
Non-taxpayer	0%	No tax due	Tax at 20% will have been deducted and can be reclaimed
Starting rate of tax	10%	Tax at 10% on the gross amount received is due	Tax at 20% will have been deducted and the additional 10% tax can be reclaimed
Basic rate tax	22%	Tax at 20% on the gross amount received is due	The 20% tax deducted is treated as settling any further liability
Higher rate of tax	40%	Tax at 40% on the gross amount received is due	Tax at 20% will have been deducted and a further 20% tax will be due

a series of interest payments and a final redemption payment. When a gilt is stripped, each of these payments is treated as a security in its own right and can be traded separately. So, for example, an investor can purchase just the redemption payment element, such as 4% Treasury Principal Strip 07Mar2009 or just a coupon strip such as Treasury Coupon Strip 07Dec2007.

Gilt strips and zero coupon bonds have a useful role to play in private investor's portfolios. If an investor needs to fund a known future liability such as school fees, they could purchase a gilt that is due to mature near the time to ensure that they have sufficient funds to meet the liability. The gilt will, however, pay interest which the investor will have to reinvest at whatever rates are available at the time. Although there is certainty about the amount that will be repaid at maturity, the rate that can be earned on the interest payments is uncertain.

An alternative strategy is to purchase a gilt strip that is due to mature when needed and which will give a more certain return. So for example, if an investor needed to invest funds to pay school fees and wanted £5000 to be available each year they could buy a range of strips as shown in Table 5.10.

Because neither type of bond carries a regular coupon, they are subject to tax rules that aim to ensure that income tax is not avoided.

Although any gain on the gilt strip will not arise until redemption, they are instead taxed as income on an annual basis. Gilt strips are treated as having been disposed of on the 5 April and reacquired on the 6 April and any resulting gain or loss is taxed or relieved as income.

Accrued income scheme

When an investor trades in bonds, the cost or proceeds will be composed of the consideration, which is the nominal value times the price of the bond, and a payment in

Table 5.10 Gilt strip funding schedule

Year	Nominal	Stock	Price	Cost	Redemption date	Redemption proceeds
2008	£5000	Treasury 5% Principal Strip 07March2008	95.05	£4752	07/032008	£5000
2009	£5000	Treasury 4% Principal Strip 07Mar2009	90.28	£4514	07/12/2009	£5000
2010	£5000	Treasury 4³/₄% Principal Strip m07June2010	84.82	£4241	07/06/2010	£5000
2011	£5000	Treasury 4¹/₄ Principal Strip 07Mar2011	81.85	£4092	07/03/2011	£5000
2012	£5000	Treasury 5% Principal Strip 07Mar2012	78.12	£3906	07/03/2012	£5000

respect of the interest that has accrued since the last interest payment.

Bond prices can be quoted clean or dirty. In most markets, bonds will be priced clean, which is the price without any accrued interest, but will settle dirty, which is including accrued interest.

There are tax rules surrounding accrued interest which are aimed at ensuring that any accrued interest included in a trade does not avoid being liable to income tax. Although it will be the responsibility of the investor to return this to the tax authorities, it is necessary to understand how the rules operate as they affect how it is processed across an investor's account.

When an investor undertakes a trade in a bond, a calculation of the accrued interest from the day after the last interest payment date to the settlement date inclusive is made. The seller will receive the accrued interest and will be liable to income tax on that amount. The purchaser will have made the payment and so when the next interest payment is received, a part of it will be a return of his capital and so will be able to claim relief for the amount paid to the seller.

Where a stock is traded ex-dividend, the position will be different as accrued interest will be deducted from the sale proceeds paid to the seller. This is known as rebate interest. The principle is the same, so this time the seller can claim relief and the purchaser will be liable to tax on the accrued interest.

The other key point to note is when the liability to tax is due. The charge to tax or the relief does not relate to the tax year in which the transaction takes place but the tax year in which the next interest payment is made. This may well be the same year, but that is not always the case.

Table 5.11 demonstrates this by showing transactions in a gilt and the year in which the charge to tax or relief will be assessed.

It is important to ensure that the next pay date is taken into account when processing an accrued interest transaction so that the charge or relief will appear on the correct year's composite tax certificate that will be sent to the client.

Dividend payments

A dividend represents a payment by the company to its shareholders of a proportionate amount of the profits it has made and that it has determined will be distributed. It is the reward that investors receive for taking the risk of investing in the company.

Shareholders do not have any right to a dividend, instead the board of directors of the company must determine whether a dividend is to be paid and how much. They do, however, need to seek approval for its proposal from the shareholders at an annual general meeting.

Table 5.11 Accrued income scheme

Holding	Transaction date	Transaction in tax year	Next coupon due	Received in tax year	Year of assessment
Treasury 8% Stock 2021	31 March 2006	2005–6	7 June 2006	2006–7	2006–7
Treasury 4¾ Stock 2015	28 November 2006	2006–7	7 December 2006	2006–7	2006–7
Treasury 8% Stock 2015	5 April 2007	2006–7	7 June 2007	2007–8	2007–8

In order to ensure that there is clarity over who is entitled to a dividend, especially for trades close to the dividend date, there are standard market rules. There are four key dates:

- Announcement date – the date the company announces the rate of dividend to be paid.
- Ex-dividend date – to enable the share register to be updated for payment of the dividend, a share will be traded as ex-dividend, that is without the dividend, a few days before the books are closed on the record date.
- Record date – shareholders recorded on the register at this date will receive the dividend.
- Payment date – the date the actual payment is made.

The London Stock Exchange and Crest have agreed a standard timetable that company registrars are expected to adhere to. Each year, the London Stock Exchange will issue a dividend procedure timetable which sets out the date which should be used for the announcement date, ex-date and record date.

With some exceptions to allow for bank holidays, announcements are to be made no later than a Thursday of each week, with the ex-date being set for the following Wednesday and the record date being set for the Friday. This provides some consistency as to when the ex-date and record date of a share will take place.

The actual payment date is at the discretion of the company but the London Stock Exchange would expect any sizeable company, which is one with more than 100,000

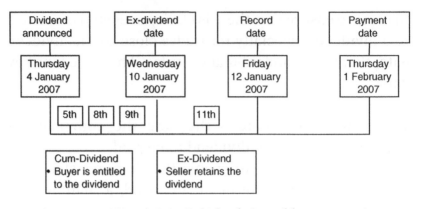

Figure 5.4   Dividend timetable

shareholders, to make the payment within 30 business days of the record date.

The timetable for a dividend payment can be seen in Figure 5.4.

A company will usually pay an interim and final dividend which will be expressed in pence per share. When the dividend is paid it will be accompanied by a tax voucher which will show the tax credit of 10% that is associated with the payment.

For lower rate and basic rate taxpayers, the tax credit satisfies any further liability to income tax that might arise. Importantly, it cannot be used to reclaim tax if the investor is due to a repayment. For higher rate taxpayers, the tax credit can be used to offset the tax of 32.5% that is due on dividend income so that any dividends received will be taxed at a further 22.5%.

Table 5.12 Tax treatment of dividends.

Tax band	Rate	Liability
Non-taxpayer	0%	No more tax due but 10% tax credit cannot be reclaimed
Starting rate of tax	10%	Tax credit satisfies the tax liability and no further tax due
Basic rate tax	22%	Tax credit satisfies the tax liability and no further tax due
Higher rate tax	40%	Dividends are treated as the top slice of income and any amounts in excess of the basic rate band and after deducting any personal allowances are taxable at 32.5% The 10% tax credit is used to offset the tax liability, so that a further 22.5% tax is due

The different tax treatment of dividends can be seen in Table 5.12.

Scrip Dividends and DRIPs

Instead of paying cash dividends, companies will often offer the alternative of receiving shares instead.

The two main schemes are scrip dividends and DRIPs. Scrip dividends are where the company issues new shares to the investor instead of a cash dividend. DRIPs stands for dividend re-investment plans. Under these, the company pays the cash dividend to an administrator and the cash is used to purchase additional shares.

They are attractive to private investors who do not need the dividend income and who instead can use the dividends to periodically increase their stake in a company. It is also attractive for companies as they are providing an option that investors find attractive which can increase shareholder loyalty and can retain the cash that would otherwise have been paid out for reinvestment.

Scrip dividends and DRIPs are similar in that instead of receiving a cash dividend, the investor receives shares instead. Where they differ is in the mechanics of how this is achieved.

Under a scrip dividend, the company uses the cash dividend that would otherwise have been paid to acquire shares for the investor. It will use an average share price to calculate the additional shares to be allocated and the cash equivalent of the dividend is then used to acquire these shares. The shares are issued by the company, so there is no stamp duty or other charges to pay.

With a DRIP, the company will pay the cash dividend to a plan administrator who will then purchase shares in the open market and allocate them to the investor. The number of shares to be acquired is therefore not known until the purchase has been made.

Charges will usually be levied for the shares purchased under a DRIP. The amount will vary but will incorporate a charge of 0.5% for the stamp duty payable on the purchase and any administration charge levied by the plan administrator.

Processing scrip dividends and DRIPs takes longer than normal cash dividends due to the time difference needed for either the shares to be added to the account or to be purchased in the market. Typically it can take an extra week for a scrip issue and up to three weeks for DRIPs.

Inevitably, there will be a small amount of the cash dividend left over which could not purchase a whole share. In those cases, the company will retain the cash until the next dividend payment and add it to the amount available to acquire further shares then.

Interest and dividends on collective investment funds

Collective investment funds, such as unit trusts and OE-ICs, can pay either interest or dividends and they are processed and treated in exactly the same way for tax purposes as any other dividends and interest payments.

The areas where they differ that are worth noting is when a fund can make an interest distribution, under what circumstances interest can be paid gross and the treatment of equalisation.

An authorised unit trust or an OEIC can make an interest distribution when the market value of the interest-bearing assets it holds has exceeded 60% for the entire distribution period. If that test is satisfied, the fund can choose to treat the distribution as an interest distribution and pay it subject to deduction of the lower rate of tax of 20%. The fact that part of the underlying income may consist of equity dividends is ignored. In the investor's hands, the interest distribution is treated exactly the same way as any other interest payment.

Funds can only pay interest distributions gross under certain circumstances. The most notable are for gross entities such as pension funds and charities and to ISA and PEP managers.

At the moment, it is not possible for UK investors to request that interest is paid gross as is the case with other interest distributions, such as gilt interest or bank interest. The government has announced plans to extend the existing facility for gross payments to non-taxpaying investors and are consulting on the practical implications of this with industry representatives.

Equalisation payments are seen in many but not all investment funds. When units in a fund are purchased, the price paid may include an amount of income that has accrued up to the date of purchase. This accrued income is referred to as equalisation.

Units that are purchased part way through a distribution period are referred to as group 2 units. When the next distribution is made, the payment made to investors is made up of income since the date of purchase and this accrued income.

The equalisation part of the payment is a return of capital and is not taxable. It should instead be posted to the client's capital account and deducted from the cost of purchase for capital gains tax purposes.

Individual savings accounts

Processing income events to ISAs and PEPs is essentially the same as for a client's taxed account. The differences that arise between the two principally relate to the different tax treatment of an ISA and PEP and the need for the ISA and PEP manager to report details of income arising to HMRC.

Dividends arising in an ISA or a PEP can be processed in exactly the same way as the tax credit is no longer reclaimable. Where interest payments are received that have had tax deducted, the plan manager is able to reclaim the tax as part of its regular submission of return to HMRC.

Part

III

....

OTHER CONSIDERATIONS

Chapter

6

....

CUSTODY

6.1 INTRODUCTION

When an investor uses the services of an investment firm it will clearly expect that the firm will make appropriate arrangements to ensure that any investments held with it are adequately safeguarded.

Many investment firms will use the services of a custodian to achieve this. A custodian will undertake the safekeeping of assets given to its control and arrange to settle trades, collect dividends and interest and manage corporate actions on the underlying investment portfolio.

In this chapter, we will look at the rules surrounding the safeguarding of a client's investments, the services provided by custodians and how a firm should select a custodian and review their ongoing suitability.

6.2 PROTECTION OF CLIENT ASSETS

Under FSA rules an investment firm is expected to arrange protection for client assets where it has responsibility for them.

This is enshrined in FSA Principle 10, which states: 'A firm must arrange adequate protection for clients' assets when it is responsible for them'.

The detailed rules are contained in CASS, the *Client Assets Sourcebook*, and their purpose is to minimise the risk that the client's assets could be used by the firm without the client's knowledge or that they could be treated as the firm's assets in the event of insolvency.

Assets is a term used to include not just quoted investments but any other investment that a client might hold, including items as diverse as passbooks for savings accounts, national savings certificates, unquoted shares and deeds to property.

6.3 SEGREGATION OF SAFE CUSTODY ASSETS

The rules in the *Client Asset Sourcebook* require a clear distinction to be maintained between investments held for clients and the firm's own investments.

This therefore requires:

- Where the firm holds client assets that the title of the account makes it clear that they belong to the client.
- Where a custodian is used that the title of the account at the custodian makes it clear that the account holds client assets.
- Where a nominee is used that appropriate standards of care are adopted.

The purpose of these requirements is to ensure that the client's assets are fully protected in the event that the firm, its custodian or any third party might go into liquidation.

Where an investment firm is part of a larger organisation that has its own custodian, then this has to be disclosed in writing to the client. This disclosure is usually made by including a statement to that effect in the terms and conditions or in the account agreement.

The requirement to protect the client's assets goes beyond segregation and requires a firm to ensure that the safe custody arrangements are appropriate to the value and risk of loss of the investments concerned. It must also ensure that adequate controls are in place to safeguard these documents from damage, misappropriation or other loss.

6.4 USE OF A CUSTODIAN

As a result of these requirements, a firm must arrange to segregate client assets from its assets.

An investment firm clearly has a choice in how it organises its custody arrangements. It might act as its own custodian in the UK and appoint a local custodian in each of the foreign markets in which it invests, or it might appoint a global custodian to manage custody arrangements across the full range of foreign markets in which it has invested assets.

In these days of outsourcing, most investment firms will appoint a separate custodian, leaving the firm to concentrate on its core business activities.

The services that a custodian would typically provide include:

- safe keeping of assets;
- arranging settlement of trades;
- collecting interest and dividend income;
- identifying and taking action on corporate actions;
- managing tax reclaims.

The primary function is the safekeeping of the client's assets and the custodian must have robust processes that protect the assets and only allow those assets to be released in accordance with authorised instructions from the client.

It must also ensure that the client's assets are segregated from its own and that there are legal arrangements in place that protect the client from claims by creditors or others.

To achieve this, title to these assets will usually be registered in the name of a nominee company.

6.5 NOMINEE COMPANIES

Custodians have subsidiary nominee companies that they use for the custody of client assets.

In fact, the CASS rules require that the custodian has a separate nominee company to hold clients' investments, thus ensuring that a client's investments are kept separate from those owned by the firm itself.

Its corporate structure means that it is a legal entity that can be registered on a share register. Client investments will be registered in the name of the nominee company so, as far as the registrar of the company is concerned, the legal owner of the shares is the nominee.

The beneficial ownership, however, remains with the client.

An investment firm will need to decide what type of nominee account structure is appropriate for its business. There are three types of nominee account:

- pooled nominees;
- designated nominees; and
- sole nominees.

A pooled nominee account is where the client's assets are grouped together into one omnibus account with other clients' investments and so only one entry appears on the register.

A designated nominee account is where each client's assets are registered in the nominee's name but are designated with a unique account number, such as HSBC Nominees Account 12345.

A sole nominee account is where a separate nominee company is created solely for the purpose of holding the assets of a client.

6.6 GLOBAL CUSTODIANS

A global custodian will provide safe custody and investment administration activities for the full range of markets that a firm wishes to invest in.

The standard range of services that a global custodian provides includes safekeeping, settlement, asset servicing and tax reclaims. As a result of intense competition, the charge for these services is finely priced and has led to global custodians extending the range of services they provide to areas such as cash management, securities lending and performance analysis.

Some global custodians maintain an extensive network of branches globally so that they can meet the local custody needs of their clients. In areas where they do not have a branch, however, they will appoint a local agent bank to meet their needs for clearing and settlement, asset servicing and cash management.

The local agent bank is referred to as a subcustodian and it can either be a local custodian or regional custodian. A local custodian specialises in providing subcustody services in its home market. They are likely to be used where a country specialist is needed who has expert knowledge of local market practice, language and culture. More usual is the appointment of a regional provider that can offer subcustody services across a range of markets in a region.

The charges that a custodian may make are usually made up of two components:

- a basis point fee charged against the value of assets that the investor holds with the custodian – a basis point is 0.01%; and
- a transaction fee which will be charged according to the number of settlement transactions that the custodian processes on the client's behalf.

The basis point charge is intended to cover the cost of the underlying investment administration that the custodian has to undertake, while the transaction fee represents a charge for the clearing and settlement of trades.

The charges paid by a firm will therefore depend on the value of the funds they place with the custodian and the volume of trades they undertake.

The basis point charge made will depend upon the client and can vary between 0.5 basis points to 2.5 basis points in major markets and can be considerably more elsewhere. For the transaction fee, there will usually be a different tariff for trades in different markets to reflect the differing cost of settlement in each of those markets.

6.7   SELECTING A CUSTODIAN

When selecting a global custodian, the normal process is to invite custodians to provide a detailed proposal for consideration.

There are accepted ways in which tendering for business takes place. The investment firm seeking custody services completes a standardised request for proposal, an RFP, which requests custodians to submit a proposal. In response, the custodian will prepare a response which will detail the services that can be provided and the costs. The investment firm will use the RFP to determine which custodians it will investigate further in order to identify the most suitable candidate for its business.

The type of information that the firm will need to supply to a custodian in an RFP includes:

- background information on the firm and the investment business it undertakes;
- details of the investment funds held including value, types of instruments and markets;
- the markets the firm invests in and the likely volume of trades;
- the services the firm requires;
- the information it expects back from the custodian and the selection criteria it will use.

In response, the custodian will prepare a thorough response which will detail the services it can provide. The type of information provided will include:

- background on the custodian, the number of clients it has, the value of the funds it administers and the number of clients it has gained and lost over the last few years;
- the range of custodian services it can offer and how its accounting and reporting operate;

- the arrangements it has for safekeeping and segregation of assets, the markets it operates and its network of subcustodians;
- the control methodology it operates to ensure its service delivery;
- the strategy it will use to transition the movement of assets to itself;
- costs for custody and transaction charges.

The investment firm can then use the information provided to produce a short list that it will investigate further until it reaches a decision on which custodian has the most appropriate service offering that matches its criteria.

6.8 CUSTODY AGREEMENTS AND SLAs

Once a decision is made as to which custodian to appoint, the investment firm will need to enter into a legal agreement with the custodian and agree a service level agreement (SLA).

The agreement will document, among other items:

- How the assets will be held and registered and how they will be segregated from the assets of the custodian.
- The responsibilities and obligations of the custodian.
- The basis on which instructions will be provided and acted on.

- The reporting that will be made to the client and the deadlines that will apply.
- The service standards that will apply.

As well as a legal agreement, it is normal for an SLA to be put in place. The purpose of an SLA is to document the detail of each service that will be provided and the standards that the parties expect to meet. Examples might be the timescales for when reports will be provided and how quickly queries will be responded to.

The purpose of an SLA is to provide a tool to manage the service provided. To be useful it needs to record the key processes that matter to the client, the performance standards that will apply and how data on actual performance will be captured. To be valuable, it requires clear and timely reporting to the client combined with an effective dialogue between the parties on addressing any areas where standards are not being met.

An SLA would typically contain the details shown in Table 6.1.

The key element within an SLA is to define the key performance indicators (KPIs) that will apply and the reporting and escalation process.

KPIs will typically cover:

- delivery timescales;
- completeness;
- error rates;
- response times;
- meeting benchmarks.

Table 6.1   Typical contents of an SLA

Service	Example
Description of services to be provided	Cash and stock reconciliation
Timescales for delivery or deadlines to be met	Within FSA 25-day limit
Reports to be provided	Reconciliation breaks
Error correction	Timescales and cost allocation
Response times to queries	By type of query
Escalation process	Items over x days old
Disputes process	Heads of department
Review meetings	Formal quarterly review
Regulations	Rules that have to be met, e.g. CASS

Selecting the correct KPIs is critical to managing the service delivery and where possible should be measurable against industry benchmarks. It is important to remember though that they are an indicator of performance and not an end in itself and that the focus should be on service breakdowns and escalation of issues before they become significant.

Issues will arise and these could impact on investment performance or create financial loss, regulatory breaches, fines or negative publicity. It is important therefore that the SLA defines the mechanism for dealing with service breakdowns and specifies:

- the error correction process that will be used;
- the approach that will be adopted where a third party is at fault;

- the escalation process that will be used for service failures;
- the basis for who bears costs;
- a disputes process in the event of non-agreement;
- and finally relevant law in case serious legal action results.

6.9 REVIEWING THE SUITABILITY OF CUSTODIANS

Under FSA rules, it is necessary for a firm to satisfy itself that the custodian it uses can satisfactorily discharge its responsibilities. An investment firm is required is to do this before it appoints a custodian and periodically thereafter.

The rationale behind these rules is to ensure that the interests of investors will be protected by requiring the firm to make sure that the arrangements for safekeeping and segregation will adequately protect the clients' assets.

As a result, a firm is expected to keep records that show the criteria they have used to assess the suitability of a custodian and the rationale behind their decision to appoint a custodian.

Where they continue to retain the services of a custodian, an investment firm is required to undertake regular reviews to ensure that they continue to remain suitable. This requirement applies even where the firm is part of a larger organisation and uses an in-house custodian.

The frequency at which they should review the continued suitability of a custodian will depend on such things as the type of services they use and the markets they invest in but should be at least annually.

The areas that should be considered when reviewing the suitability of a custodian include:

- Safekeeping arrangements – whether the assets of the clients are adequately protected.
- Safety of the client assets – whether the assets would be adequately protected in the event of default by the custodian or any of its subcustodians.
- Service performance – whether the custodian has the expertise to effectively deliver the services required, their market standing as judged in publicly available custody surveys and whether the service delivery has met the required performance standards.
- Regulatory position – who the custodian is regulated by and whether it has been censured or fined by the regulatory authorities.
- Control processes – whether the control processes the custodian has are adequate to protect the client assets and deliver the required standards of service.
- Disaster recovery arrangements – what arrangements the custodian has to continue to operate in the event of disruption and the effectiveness of any contingency testing.
- Financial stability – whether the financial resources of the custodian will allow it to continue to deliver its services.

This will involve a detailed assessment of the services the custodian proposes to provide or has provided in the last year and investigation into surrounding areas.

The information will need to come from variety of sources such as:-

- Information from the custodian on how assets are safeguarded and the CSDs it uses.
- Legal opinion on the effectiveness of the custody and subcustody arrangements and the investor protection it provides.
- Data on how effective the custodian has been in meeting its key performance indicators and the number and severity of service breakdowns.
- Notices published by the FSA and other regulators on their websites censuring or fining the custodian.
- Market survey reports issued by Global Custody, a market survey organisation, on the service performance of custodians.
- An audited report on the effectiveness of the control environment known as a FRAG 21 report.
- Details of the financial position of the company can be obtained from the report and accounts of the company.

To assist with this process, the custody industry has developed a set of reports that are intended to assist clients when making assessments of their custodians.

These reports address the internal controls that custodians have in place to monitor and mitigate risks. Those controls are audited and reports are produced which custodians make available to their clients. The reports are known as a FRAG 21 in the UK and a SAS 70 in the US.

A FRAG 21 is an independently audited report on the effectiveness of internal controls used by investment custodians. The Financial Reporting Action Group (FRAG) has developed standards on a range of accounting issues for the Institute of Chartered Accountants including reporting on custodians.

A formal report recording the assessment and the results of the review should be prepared. There should be a formal process whereby the results of the review are considered and accepted by the board of the investment firm.

This might be undertaken by submitting it to a subcommittee of the board, such as an investment or operations committee who would assess the report and if approved, recommend to the board that the results are accepted.

Good corporate governance practice would suggest that this recommendation and the acceptance of the findings are recorded in the board minutes.

Chapter

7

. . . .

TAX

7.1 INTRODUCTION

While tax is a specialist subject in its own right, individuals who are involved in investment administration need to have an understanding of the various taxes and how they affect the investment portfolios of their clients.

Investment firms will process dividend and interest payments to clients' investment accounts and need to know that the way they are dealing with these payments is correct. Firms will need to have an understanding of how capital gains tax is calculated as it will affect the entries they pass for trades and corporate actions, and they may need to have a detailed understanding if they take the impact of CGT into account when managing a client's portfolio.

Tax will also be involved in dealing with income arising from overseas investments and an understanding of how withholding tax operates is needed so that the client receives the correct amount of income and the firm issues an accurate tax certificate.

A detailed understanding of tax is beyond the scope of this book, so this chapter will focus on understanding the principles that are needed to undertake investment administration.

7.2 INCOME TAX

Before looking at how dividends and interest payments are treated for income tax purposes, we need to first consider some general principles surrounding how income tax is charged.

Liability to tax

Individuals are liable to tax on the income they receive in each tax year. The tax year runs from 6 April in one year to 5 April in the following year. The income that is taxable includes earnings from employment or self- employment and, of course, income from investments.

The income an individual receives needs to be grossed up and then is divided between three sources of income:

- non-savings income such as income from earnings or pensions;
- interest on savings such as bank interest or interest payments on a fixed income security; and
- dividends income.

Grossing up means identifying the amount of income that was received before any tax was deducted. For example, an investor might receive net interest on a government stock of £80 but tax of £20 will have been deducted and it is the sum of the two figures £100 that is called the gross amount.

The total grossed up income is the amount on which income tax will be assessed. From this total figure, an individual can deduct any personal allowances that they have available before any tax that is due is calculated.

Non-savings income is taxed first, followed by savings income and then dividends.

How this operates can be understood by taking an example of individual's income and looking at how the personal allowance and the tax bands are allocated and the liability to income tax that each type of income then attracts.

For this example, we will ignore national insurance contributions and assume that the individual has the following sources of income:

- income from employment of £50,000;
- interest income of £10,000 from which tax at 20% has been deducted;
- gross dividends of £20,000 which have a tax credit of £2,000.

And use the tax allowances and rates for the 2007/8 tax year which are:

- personal allowance – £5,225;
- starting rate – first £2,230 of taxable income is charged at 10%;
- basic rate – taxable income between £2,231 and £34,600 is charged at 22%;
- higher rate – any taxable income over £34,600 is charged at 40%.

The first step is to divide the total income received between the three types of income with the personal

Table 7.1 Calculating tax liability (1)

Taxable income	Non-savings income	Savings income	Dividends	Total
Earnings	50,000			
Interest income		10,000		
Dividends			20,000	
Total income	50,000	10,000	20,000	80,000
Personal allowance	(5,225)			(5,225)
Taxable income	44,775	10,000	20,000	74,775

allowance being deducted from the non-savings income as shown in Table 7.1.

The next step is to calculate the tax due using the tax bands and starting with non-savings income so that the lower rates of tax are applied against this source first. The way this calculation is undertaken is shown in Table 7.2.

The savings income is taxed next and as the lower and basic rate bands have been fully utilised, then it will be taxable at 40% as shown in Table 7.3. As the calculation shows, the tax already paid can be set off against the amount due.

Table 7.2 Calculating tax liability (2)

Non-savings income	Income	Tax rate	Tax
Starting rate band	2,230	10%	223
Basic rate band	32,370	22%	7,121
Higher rate band	10,175	40%	4,070
Total	44,775		11,414

Table 7.3   Calculating tax liability (3)

Savings income	Amount
Gross interest received	10,000
Tax due at 40%	4,000
Less: tax already deducted	(2,000)
Additional tax due	2,000

Finally, the tax on the dividends is calculated as shown in Table 7.4. The tax treatment of dividends is explained in more detail in the next section, but it should be noted that the higher rate of tax applicable to dividends is 32.5%.

The same approach applies, however, in that as the lower and basic rate band have been fully used up the gross income is taxable at the higher rate of tax due on dividends and the tax credit can be used to offset the tax due.

The key points to note from the above are that savings and dividend income are treated as the top slices of income when calculating the amount of income tax due. In the next sections, we will consider these in more detail.

Table 7.4   Calculating tax liability (4)

Dividend income	Amount
Gross dividends received	20,000
Tax due at 32.5%	6,500
Less: tax already deducted	(2,000)
Additional tax due	4,500

7.3 TAX TREATMENT OF DIVIDENDS

Dividends are paid to shareholders out of the profits that a company makes. That profit is liable to corporation tax and when it is distributed to shareholders, the dividend that is paid is treated as having already paid tax.

When the investor receives the dividend, it carries a 10% tax credit that the investor can use to set off against any income tax that might be due on the dividend.

The gross amount of dividend that an investor receives is treated as the net payment plus a tax credit of 10%. In practice this means that if an investor receives a dividend of £90 from a company this amount is treated as the net amount and carries a tax credit of 10% or £10 to give a gross amount of £100.

When the dividend is paid, it will come with a tax voucher that shows the net payment and the tax credit as shown in Figure 7.1.

Whether any further income tax liability will arise will depend upon the investor's personal tax position. The extent of any liability was shown in the Chapter 5 and is shown again in Table 7.5.

Where an investor is not liable to income tax because their income is below the tax threshold, if they receive a dividend they will have no further liability to tax but equally they cannot reclaim the tax credit.

Tax Voucher	ABC Holdings Ltd			
	Ordinary £1 Shares			
	DIVIDEND FOR THE YEAR ENDED 30 JUNE 2006			
	PAYABLE 12 OCTOBER 2006			
PAYABLE TO	HOLDING	RATE PER SHARE	TAX CREDIT	DIVIDEND PAYABLE
J Smith	1,000	9p	£10.00	£90.00
				Company Secretary

Figure 7.1 Dividend voucher

This also applies to dividends received within an ISA or PEP.

An investor may be liable to pay tax at the starting rate of tax of 10%. Where this is the case, the tax credit is treated as meeting the liability that is due and no further income tax is due.

Table 7.5 Tax treatment of dividends

Tax band	Rate	Liability
Non-taxpayer	0%	No more tax due but 10% tax credit cannot be reclaimed
Starting rate of tax	10%	Tax credit satisfies the tax liability and no further tax due
Basic rate tax	22%	Tax credit satisfies the tax liability and no further tax due
Higher rate tax	40%	Dividends are treated as the top slice of income and any amounts in excess of the basic rate band and after deducting any personal allowances are taxable at 32.5% The 10% tax credit is used to offset the tax liability, so that a further 22.5% tax is due

Where the investor is a basic rate taxpayer, they will pay tax at 22% on their non-savings income and 20% on any interest income. By concession, the tax credit is, however, treated as satisfying any tax liability that is due so that no further tax is payable.

It is only higher rate taxpayers who will suffer any additional tax. Although the higher rate of tax is 40%, the amount of tax due on dividends is different and is set at 32.5%. Investors who are higher rate taxpayers can set off the tax credit against that liability and so will be due to pay an additional 22.5% tax on the gross amount of dividends received.

Where an investor receives a dividend from a unit trust or an OEIC, it also will be paid with a tax credit attached and the income tax treatment will be the same except when they receive equalisation.

When the investor buys units in a fund, the price paid may include an amount of income that has accrued up to the date of purchase. When the next dividend is paid, the dividend is made up of income since the date of purchase and this accrued income. This accrued income is referred to as equalisation.

The equalisation part of the payment is treated as a return of the investor's capital and so is not taxable.

Tax treatment of bond interest

Where an investor receives interest, the tax treatment is different.

An investor will receive interest on any savings accounts that they hold and where they have a holding in a government bond or corporate bond. They may also receive an interest distribution from certain types of unit trusts and OEICs.

The tax treatment of each is the same and whether any additional tax is due or can be reclaimed will depend upon whether the interest was paid gross or net. If the payment is made net, then tax at 20% will have been deducted. It will also depend upon what tax band the investor falls into as shown in Table 7.6.

For non-taxpayers, the position is different than with dividends. If they receive interest gross then there will obviously be no tax due, but if the interest has been paid net then the investor will be able to reclaim the tax deducted. This also applies to interest distributions received with ISAs and PEPs.

The position is also different for investors paying the starting rate of tax of 10%. If they receive the payment gross, then they will be liable to pay tax at 10% on the gross amount received. Alternatively, if they receive the payment net, then tax at 20% will have been deducted and they will be able to reclaim the additional tax that has been deducted.

The position is straightforward for basic rate taxpayers. They are liable to pay tax at 20% on savings income and so if the interest is received gross they will be liable to pay tax at 20% on the gross amount and if

Table 7.6 Tax treatment of bond interest

Tax band	Tax rate	Gross interest	Net interest
Non-taxpayer	0%	No tax due	Tax at 20% will have been deducted and can be reclaimed
Starting rate of tax	10%	Tax at 10% on the gross amount received is due	Tax at 20% will have been deducted and the additional 10% tax can be reclaimed
Basic rate tax	22%	Tax at 20% on the gross amount received is due	The 20% tax deducted is treated as settling any further liability
Higher rate of tax	40%	Tax at 40% on the gross amount received is due	Tax at 20% will have been deducted and a further 20% tax will be due

they have received it net, then no further liability will arise.

Higher rate taxpayers are liable to tax on savings income at the higher rate of tax of 40%. As a result, if they receive gross interest they will pay tax at 40% on the amount received. If they receive the interest payment net, then tax of 20% will have been deducted and a further 20% tax will be due to bring the amount paid up to 40%.

Apart from the conventional tax treatment of a bond, we also need to consider the tax that may be due on bond interest under the accrued income scheme, how gilt strips are treated and the tax treatment of bond interest received in an ISA.

Where an investor has undertaken trades in government stocks or other bonds, the accrued interest that is included in the purchase or sale cost has to also be brought into account for income tax.

This is known as the accrued income scheme and the way in which it operates is explained in Chapter 5. In brief, a seller will receive accrued interest and will be liable to income tax on that amount. The purchaser will have made the payment and so when the next interest payment is received, a part of it will be a return of his capital and so he will be able to claim relief for the amount paid to the seller.

Where a stock is traded ex-dividend, the position will be different as accrued interest will be deducted from the sale proceeds paid to the seller. This is known as rebate interest. The principle is the same, so this time the seller can claim relief and the purchaser will be liable to tax on the accrued interest.

We can now turn to how gilt strips are treated. The features of a gilt strip are explained more fully in Chapter 5.

If an investor purchases a conventional government stock, they will receive a series of interest payments and a final redemption payment. When a government stock is stripped, each of these payments is treated as a security in its own right and can be traded separately.

A gilt strip does not generate any income therefore and instead is bought at a discount to the amount it will be repaid at. To ensure that they are not used to avoid income tax, gilt strips are subject to different tax treatment. This involves all gains and losses on gilt strips being taxed as income on an annual basis.

At the end of the tax year, individuals are deemed for tax purposes to have disposed of, and reacquired, their holdings of gilt strips at the prevailing market value. Any gain or loss arising as a result of this is added to the gains or losses on any strips that mature in that tax year. The overall gain is then taxed as income or relief given if a loss is created.

If bonds are held in an ISA or PEP, then any interest arising is not liable to tax. If tax has been deducted, the ISA manager can reclaim this from HM Revenue & Customs and credit it to the investor's account.

Tax certificates

Where a client has an investment account, the firm will receive the dividends and interest payments and any associated tax vouchers on behalf of the investor.

Details of all income received will be included in the income statements that the firm sends to the client but the firm will also need to issue a tax certificate.

Instead of providing the client with a tax voucher for each dividend and interest payment received, the firm will instead provide an omnibus tax certificate that summarises the income received on behalf of the client. To be able to issue a tax certificate, the firm must agree the format with HM Revenue & Customs.

The omnibus certificate will need to break the total income received on behalf of the client into a number of categories. These categories will correspond with the information that the client needs to enter onto their tax return namely:

- interest distributions;
- interest distributions from UK authorised unit trusts and OEICs;
- dividends from UK companies;
- dividend distributions from UK authorised unit trusts and OEICs;
- stock dividends from UK companies.

Depending upon the type of investments held by the client, further categories may also be needed to record income from overseas companies or unit trusts and the amount of withholding tax deducted.

7.4 CAPITAL GAINS TAX

Capital gains tax (CGT) is the tax that is charged when an individual disposes of an asset and would typically arise on the gain made when shares are sold or when a gift is made.

Individuals who are resident or ordinary resident in the UK are liable to CGT, the assets which are liable to CGT are known as chargeable assets and the disposal of an asset that is liable to CGT is known as a chargeable disposal.

Chargeable and exempt assets

The charge to CGT arises when an asset is disposed of, either by way of sale or gift. Most assets are chargeable to CGT but there are occasions where CGT is not payable and some assets are exempt from CGT.

The occasions where CGT is not payable include the following:

- Transfers between husband and wife.
- When an investor dies – the assets are treated as being disposed of at the date of death because they will be transferred to the beneficiaries but the event is exempt from CGT. This exemption avoids what would otherwise be a double charge to tax as there would be a charge on the gain to the date of death and an inheritance tax liability as well.
- The gains made on any investments held in an ISA or PEP.
- Gifts to charities.

The assets that are exempt from tax include:

- UK government stocks.
- Qualifying corporate bonds which are nonconvertible, sterling denominated bonds that pay a commercial rate of interest.
- Principal private residence.
- National Savings Certificates and Premium Bond prizes.
- Assets known as chattels which include a private car.
- Shares in a venture capital trust or enterprise investment scheme provided certain conditions are met.

Tax charge

Capital gains tax is chargeable on the net gains that an individual makes during a tax year, which are the total gains less any losses that arise.

There are some quite complex rules surrounding how the gains are calculated but once calculated, there is an annual allowance that can be deducted. This is one of the tax allowances that are changed each year in the budget and for the tax year 2007/08 it has been set at £9200.

If the total gains exceed the personal allowance, then the excess is liable to tax. The way that this is calculated is to treat the gain as the top slice of income and tax it accordingly. So, if we return to the example used before, if the same investor had net gains after the annual allowance of £10,000 then this would be added after the dividend income and taxed at 40%.

The key point to note is that any gains are added after any other income and so the rate they are taxed at depends upon the other sources of income of the investor. So gains can be taxed at either the 10% starting rate, the 20% savings rate or the 40% higher rate or a combination of these.

How CGT is calculated

The gain that is chargeable to capital gains tax is arrived at by deducting the cost of acquisition from the sale proceeds.

If a client has held a share for a relatively short time and there have been no corporate actions then this can be a relatively simple calculation. Where the client has held it for some time it can be quite complex. The main stages of a CGT computation are shown in Table 7.7.

The meaning of the terms in Table 7.7 is as follows:

- Allowable costs – this is the cost of acquisition plus certain other allowable items such as the costs of enhancing the asset.
- Indexation – this is an allowance which reduces the gain to allow for the effects of inflation. It only applies to assets acquired before April 1998 and cannot be used to turn a gain into a loss or increase a loss.

Table 7.7 Steps in a CGT calculation (1)

Calculation:	£
Proceeds of sale	
Less: Allowable costs	
Gain before indexation	_____
Less: Indexation	
Indexed gain	_____
Less: Other reliefs	
Chargeable gain	_____
	_____

- Other reliefs – these are other allowances that can be used to reduce the gain, such as business asset roll-over relief.

This computation produces the gain or loss on the disposal of an individual asset. It is then necessary to add together all of the individual disposals to produce a total for the year. Table 7.8 shows how this is calculated.

Allowable losses are created when an asset is sold at a loss. Losses that arise in a tax year must be set off

Table 7.8 Steps in a CGT calculation (2)

Total chargeable gains	
Less: Allowable losses	
Chargeable gains after losses	_____
Less: Taper relief	
Tapered chargeable gains	_____
Less: Annual exemption	
Amount chargeable to CGT	_____

against gains to produce a net gain for the year. If the allowable losses are greater than the gains they can be carried forward and deducted from gains in subsequent years.

Once losses have been deducted, taper relief can be applied if the gains for the year then exceed the annual exemption. Taper relief is used to reduce the chargeable gain based on how long the asset has been held.

If there is still a gain after applying taper relief, the annual exemption is deducted to give the chargeable gain for the tax year.

In the following sections, there is a fuller explanation of indexation allowance and taper relief as well as the rules that are applied when a part disposal takes place.

Matching rules

Issues can arise in calculating the gain on disposal of shares because only part of the holding is disposed of. This is because you need to determine which shares were sold and what acquisition cost to use.

There is a set of rules, known as the matching rules, which determine the order in which shares are sold. The rules are designed to identify which shares have been disposed of and what acquisition cost can be deducted when calculating the chargeable gain.

Shares are treated as having been disposed of in the following order:

- Any shares purchased on the same day as the sale.
- Any purchases made in the 30-day period after the sale.
- Purchases made after 5 April 1998 on a last-in, first-out basis.
- Then a pool of shares acquired between 6 April 1982 and 5 April 1998.
- Then any shares acquired between 6 April 1965 and 5 April 1982.
- Finally any shares acquired before 6 April 1965.

The second bullet point, which requires matching share disposals with acquisitions within the following 30 days, prevents a shareholder from carrying out 'bed and breakfasting' of shares, as used to be possible several years ago.

Indexation allowance

Indexation was introduced in 1982 to allow investors to make an adjustment to their acquisition cost as a result of inflation.

At the time, inflation had been running at high levels for many years and many investors were becoming liable to CGT on share sales simply because of inflation. The government of the time introduced an indexation allowance that allowed the effects of inflation to be removed so that the investor was taxed on the true underlying gain.

The allowance operated by adjusting the acquisition cost of an investment by a factor that represented the increase in the retail price index. The indexation allowance was subsequently withdrawn but investors are able to apply indexation to any investments they acquired from the date the allowance started on 31 March 1982 up to the date it was withdrawn on 6 April 1998.

To do this, the indexation allowance is calculated on each investment acquired after 6 April 1982 and before 5 April 1998 and they are then pooled into one group. The allowable acquisition cost is then treated as the average acquisition cost of the pool.

Pre-1982 assets

Where part of a holding was acquired before 31 March 1982, investors have a choice of how they calculate the gain.

They can, if they wish, use the actual original cost or, if it is advantageous, they can use the market value of the asset at 31 March 1982. It is usually the case that the March 1982 value is the greater and so this is chosen.

Doing this means that the acquisition cost used is higher and so the gain that is chargeable to tax is reduced and less tax is payable.

Taper relief

Taper relief was introduced in April 1998 to replace the indexation allowance. It only needs to be calculated if the chargeable gains after allowable losses are more than the annual exemption.

Taper relief reduces the amount of chargeable gain according to how long the asset has been held for periods after 5 April 1998 and is more generous for business assets than for non-business assets.

The relief is applied to the net indexed gain on the basis of the number of complete years since 6 April 1998 the asset has been held and has the effect of reducing the indexed gain by a set percentage. These percentages are set out in Table 7.9.

Non-business assets are typically quoted shares and unit trusts or OEICs. If they were held when on 17 March 1998 then a bonus year is applied.

Table 7.9 Taper relief

Business assets		Non-business assets	
Number of complete years asset owned after 5 April 98	% of gain chargeable	Number of complete years asset owned after 5 April 98	% of gain chargeable
Less than 1	100	Less than 1	100
1	50	1	100
More than 1	25	2	100
		3	95
		4	90
		5	85
		6	80
		7	75
		8	70
		9	65
		10 or more	60

7.5 RESIDENCE AND DOMICILE

The residence and domicile of an individual will determine how any income or gains are taxed in the UK.

Broadly, an individual who is resident and ordinarily resident in the UK will pay tax on their worldwide income. For others, special rules apply depending upon where they are resident or domiciled. The first parts of this section look at the meaning of residence and domicile and are followed by an explanation of the treatment of investment income.

Residence

The residence of an individual will determine how HM Revenue & Customs treats their income and gains for tax purposes. Under HM Revenue & Customs rules, tax is charged on:

- Income arising in the UK, whether or not the person to whom it belongs is resident in the UK.
- Income arising outside the UK which belongs to people resident in the UK.
- Gains accruing on the disposal of assets anywhere in the world which belong to people resident or ordinarily resident in the UK.

Generally, the amount of income tax and capital gains tax that an individual has to pay depends on whether they are resident or ordinarily resident in the UK, and in some cases on their domicile.

The types of residency are:

- Resident and ordinarily resident – this is where an individual is resident in the UK year after year.
- Resident but not ordinarily resident – this is where an individual normally lives outside the UK but is in this country for 183 days or more in the year.
- Ordinarily resident but not resident – this is where an individual normally lives in the UK but has gone abroad for a tax year.

The relevance of the term residence is that tax is payable by UK residents. So, someone who is resident and ordinarily resident in the UK will clearly pay tax on their worldwide income and gains. Where an individual spends six months out of a tax year in the UK they will normally be resident in the UK and they too will be liable to tax on their income and capital gains.

Domicile

When a person is born, they acquire a domicile of origin, which is the country in which they are born or the domicile of their father if that is different. Once a person reaches the age of 16, they can change their domicile but this requires a deliberate breaking of all ties with the previous country, combined with an intention to live there permanently. The new country is termed a domicile of choice.

Individuals who are resident in the UK but not domiciled here receive special tax treatment in respect of income and gains arising outside the UK.

An individual can only have one country of domicile at any given time, whereas they can be resident or ordinarily resident in more than one country in any one tax year.

Tax treatment of investments

A different tax treatment applies to investment income depending upon how the individual is classified for residency purposes.

Where an individual is classed as resident, they will normally be liable to UK tax on all of their investment income. If, however, they are resident but not domiciled in the UK or resident but not ordinarily resident in the UK, they will be liable to UK tax on their UK investment income but only on their overseas investment income if it is remitted to the UK.

This approach is known as the remittance basis and essentially means that overseas investment income will only be liable if it is remitted to the UK. Income is remitted to the UK if it is paid here or brought into the UK in any way.

Where an individual is not classed as resident in the UK, tax will only be charged on income arising in the UK. A personal allowance will be available and a double taxation treaty may provide exemption or partial relief.

Individuals who are not ordinarily resident can have bank interest paid gross by completing a not ordinarily resident declaration. Special rules apply where investment income arising outside of the UK is paid through a paying or collecting agent in the UK. As long as the individual is not resident, the tax can be reclaimed or arrangements made for it to be paid gross.

There are similar rules for capital gains tax.

The rules are summarised in Tables 7.10 and 7.11. They show the different tax treatment of income and capital gains that takes place depending upon how the individual is classified for residency and domicile. It has been compiled from information in the HM Revenue & Customs publication IR20, entitled *Residents and Non-residents*.

7.6 WITHHOLDING TAX

Where investors hold shares in overseas companies, they will receive dividends that may be subject to the tax of that country. The tax that is deducted is known as withholding tax.

In many countries, local tax regulations require that any income payments that are made to non-residents should be taxed at source before payment. Withholding tax is usually deducted at source by the issuer or their paying agent and has to be reclaimed by investors from the tax authorities in that country.

Table 7.10 Tax treatment of individuals domiciled in the UK

| Status | Investment income | | | Gains on disposal of | |
	Arising in the UK	Arising outside the UK	UK government stock	UK assets	Overseas assets
Resident and ordinarily resident	Liable	Liable	Liable	Liable	Liable
Resident but not ordinarily resident	Liable	Liable	Not Liable	Liable	Liable
Not resident but ordinarily resident	Liable	Not Liable	Liable	Liable	Liable
Not resident and not ordinarily resident	Liable	Not Liable	Not Liable	Not Liable	Not Liable

Source: HM Revenue & Customs

Table 7.11 Tax treatment of individuals not domiciled in the UK

Status	Investment income			Gains on disposal of	
	Arising in the UK	Arising outside the UK	UK government stock	UK assets	Overseas assets
Resident and ordinarily resident	Liable	Liable if received in UK	Liable	Liable	Liable if received in UK
Resident but not ordinarily resident	Liable	Liable if received in UK	Not liable	Liable	Liable if received in UK
Not resident but ordinarily resident	Liable	Not liable	Liable	Liable	Liable if received in UK
Not resident and not ordinarily resident	Liable	Not liable	Not liable	Not liable	Not liable

Source: HM Revenue & Customs

This reclaim of tax is one of the services that a custodian will usually be responsible for.

Double tax treaties

Where an investor receives a dividend from an overseas company that has had withholding tax deducted, it will still remain liable to UK income tax and that raises the risk of the double taxation of the dividend or interest income.

To address this issue, governments enter into what are known as double taxation treaties to agree how any payments will be handled. The UK has the largest number of double tax treaties covering more than 100 countries and they are available for inspection on the HM Revenue & Customs website. The *Double Taxation Relief Manual* is also available and for each country provides the rate of withholding tax that is applied and information on how any excess tax can be reclaimed where it has not been given automatically.

In very simple terms, the way that a double taxation agreement operates is that the two governments agree what rate of tax will be withheld on any interest or dividend payment. The rate of tax will usually be less than the rate that the investor is due to pay in the UK, so that the UK tax authorities can collect the balance. This prevents double taxation and shares the tax revenue between the two countries.

For some markets that a private investor is likely to deal in, relief at source is available and the reduced rate of withholding tax that applies to dividends is 15%. The exceptions are Ireland, Finland, Australia and South Africa where no withholding tax is deducted and Belgium and Sweden where the rate is 5% and 10%, respectively.

In these markets, it is possible for this reduced rate of withholding tax to be deducted instead of the normal domestic rate by making appropriate arrangements in that country and obtaining the necessary documentation. In some countries, such as the US and France, significant documentation is required to put this into place. The requirements for the US are covered below in the section on 'Qualified intermediaries'.

Where relief at source is not available or the arrangements cannot be put in place in time before the dividend is paid, relief can only be obtained by making a repayment claim.

To be able to claim relief from foreign tax or a repayment, however, requires a detailed understanding of the relevant double taxation treaty, the tax laws of the country concerned and how the tax authorities in that country operate. This is why the specialist tax services of a custodian are usually used as they have the knowledge required to manage this and access to their network of subcustodians to make the claim.

Qualified intermediaries

Regulations were introduced in the US in 2001 to clamp down on US citizens that attempted to evade tax by holding securities outside of the US and then not declaring the income.

These regulations also impacted on foreign investors who invested in US stocks and brought in new rules governing the withholding of US income taxes from the payment of interest and dividend income to foreign investors.

The effect of these regulations is that non-US investors holding US stocks are required to prove that they are not US citizens by lodging proof of their domicile with their custodians. The custodian is then obliged to report this to the US Inland Revenue Service.

Custodians have had to apply for qualified intermediary (QI) status so that they can undertake this service on behalf of their customers. As a QI, the custodian is required to determine the eligibility of its account holders to receive income with a reduced rate of withholding tax deducted.

The custodian is required to obtain from its customer a form W-8BEN under which the customer states that he is the beneficial owner and is not a US person and certifies his qualification for the benefits of the double tax treaty.

7.7 EU SAVINGS DIRECTIVE

The EU Savings Directive became effective in 2005 and is intended to counter cross-border tax evasion.

It involves each EU country collecting information about the payment of savings income to residents of other EU countries and then exchanging this information with that EU country.

The scheme mainly affects banks, registrars, custodians and other financial institutions that make interest payments. They are required to report information regarding the savings income that is paid to their own tax authority, which will then pass it on to the tax authority of the country or territory in which the individual is resident.

The firms who make these payments are known as paying agents and they are required to make an annual report to HM Revenue & Customs. They are required to report interest earned on bank deposits, bond interest, the proceeds of sale or redemption of certain bonds and income from certain types of investment funds, principally open-ended money market retail funds.

Other types of income, such as dividends on ordinary or preference shares fall outside the definition and are therefore outside the scope of the directive.

Where the firm believes the investor is a resident of another EU state, they are required to establish their identity and residence. If the individual is resident in another member state, they have to obtain the individual's name, address and tax identification number (TIN). If there is no TIN or the TIN is unavailable, they need to obtain the date and place of birth instead.

Chapter

8

POWERS OF
ATTORNEY

8.1 INTRODUCTION

Powers of attorney are used throughout the financial services industry in a variety of scenarios from authorising individuals to carry out activities for a firm to acting on behalf of private individuals who are incapable of managing their own affairs.

When a client becomes incapable of managing his own affairs, it has serious ramifications for the administration of any investments. An understanding of the background and rules surrounding what happens when someone becomes incapable is therefore essential when managing investments for private clients.

In this chapter we will take a detailed look at some key features of how an individual's financial affairs are dealt with once an individual loses mental capacity, review the changes that will take place in 2007 as a result of new legislation and consider the ramifications for investment administration.

8.2 BACKGROUND

When a client uses the services of an investment firm he will usually enter into some form of agreement for the provision of investment management or investment administration services.

By signing the agreement, the client authorises the firm to undertake certain agreed activities on his behalf. What it is essential to appreciate is that the authority to act on behalf of the client can continue only so long as the client can change his mind and cancel the contract or agreement. Once a client becomes incapable of managing his own affairs, the authority to act ceases and alternative arrangements need to be made.

This principle extends beyond investment management services to everyday financial products, such as bank accounts.

Once an individual becomes incapable of managing their own affairs, someone else needs to be appointed to act on their behalf. This may be either a member of the family, a solicitor or even the investment firm itself.

How they are appointed will depend upon whether the individual makes arrangements in advance or not, but either way there is a series of rules and legal procedures that have to be followed.

It is important to understand, therefore, what these rules and procedures are and how they impact on the provision of investment services.

8.3 PARTIES AND TERMINOLOGY

Before we look in detail at the legal rules surrounding what happens when a person becomes incapable of managing their own affairs, we firstly need to understand the role and responsibilities of the parties that are involved and appreciate what some of the legal terminology means.

First, once an individual becomes incapable of managing their own affairs they are described as *non compos mentis*, a Latin term meaning not being of sound mind.

Once that occurs, someone needs to be appointed to manage their affairs. This is a highly responsible position and to ensure the financial interests of the individual are protected, the legal system through the Court of Protection and the Public Guardianship Office becomes involved.

The Court of Protection is responsible for assisting people who are unable to manage their affairs due to lack of mental capacity. The Public Guardianship Office is the administrative arm of the Court of Protection and regulates and monitors those people the court approve to look after another's financial affairs to ensure they are acting in their best interests.

How someone is appointed to look after the affairs of another will depend upon whether they make arrangements whilst they are still of sound mind.

An individual may become incapable of managing their affairs and have made no arrangements for what is to happen in that event. If that occurs, someone else will need to apply to the court to have authority to act. That person is known as a receiver and the person whose affairs they are looking after is referred to as the client.

An individual can execute a power of attorney during their life whilst they are of sound mind and appoint someone to carry out certain activities. Once they are no longer of sound mind, their authority to continue to act ceases and that person will need to apply to the court to be appointed as a receiver.

Alternatively, an individual can execute what is known as an enduring power of attorney (EPA), which will appoint someone to manage their financial affairs in the event that they can no longer do so.

The person executing the EPA is known as the donor and the person appointed to act on their behalf is known as an attorney. Once the individual loses their mental capacity, the attorney must register the EPA with the Court of Protection before they can legally use it.

8.4 ENDURING POWER OF ATTORNEY

What is an enduring power of attorney?

An enduring power of attorney, usually referred to as an EPA, is a legal document by which the donor appoints one or more people to act as their attorney and which gives them legal right to manage that person's financial affairs and assets.

When creating an EPA, the person executing it can specify that it is to come into effect once he or she is incapable of managing their own affairs or alternatively, that it should come into effect immediately.

The key difference between an enduring power of attorney and an ordinary power of attorney is that the authority to act does not cease when the individual becomes mentally incapable.

This allows an individual to plan for the future and execute an EPA now, continue to manage their own financial affairs and only hand over responsibility later. The enduring nature of the power of attorney means that their attorney can be authorised to manage their financial affairs with minimal delay compared to the lengthy delays that can be involved in appointing a receiver.

Creating an enduring power of attorney

Anyone aged over 18 can create an EPA provided they are still of sound mind and understand the implications of what they are doing.

Given the importance of the document and the protection it can provide to an individual's financial affairs, most people will take legal advice when creating an enduring power of attorney. Where there is any doubt about mental capacity, it is also usual for medical advice to be obtained to ensure that the power will be valid.

The Court of Protection provides a standard form to create an EPA, but solicitors will often prepare their own forms especially when an individual's affairs are complex.

To execute the EPA, the donor's signature must be witnessed by someone other than the attorney. The attorneys must also sign the EPA and have their signatures witnessed.

Who can be an attorney?

With a few exceptions, an attorney can be anyone over 18 provided that they are not bankrupt when they sign the EPA document or at any later date.

Granting an enduring power of attorney to someone gives them complete power over the donor's financial assets and so selecting someone who the individual can trust and who has the necessary financial acumen is essential. As a result, solicitors regularly act in this capacity as do some wealth management firms.

It is possible to appoint more than one attorney and they can be authorised to act either jointly or jointly and severally. If they are authorised to act jointly, it means that they have to act together and, for example, be joint signatories on a bank account or be both registered for a shareholding. If the attorneys are appointed to act jointly and severally, then this provides flexibility by allowing them to act separately or together.

As well as appointing more than one attorney, it is also possible to create more than one EPA with each appointing different people to do different things.

Powers and restrictions

When completing an EPA, the donor will need to consider what powers they will give to their attorney and what restrictions they may wish to place on them.

The donor can give a general power which means that they will be able to deal with that individual's financial affairs in exactly the same way that the individual could have done. This includes, for example, signing cheques, paying bills, undertaking stock market trades or selling that person's house.

Alternatively, the donor can decide to restrict the powers that the attorney has and only provide authority for them to carry out specified activities. The EPA can also be in relation to all of the donor's property and affairs or restricted to certain assets and arrangements.

Conditions can also be added to the EPA that restricts the authority of the attorney. Restrictions might include preventing the attorney from selling their house or requiring the attorney to provide accounts to someone independent such as a solicitor or accountant. The conditions could also require them to get written medical evidence and register the EPA with the Court of Protection before they use it.

Depending upon any restrictions, the attorney will have the power to use any of the donor's assets to make provision for the donor or to make gifts, subject to the limitation that they are reasonable in relation to the total value of the donor's assets.

Registering the EPA

The enduring power of attorney will come into effect either immediately or when the individual is no longer capable of managing his own affairs depending upon the terms of the document.

Either way, once the attorney believes that the individual is or is becoming mentally incapable they are under a duty to apply to the court to register the EPA. As part of that they are obliged to serve notice on the donor and at least three relatives of their intention to apply to the court.

The court will take a minimum of 35 days to consider the application in order to allow time for any objections.

It is only when the application to register the EPA has been accepted that the attorney will have full powers to administer the donor's financial affairs. Whilst the application is being considered, the attorney's powers are limited to maintaining the donor and preventing any loss to their assets.

Once the application is accepted, the court will return the EPA with a Court of Protection stamp to say when it was registered. The court will also supply certified copies of the stamped EPA for registration with financial institutions such as banks.

Managing the donor's affairs

Once the EPA has been registered, it is then the responsibility of the attorney to manage the affairs of the donor.

The EPA should be registered with each financial institution and the title of the accounts changed to clearly reflect that the attorney is holding the asset on behalf of the donor. The attorney will then have full powers to manage their affairs including the right to sell their house.

Their role is a fiduciary one which means that they must act in the best interests of the donor, not take advantage of their position and keep the assets separate from their own.

The Court of Protection will not actively oversee the activities of the attorney but they are required to answer to the court if anyone questions their actions.

The attorney does, however, have a duty to keep accurate accounts of all of their dealings and be ready to produce these at any time. The accounts should include an initial list of the assets of the donor and record all subsequent income and expenditure and be supported by any necessary vouchers and statements.

When the donor dies, the EPA will come to an end and the attorney is required to send the original EPA and the death certificate to the Court of Protection. They will then have to account for the assets that they hold and any transactions they have undertaken to the executors.

8.5 RECEIVERSHIPS

If a person becomes incapable of managing their affairs and has not executed an enduring power of attorney, then it will be necessary for someone to apply to the Court of Protection to be appointed as receiver.

The Court of Protection takes a greater supervisory role with receiverships than it does with an attorney acting under an EPA. This reflects the simple fact that with an EPA, the donor selects the attorney as someone they trust to take control of their financial affairs.

The individual appointed as receiver was not directly chosen and so the court assumes a greater role of financial protection.

What is a receiver?

When someone becomes incapable of managing their own affairs, they will obviously be unable to legally pass responsibility for this management to someone else. The only body who can legally appoint someone to do this is the Court of Protection.

The person the court appoints will be known as a receiver. A receiver is only appointed for people who haven't already made an enduring power of attorney.

As with an EPA, the person who will undertake the day-to-day activities of managing their affairs will usually be a member of the family or a solicitor acting on their behalf.

The activities they will undertake will be the same as an attorney, such as paying bills, receiving income and managing assets, as well as looking after the day-to-day needs of the individual.

Their role and responsibilities will therefore be the same and the major differences arise in how they are appointed and subsequently supervised by the Court of Protection.

Appointing a receiver

To become a receiver, requires an application to the Court of Protection. The application can be made by a relative, a friend, a solicitor or an officer from a local authority. Sometimes there may be nobody willing or able to act and in such cases the court can appoint a public receiver or a receiver from an approved panel.

The court will either make what is known as a short order or an order appointing a receiver but in both cases will clearly list what is expected of the receiver in undertaking the role. A short order is usually made when the value of everything the client owns is no more than £16,000 and there is no property to be sold.

When making the application, the proposed receiver is required to complete a declaration form that is designed to make them aware of their duties and provide a written confirmation that they will carry them out. The court will use that form to assess the suitability of the individual to act as a receiver.

A medical certificate also needs to be submitted, along with a statement of the client's assets and income and confirmation that notification letters have been sent to anyone who has a close relationship with the client that an application is being made.

The process of appointing a receiver can be lengthy. When the application is lodged, the court will set a hearing date which will be at least 28 days later to allow time for objections. If the application is approved, the order will then usually be issued within six weeks.

Urgent matters may need to be dealt with during this time and if so, the court can be requested to make interim directions authorising action to be taken.

Managing the client's affairs

Once the application is approved, the court will issue an order which confirms the appointment as receiver. The order is called a First General Order or an Order Appointing a New Receiver and sets out details of the role and the powers that have been granted.

The court will send a copy of the order which the receiver has to retain and a number of sealed copies for lodging with banks, building societies, company registrars and the Benefits Agency and anyone else who needs proof of the appointment.

The receiver is required to open a receiver's bank account and use this for all income and expenditure transactions. They are also required to take out insurance to cover any losses in case they fail in their duties.

The receiver is then expected and able to manage the client's financial affairs. They do not have unfettered discretion to do so, however, and have to seek court approval to undertake certain transactions such as switching investments, selling the property or making gifts.

Accounts

As is the case with an attorney acting under an EPA, the receiver is required to keep detailed accounts of all transactions undertaken on behalf of the client.

Unlike an attorney, however, the receiver is required to provide an account to the court each year of how they have dealt with the money they have received and spent on the client's behalf.

The annual receiver's account requires a detailed analysis of income and expenditure and details of all assets and how any balances have changed during the year. Bank statements and copies of any portfolio valuations need to be provided in support of the accounts.

As part of the annual accounts, the receiver is also required to provide information in response to a series of enquiries and make proposals for expenditure in the coming year that will improve the quality of life of the client.

8.6 MENTAL CAPACITY ACT 2005

The Mental Capacity Act 2005 comes into force during 2007 and will bring about a number of changes including introducing a new lasting power of attorney and a new Court of Protection.

The new Court of Protection will have powers to make declarations about whether someone lacks the mental capacity to manage their own affairs and make orders to appoint individuals to manage their affairs who will be called deputies

A new public guardian is to be created and the Office of the Public Guardian will be responsible for registering lasting powers of attorney and supervising the deputies appointed by the Court of Protection.

Lasting power of attorney

From October 2007, the Act will allow a new type of power of attorney to be created. This is similar to an enduring power of attorney but will allow an attorney to make decisions concerning the donor's health and welfare.

There will be two types of lasting power of attorney (LPA): a property and affairs LPA and a personal welfare LPA.

A property and affairs LPA is similar to the existing enduring power of attorney and allows the donor to choose someone they trust to make decisions about how their financial affairs are managed and how their money is spent.

The personal welfare LPA once registered will allow the attorney to make decisions about the donor's personal healthcare and welfare including decisions to give or refuse consent to medical treatment.

Impact on existing arrangements

It will not be possible to make any new enduring powers of attorney after October 2007 as they will be replaced by the new lasting power of attorney.

Existing enduring powers of attorney will continue to be valid and attorneys will still be able to register them once the donor becomes incapable of managing their own affairs.

When the Act comes into effect, receivers will be called deputies but this change of name will not have any effect on the powers they have been given by the court and will remain exactly the same as set out in the order appointing them.

What will change for receivers is the process for obtaining court approval for access to funds to meet care costs and other outgoings. Many of the current restrictions will be relaxed and many receivers will be given the power to manage and administer all cash and investments without needing permission to undertake specific transactions.

The supervision of receiver's will also change and there will be two types of supervision, one a 'light touch' approach which will apply for most cases and the second for cases where a greater degree of support and supervision is appropriate.

8.7 ADMINISTRATION

The level of involvement in the administration of someone's affairs under an enduring power of attorney or as receiver will depend upon the services offered by a firm.

Their client may no longer be capable of managing their affairs and the firm will need to deal instead with the attorney or receiver. Alternatively, the firm may act as the attorney or receiver and need to undertake a wide range of administration activities.

Figure 8.1 contains a process flow that describes how the process works and in the following sections, we will look at some of the main administration activities that might be required.

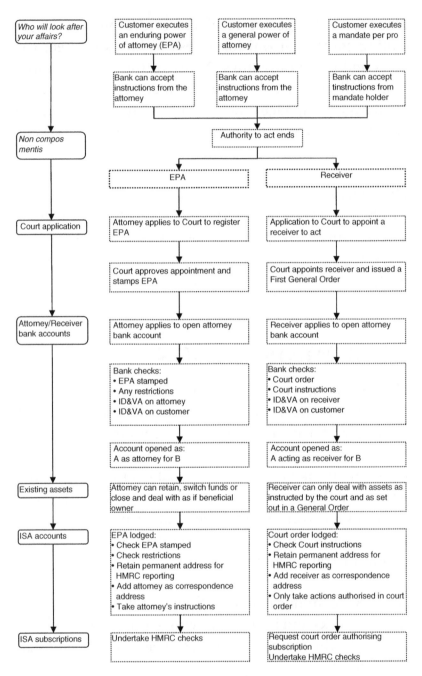

Figure 8.1 Powers of attorney

Authority to act

In looking at the impact on investment administration activities, it is important to remember the key difference between an attorney and a receiver.

With an EPA, the attorney gains authority to deal with the client's assets freely, subject to any restrictions in the document. A firm having satisfied itself as to the validity of the document can then take instructions from the attorney as if those assets were their own.

With a receiver, the actions they can take are determined by the court and will be detailed in the General Order or any further orders that are issued. A firm needs to inspect the court order each time it is asked to undertake an action to make sure that the receiver has the authority to request the action to be taken.

Bank accounts

An attorney or receiver will need to open a banking account to be able to manage the funds of the individual.

The range of accounts and services available will be the same as if the customer were operating the account as banks need to comply with the requirements of the Disability Discrimination Act.

The account opening process will differ, however, as the attorney or receiver is operating the account on behalf of someone else.

An attorney will need to provide the usual evidence so that their identity and address can be verified but will also need to do the same for the donor. Banks will also need to make checks on the EPA for any restrictions and to see whether it is has been registered with the Court of Protection and take a copy for their records. The account can then be opened and should be designated as Mr(s) A as attorney for B.

The Court of Protection requires all receivers to open receivership bank accounts. The same account opening process applies for receivers, other than the authority will be the Court of Protection order which will specify which accounts the receiver can manage and any restrictions that are imposed. The account should be designated as Mr(s) A acting as receiver for B.

Both the attorney and the receiver will also need to deal with existing accounts.

Once the bank has accepted the EPA, then the attorney can provide directions as to what they wish to do and the bank can safely accept their instructions.

Where a receiver is appointed, the court order will direct what is to happen. The order may direct that the account be closed and paid to the receiver or even to the court. If the account is not to be closed, then the order will usually direct that the account remains in the name of the client and that any interest is paid to the receiver. Any other payment will need to be expressly authorised by a court order.

ISAs

With an ISA or PEP, there are two scenarios that need to be considered, namely the operation of the account and further subscriptions.

A power of attorney gives authority to the attorney to act on behalf of the individual and so once the attorney registers it with an ISA provider, they will be able to deal with the ISA or the PEP.

From the perspective of the firm, once they receive a power of attorney or an EPA they should undertake checks of the document. These checks should establish whether it is a general power of attorney or an enduring power of attorney.

They should also carefully check for any restrictions that might be placed on the attorney. Apart from that, registration of the power of attorney or EPA provides the firm with authority to accept instructions from the attorney.

Once a firm becomes aware or believes that the client may be *non compos mentis*, then they must require the attorney to approach the court as they will no longer have authority to accept instructions from the attorney.

If it is a power of attorney, then the firm should advise the attorney that they can no longer accept their instructions to manage the account. They should request the attorney to apply to the court to seek an order appointing them as a receiver. That court order will then give the firm the authority to accept instructions from the receiver on the account.

If it is an enduring power of attorney, then the firm should advise the attorney to register the EPA with the court.

In both cases, the firm can continue to operate the ISA or PEP. It cannot accept instructions from the attorney to make payments but can take all reasonable steps to protect the asset. If any urgent action is needed, then consideration should be given to asking the attorney to apply to the court for an interim direction order.

Instructions can then continue to be taken on the ISA or PEP until the client dies, when the authority finally ceases.

The second consideration relates to applications to subscribe to an ISA, in other words scenarios where an attorney wishes to either open an ISA or subscribe to an existing one.

HMRC rules allow an ISA manager to accept an application from someone who is legally appointed or authorised to act on behalf of the investor. The investor must be incapable of completing the application form by reason of mental disorder or incapacity or physical disability, illness or old age.

The firm will therefore need to see the document authorising them to act on behalf of the investor.

Investment management

Where a receiver is appointed the Court of Protection will normally take a more active role in how the financial affairs of the client are managed. This particularly extends to the investment of the funds in quoted securities.

It should be noted that the first general order that appoints the receiver does not usually cover investment matters beyond authorising that all funds are invested in cash assets. Subsequently, the Investment Branch of the Public Guardianship Office will look to agree a more appropriate investment strategy.

If the client already had investment managers before the receiver was appointed then, subject to the court's agreement, those advisers can be given authority by the court to continue to act if the receiver wishes.

If there is no existing adviser the receiver may consult an adviser of their choice or use one of the panel fund managers who are under contract with the court. Although the receiver does not have to use these panel fund managers, the court uses their services as a benchmark to make sure that any other arrangements that are made are of at least equal value for the client.

If a panel fund manager is to be appointed this is done by the Public Guardianship Office. If alternative advisers are to be used, then the court will need to see and approve the content of the client agreement and terms and conditions before the receiver can sign the agreement which should be in the name of the person as receiver for the client.

An authority, known as a General Powers Authority, an Investment Management Authority or an Investment Powers Authority, is usually issued so that the receiver can deal direct with the fund manager without needing to get a specific court order for every transaction.

The investment firm will need to send copy contract notes for all transactions that are carried out, along with, at minimum, a yearly review and valuation of the investments, together with a performance assessment. The performance report will be used to assess how the adviser is performing against the benchmarks that the court uses.

Stock exchange transactions

If no adviser is appointed and the receiver wants to sell any of the client's investments and reinvest the proceeds, they will need a court order before doing so.

Holding investments in court

There may be occasions where the investments may be held in court as it is advantageous for benefit purposes.

In those circumstances the investments are held in the name of the Accountant General of the Supreme Court through the Court Funds Office (CFO), and are known as funds held in court. This is because the Benefits Agency may take account of funds held out of court when assessing entitlement to these benefits, whereas they will ignore funds held in court.

This is not possible for ISAs and PEPs because they have to be held in the name of the client and not of the Accountant General.

Chapter

9

....

OUTSOURCING

9.1 INTRODUCTION

Outsourcing is where a firm transfers investment administration or other functions to a third party and has been one of the major features of investment operations for the last few years.

Outsourcing activity has grown as firms decide that they can operate more effectively if they focus on their areas of core competence, such as management of investment funds. In order to focus on their strengths, they transfer responsibility for functions such as investment administration to third parties who are able to make that activity their core competence.

The key point to remember with any outsourcing arrangements is that what is taking place is delegation of the investment administration activities. The firm may have appointed another firm to undertake some or all aspects of its investment administration activity but that does not mean that it has delegated responsibility for what takes place.

In making outsourcing arrangements, it is essential that the firm and the individuals responsible for managing the arrangement remember their responsibilities to their clients. They have a regulatory and fiduciary responsibility that can be summarised as: 'you can delegate activity, but you cannot delegate responsibility'. This requires them to ensure that they have effective oversight on the performance and delivery of their supplier.

Many firms will have outsourcing arrangements in place and staff within the investment operations function are likely to be involved in both outsourcing activities and subsequently managing the service delivery.

As a result, we will consider how the market for outsourcing has developed over recent years and then consider the risks associated with outsourcing that need managing, and the regulatory principles that need to be followed.

9.2 DEVELOPMENT OF OUTSOURCING

Outsourcing has been a feature of the financial services industry for many years, the obvious example being the use of global custodians. It has extended over recent years, however, to the outsourcing of mainstream investment administration activities and to outsourcing to offshore centres.

A major impetus for firms to consider outsourcing or offshoring came with the three years of market downturn at the beginning of this century when the market slump hit investment revenues and forced firms to consider how they could reduce their cost base to match these falling revenues.

After the slump, the need to reduce their cost base did not go away; indeed the importance of outsourcing became seen as a tool that could help address how the firm could prosper in an environment of low interest rates and increasing pressure on margins. This coupled with a tightening of the regulatory control environment if anything accelerated the move to outsource non-core activities including investment administration.

Cost reduction was the initial driver behind this development and led to many firms seeking locations which offered cheap labour and operating costs, bringing about the major growth that has been seen in offshoring. Today, there is hardly an investment bank that has not set up its own operations offshore or contracted a third party to provide the service.

The transfer of work to offshore centres has, however, not been without its problems. The experience of many firms has been dominated by firefighting poor processing and backlogs, the need for greater supervision than expected, business case benefits not being achieved and disillusioned employees.

This has lead to a re-evaluation of the strategy behind outsourcing and the realisation that offshoring is not just a tactical fix to achieve cost reduction but has to be incorporated into a broader strategic approach that drives the business forward.

The trend to outsourcing and offshoring shows little sign of slowing down. In fact, a review of the reports and accounts for financial institutions will show that it remains a major priority for many firms.

With that background, understanding the risks associated with outsourcing and the regulatory principles that need to be adhered is essential.

9.3 RISKS ASSOCIATED WITH OUTSOURCING

A decision to outsource will bring with it risks that the firm will need to effectively manage. Some of these risks will be new, such as the political risk that arises from operating in another country and some will be variations on ones that already existed, such as how to manage the day-to-day operations, but remotely.

The types of risk that arise need to be understood so that appropriate risk management can be put in place and risk mitigation techniques applied. In the following sections, we consider the main types of risk that arise and then consider some of these in more detail.

Types of risk

The types of risk that arise when outsourcing and examples of how they might apply are shown in Table 9.1.

Project management

Outsourcing involves major change for a firm and it therefore needs to be managed appropriately.

Table 9.1 Outsourcing risks

Type of risk	How the risk might arise
Compliance risk	• Failure to undertake effective oversight of the service provider • Inadequate experience to undertake supervision effectively • Service provided is not compliant with regulations • Data cannot be provided to regulators in a timely manner
Operational risk	• Inadequate knowledge and experience leading to process failures and extensive rework • Fraud and unauthorised access to customer data • Inadequate due diligence checks due to distance and cost
Supplier risk	• Reliance on one supplier • Lack of a strategy to repatriate processes in event of disaster or service breakdown • Inadequately trained staff • Different culture and language present issues in training and supervision
People risk	• Lack of operations managers with experience of managing remote operations • Lack of experienced project managers to effectively implement change programme • Disillusionment of existing staff leading to deteriorating performance and staff attrition
Reputational risk	• Poor service translates into customer dissatisfaction
Country risk	• Political changes may make continued operations difficult or untenable
Legal risk	• Ability to enforce contract

Allocating experienced and suitably qualified people who can operate using a project management methodology is seen as a way in which the significant risks and issues involved can be effectively managed.

The role of the project team will be to execute the change management programme by transferring the functions to the supplier. To be effective, however, it will also need to:

- Review the processes that are being transferred and, where appropriate, redesign them.
- Assess the risk controls in place at the supplier.
- Assess the knowledge levels of the supplier and determine a plan to close any gaps.
- Develop quality assurance measures that can be deployed to assess the effectiveness of the services that are delivered.
- Develop a methodology for the firm to manage the outsourced processes that demonstrates how it meets it regulatory responsibilities.
- Develop plans for how the people issues will be handled.
- Manage communications regarding the intentions and progress of the project.

Service delivery

While the strategy behind outsourcing may be driven by a desire to reduce costs, it is essential to recognise that the objective is much wider. The service supplier also needs to deliver accurate and timely services to the firm.

Considerable effort needs to be applied to developing a service level agreement (SLA) that captures the key activities that have to be performed and defines the key performance indicators that describe acceptable levels of performance.

An SLA is, however, only a document and it therefore needs to be accompanied by appropriate management information and an effective escalation process that can resolve issues.

Managing the relationship is also key, especially as outsourcing arrangements are moving towards being long-term strategic partnerships.

Reducing staff numbers

Outsourcing will inevitably involve either reducing the number of staff that a firm employs or redirecting the affected staff to other activities.

This presents risks that need to be managed. A firm needs to have a clear selection process that identifies the staff it will need going forward that can add value to its business. The roles that will exist after outsourcing will be different and a clear understanding of key accountabilities and the skills needed is essential. Above all, the firm needs to ensure that it has a selection process that is clear, transparent and defensible in the event of challenges.

It is equally vital to remember that this can be a traumatic experience for the people involved and open and honest communications are essential.

An outsourcing project should have a people and communications plan that incorporates some of the following:

- Clear definition of the roles and associated skills that will be required.
- Clear and open communications that are issued on a regular basis.
- A selection process that meets employment law requirements.
- Recognition that the number of people required to supervise the outsourced activity will inevitably be greater than anticipated.
- Recognition that by the time the project is implemented, the business will have grown and need more people.

People skills

For an outsourcing arrangement to work well, it needs people with appropriate levels of skill.

In the firm that is outsourcing, this means that its operational management needs to have the experience and capability of managing geographically dispersed operations. This is a skill set in its own right and different than managing the day-to-day investment operations that take place. It needs to be recognised as such and requires the development of appropriate training and development programmes.

The right levels of skills are also needed in the area that the work is being outsourced to. When outsourcing, a training plan needs to be developed that addresses how to transfer knowledge to the supplier to ensure appropriate standards of processing can be achieved.

When managing the outsourcing arrangement, the firm should also recognise that the level of knowledge and skill that the supplier's people have will directly translate into the quality of the work that is processed. Training delivery and achievement of knowledge and skill levels should be a key performance indicator that the outsourcing firm should specify and monitor.

9.4 REGULATORY PRINCIPLES

The amount of outsourcing that is taking place globally has attracted the interest of regulators worldwide and resulted in the development of regulatory principles that a firm is required to adhere to.

There are specific rules within the FSA Handbook that have to be followed and international bodies such as the Bank for International Settlements and the International Organisation of Securities Commissions (IOSCO) have also published principles that are intended as guidelines for firms to follow.

What is notable in both the FSA rules and the guidelines mentioned, is that they are seen as being applicable both where a firm outsources to a third-party provider and equally so when the provider is part of the same organisation.

FSA principles

FSA rules recognise that a firm may choose to outsource some or all of its investment activities and where this is done, it requires firms to ensure that it has appropriate control mechanisms in place to manage the outsourced functions.

The fundamental basis for the FSA rules is that a firm may delegate activities but in doing so it remains fully responsible for the actions of the third party.

Although an investment firm may choose to delegate investment administration activities to either a third party or to another division of the group, it remains responsible for the work that the provider carries out. A client will not be interested in who the firm uses to carry out its work and if something were to go wrong, would not accept an excuse that another firm undertook the work. The regulatory rules reinforce this and place an obligation on the firm to accept responsibility.

The FSA therefore expect an investment firm to put in place appropriate controls to ensure that the delegated activities are undertaken in a compliant manner and that the interests of the customers are fully protected.

The rules relating to outsourced activities are contained in the following rulebooks:

- SYSC – *Senior Management Arrangements, Systems and Controls.*

- IPRU (Bank) – *Interim Prudential Sourcebook for Banks.*
- PRU – *Integrated Prudential Sourcebook.*

The detailed requirements are contained in Chapter 3 of SYSC which sets out the issues that the FSA expect a firm to manage.

The key points to note are:

- The rules apply even if the outsourcing is intra-group, although it does give some flexibility in how they are applied.
- A firm should take reasonable care to supervise the discharge of outsourced functions by its contractor.
- A firm should take steps to obtain sufficient information from its contractor to enable it to assess the impact of outsourcing on its systems and controls.
- Service level agreements should be used to manage the outsourced processes and should cover performance targets, service delivery reports, remedial action and escalation processes.

As well as high-level principles, the FSA has also issued detailed guidance on the standards it expects firms to meet.

When entering into an agreement with a third-party service provider, the FSA expects the firm to give consideration to the following:

- The impact of the outsourcing arrangement on the ability of the firm to meet regulatory obligations.

- How it will monitor and control its operational risk exposure.
- The need to undertake due diligence on the provider's expertise.
- The impact that the arrangements will have on the ability of internal and external auditors to access data.
- That adequate arrangements are in place to protect client data.
- The need to develop or amend their business continuity plans.
- The need for continued availability of software and how this will be achieved.
- Identification of qualitative and quantitative performance targets to assess the adequacy of service provision.
- Evaluation of performance through service delivery reports.
- Remedial action and escalation processes.

The detailed rules also strongly recommend that the provision of the services to the investment firm is managed by use of detailed service level agreements which address each of the above considerations.

Once an outsourcing arrangement is in place, an investment firm should also give consideration as to how it will demonstrate that it has adequate corporate governance procedures in place to monitor the arrangement.

Although it is not specified in the FSA rules or guidance, best practice would suggest that a firm should follow the same process as it would when using a custodian.

It should therefore consider undertaking a regular review to assess the continued suitability of employing the services of the third party, even of it is an intra-group firm.

A formal report recording the assessment and the results of the review should be prepared. There should be a formal process whereby the results of the review are considered and accepted by the board of the investment firm.

This might be undertaken by submitting it to a subcommittee of the board, such as an Investment or Operations Committee who would assess the report and, if approved, recommend to the board that the results are accepted.

Good corporate governance practice would suggest that this recommendation and the acceptance of the findings are recorded in the board minutes.

Recommendations of the Bank for International Settlements

The Bank for International Settlements (BIS) has, as part of its remit, a responsibility to review the stability of financial services business.

With the increasing use of third parties, it recognised that outsourcing has the potential to transfer risk, management and compliance to third parties who may not be regulated and who may operate offshore. It has therefore published a set of high-level principles regarding outsourcing that can provide guidance to firms on the approach they should adopt and can give the firms something that they can benchmark its proposals against.

The nine principles and a brief note of the areas that they recommend are considered and addressed are as follows:

- Outsourcing policy:
    - the firm should set specific policies and criteria for making decisions about outsourcing;
    - there should be limits on the level of outsourced activities with one provider;
    - the firm should assess its ability to effectively oversee the outsourced activity;
    - the roles and responsibilities required of the outsourced firm should be clearly defined;
    - ensure it can comply with legal and regulatory requirements;
    - the arrangement should allow regulators to still effectively supervise the firm.
- Risk management:
    - the firm should develop an outsourcing risk management approach;
    - assess the financial, reputational and operational impact of the third party not performing adequately;
    - what the potential losses to customers and counterparties would be in the event of service provider failure;
    - impact on its ability to conform with regulatory requirements and changes;
    - regulatory status of the service provider;

- o difficulties involved in repatriating the processes;
- o complexity of the arrangements;
- o data protection arrangements.
- Regulatory responsibilities:
  - o outsourcing should not impact its ability to meet its regulatory responsibilities;
  - o its obligations to its customers should not be affected.
- Due diligence:
  - o the firm should set criteria to assess the ability of the outsourced firm to meet its responsibilities before it makes its selection;
  - o due diligence should be conducted.
- Contracts:
  - o outsourcing arrangements should be governed by written contracts;
  - o services, roles and responsibilities should be defined;
  - o should provide for continuous monitoring;
  - o should contain a termination clause.
- Contingency plans:
  - o specific contingency plans should be developed for each outsourcing arrangement.
- Data protection:
  - o ensure that the service provider has adequate arrangements to protect confidential information.
- Regulatory supervision:
  - o outsourcing should be included in regulators' overall assessment risk of the firm;
  - o regulators should be able to obtain promptly any relevant books and records relating to the outsourced activity.

- Outsourced service suppliers:
  - regulators should be aware of the risks where there are only a limited number of third-party service providers

If more detail is required, it can be found in the report entitled 'Outsourcing in Financial Services' which is available from the Bank of International Settlements (BIS) website.

IOSCO principles

The International Organisation of Securities Commissions (IOSCO) worked with the Bank for International Settlements to develop the principles mentioned above.

IOSCO has also produced a set of principles on outsourcing specifically aimed at securities companies, which are designed to be complementary with the high-level principles.

The principles address the following areas:

- Due diligence on selection of the third party.
- The contract with the service provider.
- IT security and business continuity at the service provider.
- Client confidentiality.
- The risks where one provider is providing services to multiple firms.
- Termination procedures.
- Regulatory access to books and records.

As with the BIS principles, there are recommendations on how each of these areas should be addressed. The details of their recommendations can be found in their publication entitled 'Principles on Outsourcing of Financial Services for Market Intermediaries' which is available from the IOSCO website.

Part

IV

....

INVESTMENT ACCOUNTS AND PRODUCTS

Chapter

10

....

INDIVIDUAL SAVINGS ACCOUNTS (ISAs)

10.1 INTRODUCTION

An ISA is an acronym standing for an Individual Savings Account. The ISA itself is often referred to as an investment wrapper because it is essentially an account that holds other investments, such as deposits, shares and unit trusts and allows them to be invested in a tax-efficient manner.

Their tax advantages have made them very popular and as at 5 April 2006, £111 billion was held in cash ISAs and £70 billion in stocks and shares ISAs.

10.2 DEVELOPMENT OF ISAs AND PEPs

Encouraging savings and investment has been a key part of the economic policies of governments for many years. As a result, successive governments have offered tax advantages to encourage both saving and wider share ownership.

ISAs and PEPs before them have been one of the main investment products that have received preferential tax treatment.

PEPs were introduced in 1987 to encourage wider share ownership. Originally, a general PEP was allowed, which could hold a range of shares and where the income arising and any capital growth were free of both income tax and capital gains tax.

This was extended by the introduction of a single company PEP where, as the name suggests, the investor could hold an investment in just one company and benefit from the income tax and capital gains tax exemption.

Over the years, single company PEPs grew substantially but presented problems as the requirement to hold just a single investment prevented investors diversifying their portfolios efficiently.

A new government brought changes to the rules in 1999 to make investment accounts that offer tax benefits available to more of the population other than those who wanted to own shares.

No further subscriptions were allowed to be made to PEP accounts. Existing PEP accounts were allowed to continue and investors were still able to benefit from the favourable tax treatment.

Individual savings accounts were introduced in 1999 with the intention of extending preferential tax treatment to cash deposits. Two types of ISA were allowed, a maxi ISA which could hold investments and a cash ISA for cash deposits.

As mentioned above, PEPs were allowed to continue and, eventually, the tax rules were changed in 2001 to allow PEP providers to merge single company PEPs into the general PEP. This had the benefit of allowing investors to achieve diversification more easily and for providers to gain operating efficiencies. With the distinction between the two types removed, general and single company PEPs are now simply known as PEPs.

Significant changes were made to the preferential tax treatment of both ISAs and PEPs in 2005 when the government withdrew part of their tax advantage and it is now no longer possible to reclaim the tax credit on dividends. However, the tax advantage remains for investments earning interest such as cash deposits and bonds. No change was made to their capital gains tax (CGT) treatment and any growth remains exempt from CGT.

The long-term future for ISAs was also placed in doubt when the government announced that ISAs would be phased out by 2010.

This uncertainty has now been removed with the announcement in December 2006 of the government's long-term plans for ISAs. They have confirmed that ISAs will continue and have announced plans for their simplification.

At the time of writing, the government have confirmed that the simplification measures will be introduced but only from 2008 to give time for firms to undertake the necessary systems development.

10.3 ORGANISATION AND REGULATION

As ISAs provide valuable tax advantages, there is inevitably a series of rules surrounding the amounts that can be invested and the types of investments that are permitted.

In this section, we will look at the role of HM Revenue & Customs and how it controls the operation of ISAs by authorising ISA and PEP managers, requiring detailed reporting and undertaking regular audits.

Role of HM Revenue & Customs

As both ISAs and PEPs offer attractive tax benefits, their operation and use are closely controlled by HM Revenue & Customs (HMRC).

The detailed rules concerning both are contained in the PEP and ISA regulations. HMRC has, however, converted these into a set of guidelines aimed at providing ISA and PEP managers with practical guidance on how the regulations should be interpreted and what HMRC expects authorised managers to do in a variety of scenarios. The guidance notes were updated in February 2006.

HMRC also issues a series of bulletins as and when it becomes aware of issues that require guidance to managers; for example, it issued detailed guidance on what it would expect to see when transfers are made between ISA managers.

HMRC administers the PEP and ISA schemes through its office at Bootle. The audit aspects are handled by the Audit and Pension Schemes Services (APSS) and the operational aspects by the Savings Schemes Office (SSO)

ISA and PEP managers

All ISA and PEP managers need to be approved by HMRC in order to manage ISAs or PEPs. Details of all ISA and PEP managers are available on the HMRC website.

'Authorised persons' under the Financial Services and Markets Act 2000 are eligible to apply for authorisation as an ISA or PEP manager, as are a number of other institutions such as building societies and friendly societies.

Where a European institution wishes to be authorised but does not have a branch in the UK, it must appoint a tax representative who will be responsible for ensuring that the manager meets its obligations.

Applications can request approval as either an ISA manager or a PEP manager or both. Once approved, each receives a unique identification number.

Whilst a firm may voluntarily decide to cease to act as a manager, HMRC can also withdraw authorisation where they consider the manager has failed to manage the ISAs or PEPs in accordance with the regulations.

The PEP and ISA Manager Association (PIMA) is the trade association that represents the interests of the firms that act as ISA and PEP managers.

As well as lobbying on changes to ISAs, PIMA also provides valuable technical guidance to its members. It issues a series of technical bulletins ranging from developments in the industry to specific guidance on the treatment of corporate actions.

Terms and conditions

Another way in which HMRC controls the operation of ISAs is by specifying what must be contained within a firm's terms and conditions.

The types of items that must be set out include:

- ISA investments must remain in the beneficial ownership of the investor and not be used as security for a loan.
- The title to the investments will be registered in the ISA manager's name or their nominee and remain in their control.
- Copies of the annual reports and accounts for any investments will be provided on request.
- Arrangements will be made for the investor to attend and vote at company meetings if requested.
- Transfers of ISAs will be made within a defined time period not to exceed 30 days.
- The investor will be notified if an ISA becomes void.

There requirements have to be included in the ISA terms and conditions which must be handed to the investor when an account is opened.

If a firm fails to properly include them, then any ISAs opened will be invalidated and HMRC will seek to recover the tax that would otherwise have been paid, from the manager.

HMRC reporting

HMRC requires regular reporting by ISA and PEP managers so that it can monitor the activity that is taking place within accounts and identify cases where ISAs have been incorrectly subscribed to.

The returns that must be submitted are:

- Annual and interim returns and claims:
  ISA 10: interim return used to claim or pay over tax;
  ISA 14: annual return of tax to be reclaimed or paid over.
- Annual information returns:
  ISACOM100(OCR): details of all ISAs managed.
- Statistical returns:
  ISA14 (Stats): annual return of market value of ISAs;
  ISA25 (Stats): quarterly return of subscriptions.

The ISA10 and ISA14 are the mechanism by which tax is paid or claimed. A claim will be made where interest has been received net and the tax is being reclaimed; the ISA manager must have the appropriate tax voucher to support the claim.

A return will be used to pay back tax where the manager claimed tax back that was not properly due, where a subscription is made void and the interest taxed and where interest payments were incorrectly paid gross after the death of the investor.

The statistical returns provide HMRC with a high-level view of the activity that is taking place across ISA managers. The quarterly return provides details of the total number of ISAs to which subscriptions have been made, whilst the annual return provides the aggregate market value of investments and cash held.

The ISA100 is a return of information of all ISA accounts. It has to contain details of all ISAs managed during the year, including any that were transferred in and those that were closed. It contains full details of investors, the types of accounts held and the subscriptions made during the year.

HMRC is able to use this to identify cases where an investor may have subscribed to more than one ISA. Following the end of the tax year, it runs computer programs to compare the subscriptions made across all ISA and PEP managers. They then issue notices to managers requiring an investigation to determine whether the cases it has identified have been incorrectly opened and if so, for corrective action to be taken.

HMRC audits

As well as requiring returns from ISA and PEP managers, HMRC will undertake periodic checks of managers to ensure that the requirements set out in the guidance notes are being followed.

10.4 INDIVIDUAL SAVINGS ACCOUNTS

An ISA is defined by HMRC as a scheme of investment managed in accordance with the ISA regulations under terms agreed between the ISA manager and the investor.

The benefit of an ISA is that investors do not pay any tax on any of the income they receive from ISA savings and investments, nor do they pay any tax on capital gains arising on ISA investments.

In this section, we will look at the types of ISA that are available and the rules surrounding subscriptions and allowable investments.

Types of ISA

There are four types of ISA:

- maxi ISA;
- mini cash ISA;
- mini stocks and shares ISA;
- TESSA-only ISA.

The distinction between them can sometimes be confusing and is best understood by looking at the rules for investment.

In each year you can invest in one maxi ISA, which can include stocks and shares and cash. Alternatively, you can invest in two mini ISAs, that is one for cash and one for stocks and shares. You cannot invest in both a mini ISA and a maxi ISA in the same tax year.

A TESSA-only ISA was available for a short time to allow monies that had been saved in a TESSA (tax-exempt savings account) to be rolled over into an ISA. No further subscriptions can be made to these accounts.

Eligibility

To be eligible to apply for an ISA, an investor needs to meet both age and residency conditions.

The age conditions are designed to limit access to stocks and shares only to those aged 18 and over. This follows the same approach that is used for other investment products and is derived from the fact that contracts with someone under 18 are not enforceable.

As a result, individuals aged 16 and over can only subscribe to a mini cash ISA or the cash component of a maxi.

An investor also needs to meet a residence qualification requirement when they subscribe to an ISA. Under this, an ISA investor has to be resident and ordinarily resident in the UK. An exception is made for Crown employees serving overseas.

Annual limits

There are limits on the amounts that can be subscribed to an ISA each year.

At the moment, an individual can subscribe the following amounts in each tax year:

- £3000 in a mini cash ISA; and
- £4000 in a mini stocks and shares ISA

The key point to note is that you can invest in both. What you cannot do, however, is to invest in more than one mini cash ISA, or more than one mini stocks and shares ISA in the same tax year.

With a maxi ISA, the total amount you can invest each tax year is £7000. If the provider offers a maxi cash component, then the maximum that can be invested is £3000.

The annual subscription limits have not changed for several years but they will now change as a result of the conclusion of a government review of the long-term future of the ISA.

With effect from 6 April 2008, the simplification of ISAs will be introduced and after this date an investor will be able to subscribe to either a cash ISA or a stocks and shares ISA.

The annual limits will then rise which will mean that investors can subscribe:

- up to £3600 per tax year in a cash ISA; and
- up to £7200 per tax year into a stocks and shares ISA.

This will, however, be subject to an overall limit of £7200 subscribed to both ISAs in a tax year.

Subscriptions

Within these annual limits, there are rules surrounding the make up of the subscription and we will briefly look at the rules around cash subscriptions, transferring investments directly into an ISA and shares arising from employee share schemes.

Where cash is subscribed, it must be the investor's cash and it can be subscribed as a lump sum or by direct debit or standing order. The ISA manager can accept a subscription from a third party on behalf of the investor unless they hold information that shows the cash does not belong to the investor.

Parents may want to consider making subscriptions to an ISA for their children so that interest can be received gross. They need to be aware that if the total income from all of their gifts produces more than £100 gross income in a tax year, then the whole of the income from the gifts is normally taxed as that of the parent.

It is not possible to transfer existing investments into an ISA. What you can do is either to sell the existing investments and use the funds raised to fund the cost of the subscription or arrange a bed and ISA transaction. This involves a sale of the investments taking place outside of the ISA and the resulting cash being used to buy back the shares within the ISA at the open market price. Either way, the sales constitute a disposal for capital gains tax purposes.

The only exception to the rule that existing investments cannot be transferred into an ISA is where they have been acquired from a savings-related share option scheme, an approved profit-sharing scheme, or from a share incentive plan. The limitations on the maximum annual subscription still apply and the shares have to be valued at the date of transfer and only the number of shares up to the value of the maximum subscription amount can be added to the ISA.

10.5 ALLOWABLE INVESTMENTS

There are restrictions on the type of investments that can be held within an ISA or PEP.

The guidance notes specify what may be held and these include:

- qualifying shares and certain investment trusts;
- depositary interests;
- qualifying securities;
- government securities;
- UCIT funds and qualifying authorised funds and non-UCITS funds;
- cash.

To be a qualifying, a share must be quoted on a recognised exchange and so this excludes shares dealt on alternative investment market (AIM). The rules also do not allow futures and options, warrants, covered warrants or nil paid rights bought in the market to be held.

There are also rules for the type of securities that may be held. They must be quoted and so loans and loan stocks are eligible investments but unquoted ones are not. This can become particularly relevant where there is an unquoted loan note alternative as part of a corporate action which could not be validly held within an ISA or PEP.

Both securities and government bonds must have a minimum five-year period to redemption when they are purchased. Additionally, there are other rules that define whether investment trusts, unit trusts, depositary interests and new issues are eligible investments.

The rules are complex and constant reference should be made whenever a new security is to be added to a portfolio. The list of eligible investments will need to be referred to regularly to ensure any assets transferred in and that any securities that are purchased are eligible and to check that any new security available under a corporate action can be validly held.

10.6 NEW AND CLOSING BUSINESS

There are specific rules and considerations that need to be taken account of when dealing with new and closing business for ISAs. In this section, therefore, we will look at the rules surrounding new accounts transfers and the action that needs to be taken on the death of an ISA account holder.

New accounts and subscriptions

HMRC has a series of rules that must be followed when an account is opened if it is to attract the tax benefits of an ISA.

Before an ISA can be opened the investor must agree to the ISA manager's terms and conditions and apply to subscribe. This is achieved by providing the customer with a copy of the terms and conditions and completion and signature of an account agreement.

Once this is completed, the account opening process must undergo checks to ensure that all steps have been validly completed. The guidance notes for ISA and PEP managers specify in detail the various stages that an application can go through and the checks that are required to be carried out.

Figure 10.1 provides a process flow view of the stages that an application goes through. The diagram makes the point that an ISA is only validly opened after the ISA manager has received an application and the funds to invest and has undertaken checks that all documentation is correctly completed.

Where any information is missing, the ISA manager can provisionally open the account and request the details

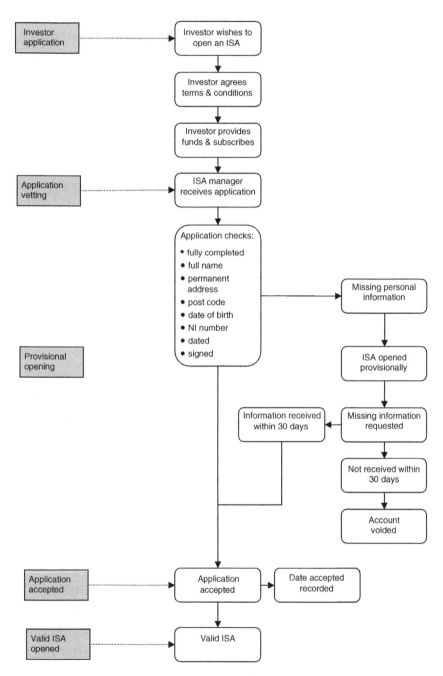

Figure 10.1 ISA subscriptions

and provided that it is received within 30 days, the ISA can be validly accepted. If it is not, the account must be voided which involves closing the account, returning the funds to the investor and taxing any interest that is earned.

Account opening is an area that the HMRC auditors will examine and so the account agreement and any associated documentation need to be stored so that they can be made available for production at audit.

Transfers in and out

Investors are able to transfer their ISAs and PEPs to another provider at any time.

They can transfer either the whole or a part of the investments representing previous years' subscriptions but are only allowed to transfer the current year's subscriptions in full.

When an ISA is transferred, the component parts will always retain their identity as a cash or a stocks and shares ISA because it is not permissible to transfer funds between them.

The designation of an ISA as a maxi or mini is important only when a transfer of the current year subscriptions is taking place. So, for example, current year subscriptions to a mini cash ISA can only be transferred to another mini cash ISA.

Where previous years' subscriptions are transferred, the position is different. The investments representing the previous years' subscriptions to a maxi stocks and shares ISA can be transferred to another maxi stocks and shares ISA or to a stocks and shares mini ISA. Similarly, previous years' subscriptions to a mini cash ISA can be transferred to another mini cash ISA, the cash component of a maxi ISA or even to an account that had been opened as a TESSA-only ISA.

HMRC has issued best practice guidelines on how it would wish to see transfers of ISAs and PEPs take place. Some of the key points to note from this are:

- The investor should be asked to complete a new application form even though it is not strictly required.
- Where the new manager requests details of an existing ISA to determine if they can accept the transfer, a response should be given within five working days.
- A transfer date should be agreed and this represents when the old manager ceases to be responsible for the investment wrapper and is the date both parties should use for HMRC reports.

Deceased customers

When a customer dies, the details of their investment in an ISA need to be included in the application that the executors make to obtain a grant of probate.

The executors are required to report not only the balance as at the date of death, but also any interest that has accrued up to the date of death or the amount of any dividend if a share or unit trust is quoted ex-dividend.

Once the grant of probate is issued, the executors will then register the grant with the bank and the balance of the account can be paid to them.

From an investment administration viewpoint, the key point to note is the need to ensure that any interest is taxed correctly.

On the death of a customer the tax benefits of an ISA cease, which means that any interest arising after death needs to be taxed.

Any interest arising on a mini-cash ISA is exempt from tax up to the date of death, including the interest that has accrued up to the date of death. Any interest arising after death is taxed in the normal way and needs to be included on the tax return that either the executors or beneficiaries will have to submit to HMRC. See Figure 10.2.

Dividends are paid with a 10% tax credit and as with all dividends the tax cannot be reclaimed. No special treatment of the dividend is therefore required.

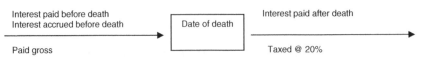

Figure 10.2   Tax treatment of interest on death

Where an interest distribution is made, however, it will be paid into the ISA gross. As a result, where the interest payment is made before death then it will have been correctly paid gross. If the payment is made after death, it needs to either be paid net or have tax at 20% deducted. If there is a delay in the ISA manager being advised of death, the interest payment may have been paid gross and will need to be taxed.

Where there is a delay between the date of death and the date when the ISA manager is advised, investigations need to be made to see whether any interest paid after the date of death needs to be taxed.

In order to ensure that tax is correctly deducted, the ISA manager needs to apportion any interest paid after death into:

- interest accrued up to the date of death which can be treated as arising in the ISA and which can be paid gross; and
- interest accrued from the date of death which is not exempt from income tax and which must have tax at 20% deducted.

Any gains made on the investments held in a stocks and shares ISA up to the date of death are exempt from capital gains tax. After death, the executors may need to sell the holdings and any gain that arises from the date of death until the date they are realised will fall to be assessed on either the estate or the beneficiaries. Details of any transaction therefore need to be provided to the executors.

It is essential that detailed records of all correspondence and action taken are retained as at audit, HMRC will check deceased cases to ensure that the correct tax treatment has taken place.

10.7 VOIDS AND REPAIRS

Occasions will arise where an ISA has been opened and later is found to be invalid. Originally when this happened HMRC required the ISA manager to close the account, return the funds to the investor and tax any interest that arose, a process known as voiding the account.

To reduce the numbers of ISAs that have to be voided, HMRC introduced arrangements whereby ISAs could instead be repaired in certain circumstances.

Repairs

There are a number of circumstances where an error can be repaired and although an exhaustive list is not provided in the HMRC guidance notes, it does include the following:

- application form not held;
- non-qualifying investments purchased or held;
- non-qualifying individual;
- disallowed combination of ISAs;
- subscription limits exceeded.

Where an ISA cannot be repaired it must be voided and the voiding procedures followed.

Where the manager discovers breaches outside of an HMRC audit, and provided the breaches are small in number and are repairable, then the manager is permitted to repair the breach. If it is unclear whether it may be repaired, the ISA manager can contact the APSS Audit Unit for advice.

A record of the accounts where repairs have taken place needs to be kept as repairing an ISA will usually involve HMRC seeking recovery of any lost tax and it may charge a penalty for errors made. It is essential therefore that detailed records of all correspondence and action taken is retained for production at an HMRC audit.

Voids

Occasions will arise when an investor may subscribe to more than one ISA in a tax year. When HMRC become aware of this and if it cannot be repaired, it will instruct the ISA manager to void the invalid subscription.

As part of the annual reporting to HMRC, ISA plan managers are required to provide details of all investors who subscribe to an ISA in the ISA(COM)100 return. From this data, HMRC will identify cases where an investor has made a subscription to more than one ISA.

HMRC will identify which ISA was subscribed to last and if it cannot be repaired, it will then write to that ISA plan manager with instructions to void the subscription.

On receipt of a void notification, the ISA manager unit is to undertake the following steps:

- Identify when the invalid subscription was made and the amount.
- Obtain details of all interest credited to the account subsequently.
- Calculate and pass the amount of tax to be deducted on all income arising.
- Pay out the invalid subscription and associated net income to the customer.
- Confirm details of the amounts withdrawn and tax deducted to the customer.

The key point to note with a void is that all subscriptions and associated interest are to be removed from the ISA.

When the amount of the subscription and interest to be withdrawn has been calculated, it should be paid to the customer and a letter sent that covers the following:

- The date and amount of any interest on the invalid subscription and the amount of any tax deducted.
- For any investment that has to be sold, details of the cost of acquisition and details of the date of sale and proceeds.
- How the amount of the invalid subscription that is being returned is made up.
- Advice to the customer to report details to their tax office.
- That tax certificates are available on request.

In the normal course of events, HMRC do not expect to receive an acknowledgement that the void notice has been received and dealt with. The only exception is when there is insufficient in the account to permit the tax liability to be settled.

Again, it is essential that detailed records of all correspondence and action taken is retained for production at an HMRC audit.

10.8 RESIDENCE

To be able to subscribe to an ISA, an investor must be resident in the UK. In this section, we will look at what the term resident means, what the rules are and the action that needs to be taken by ISA managers to ensure that they comply with HMRC regulations.

Residence

The rules surrounding residency are designed to determine whether an individual is liable to tax in the UK. They are quite complex but its relevance for an ISA is restricted to whether an investor can make any further subscriptions.

Where an individual is resident in the UK year after year, then they are treated as ordinarily resident here. Where that is the case, they will clearly be eligible to subscribe to an ISA.

Some individuals will spend significant amounts of time abroad and if they spend more than 183 days in a tax year in the UK, they are usually classed as resident but not ordinarily resident. Equally others may normally reside in the UK but be out of the country for say a tax year and then they are classed as ordinarily resident but not resident for that tax year. Depending upon their circumstances, neither of these would be eligible to subscribe to an ISA.

As we will see in the next section to be eligible to subscribe to an ISA, an investor must be resident and ordinarily resident in the UK, hence the importance of these definitions.

HMRC requirements

To subscribe to an ISA, an investor must be resident and ordinarily resident in the UK. In this context, the UK means England, Wales, Scotland and Northern Ireland. It does not include the Channel Islands or the Isle of Man.

Once an investor ceases to be resident in the UK, they can no longer subscribe to an existing ISA but that account can continue. If the investor returns, then they can recommence making subscriptions to an ISA.

There is an exception for Crown employees who can continue to subscribe whilst they are non-resident and performing Crown duties abroad. This exception also extends to the spouse or civil partner.

Residency checks

The application form that an ISA manager uses for subscriptions is required to have a declaration that the investor meets the residence qualification and that the investor will notify the ISA manager of any change in their status that will affect their ability to subscribe.

The ISA manager must therefore ensure that the investor declares that they meet the residence qualification before accepting a subscription. This would involve ensuring that the declaration has been completed and a check of the address made.

If the address used is outside of the UK, then the investor must be asked for a written confirmation that they meet the residence qualification. The confirmation needs to be kept with the ISA records so that it can be produced to HMRC at audit.

When the ISA manager receives information that suggests the investor may no longer be resident in the UK, for example by notification of a change of address, the ISA manager is required to investigate and take appropriate action.

This will involve writing to the customer and asking them to confirm whether or not they are still a UK resident. The ISA manager can continue to accept subscriptions whilst the investigations are going on, for example, by continuing to accept standing order payments.

The HMRC regulations allow a period of up to 90 days for enquiries to be made. If the investor responds and advises that they are no longer resident, or at the end of the 90-day period, the ISA manager needs to mark the ISA account that no further subscriptions are allowed.

They will also need to void any subscriptions that have been made during the period whilst the enquiries were made. This involves removing the subscriptions from the ISA account, taxing any interest that has arisen on the funds and returning them to the investor.

The ISA manager will also need to take similar action where they become aware that an investor who used the Crown employee exception is no longer married or a civil partner.

At audit, the ISA manager will need to demonstrate the action taken with residency cases and will therefore need to maintain detailed records of the action taken, the dates when the enquiries were made and when the subscriptions were voided.

10.9 INVESTOR REPORTING

An ISA manager is required to issue reports to investors providing details of their ISAs and reminding them of the rules surrounding subscriptions.

In this section we will look briefly at the types of reports that have to be issued.

Types of investor reports

There is a range of reports that an ISA manager is expected to issue. Some of the main ones are as follows:

- Annual notices – reminder to ISA investors about subscription rules.
- Contract notes – details of purchases and sales of securities and unit trusts in their stocks and shares ISAs.
- Mini-cash ISA statements – annual account statements.
- Periodic statements – valuations and transaction statements for the stocks and shares ISAs.
- OEIC and company reports – where requested by the client.

Annual notices to investors

The reports mentioned previously are common to most investment accounts with the exception of the annual notices that have to be issued to investors.

To open an ISA and make a subscription requires completion of an application form by the customer.

An ISA manager has the option of requiring customers to complete and sign an application form each year or alternatively to sign a continuous application which allows subscriptions to be made in the next tax year without the need for a further application.

Where a continuous application form is used, the HMRC rules require that customers are reminded of the subscription rules to protect investors from inadvertently opening an incompatible ISA in the next tax year.

The HMRC rules require ISA managers to choose from one of the following four methods:

- Issue the notice to customers who have subscribed during the year.
- Issue notices to customers who invested during the year and who they expect to continue to subscribe.
- Issue notices only to those who continue to subscribe in the next year.
- Issue notices to all investors.

Whichever option is selected, the ISA manager is required to ensure that notices are served on all investors where appropriate.

The option to issue blanket annual notices to all investors could confuse those investors who closed their ISAs during the year. The rule about annual notices was therefore relaxed slightly so that ISA managers can choose, as an alternative, not to have a blanket issue of an annual notice, but rather to target the annual notice more accurately at those investors who seem likely to subscribe, or who actually subscribe in the next tax year.

The annual notice must inform the investor that:

- Maxi ISA – that if they continue to subscribe to their ISA in the next tax year they are not allowed to subscribe to another.

- Mini ISA – that if they continue to subscribe to their mini ISA they cannot subscribe to another mini ISA or maxi ISA.

Where the ISA manager chooses to issue notices other than at the time of subscription, they are allowed to issue them at any time between the 6 January and the 5 May.

If the notices are issued before the end of the tax year, the ISA manager must ensure that any investor who subsequently opens an ISA receives a notice either at the time or when the first subscription is made.

Half yearly and annual reports

FSA rules require a firm to issue periodic statements to customers where it acts as investment manager or administers an account that contains investments for a customer.

As an ISA manager, therefore, it is necessary to send statements to customers who have either a mini or maxi stocks and shares ISA.

The detailed rules are contained in the FSA Conduct of Business Rules, which requires that periodic statements are to be issued at least six monthly. To meet FSA rules, the statement has to be issued to the customer within 25 business days after the end of the six-monthly period.

FSA rules detail the required content of such a report. It is also normal for the terms and conditions for the stocks and shares ISA to detail what will be issued. They will usually say that the statements will provide details of all transactions undertaken in the period including investments and withdrawals and details of any income or distributions that have been received, paid out or reinvested.

For a stocks and shares ISA this requires the information shown in Figure 10.3 to be provided:

10.10 REFORM OF THE ISA REGIME

As mentioned at the beginning of this chapter, the government has announced the results of their review of the ISA regime and will introduce the resulting changes with effect from 6 April 2008.

Changes are to be made to the regulations that will remove any remaining distinctions between PEPs and ISAs

This will allow firms to merge PEPs with stocks and shares ISAs and, by having a combined portfolio, will allow investors to have a clearer picture of their portfolio and manage their funds more effectively.

This will involve aligning the eligible investments rules and how interest on unearned cash is treated. It will also involve change to HMRC reporting as combined reports will be required in future.

As a result, PEPs will cease to exist although the government will leave the decision whether to merge PEP

Report details	• Client name
	• Account number
	• Date of the valuation
	• Period covered
Content and value of the portfolio:	• The number of shares held in each company
	• The price of each share
	• The date used for each price
	• The value of each holding
	• The amount of any cash held
	• The total value of the portfolio
Basis of valuation	• A statement of the basis on which each holding has been valued
	• An explanation if the basis has changed since the last statement
Transaction details	• Details of all transactions that have passed through the customers-related cash account including:
	• Date and amount of each cash deposit and withdrawal including any regular payments made by standing order
	• For each investment or redemption, the date, the number of shares bought or sold, the dealing price and the value of the transaction
	• Details of any dividend or interest distribution received
General statements	• An explanatory notes page that provides a straightforward explanation of terms used in the report

Figure 10.3   Investment reports

accounts into ISA stocks and shares accounts or not with the providers.

As mentioned earlier, the changes will also remove the distinction between mini and maxi ISAs and hopefully make the choices clearer for investors.

Going forward, there will be a cash ISA and a stocks and shares ISA only. Investors will be able to contribute to both types provided that they do not exceed the maximum for each or the overall combined total. Once the changes are implemented, investors will be able to transfer funds they have built up in previous years in a cash ISA into a stocks and shares ISA.

Chapter

11

. . . .

COLLECTIVE INVESTMENT SCHEMES

11.1 INTRODUCTION

Collective investment schemes are investment vehicles which allow investors to pool their assets into a single portfolio in order to gain access to the stock market generally or to specific markets or sectors.

For small investors, they can allow access to professional investment management that would not otherwise be available and enable them to spread the risk of investing in direct equities by having a share of a much larger portfolio than they could invest in on their own. By pooling their funds in this way, they also benefit from the lower dealing costs that a large fund can command.

Collective investment vehicles also have their place in the portfolios of more wealthy investors and in institutional portfolios. Even with a sizeable portfolio it is not always possible or desirable to achieve exposure to a specific market or sector by direct holdings. This can be because the percentage of funds allocated to that market or sector are insufficient to obtain a wide spread of holdings. Equally, it could be that a particular market or sector requires specialist investment experience and so makes a collective investment vehicle the most suitable way of achieving this.

Collective investment schemes are a significant and integral part of the investment landscape and a detailed understanding of their types, administration and dealing is required for almost anyone dealing with investment administration.

11.2 REGULATION OF UK FUNDS

Introduction

The administration of collective investment schemes is a regulated activity and an understanding of the regulations that affect it are important in order to appreciate why certain activities take place in the way they do.

Overview of regulation

As the UK is part of the European Union (EU), much of the regulation of collective investment vehicles derives from EU directives.

UK regulation of investment funds therefore involves tiers of rules starting with European directives, then the UK legislation that has implemented the directives and set UK specific rules and finally FSA rules which detail more specific aspects that have to be followed.

The FSA describes this as a hierarchy of rules that at each level deals with more specific aspects of collective investment scheme regulations. Diagrammatically, it can be displayed as shown in Figure 11.1.

European regulation of investment funds was first introduced in 1985 with the Undertakings in Collective Investments and Transferable Securities (UCITS) directive. This came into force in the UK in 2004 and if an investment scheme complies with the provisions of the directive, it can be marketed throughout the European

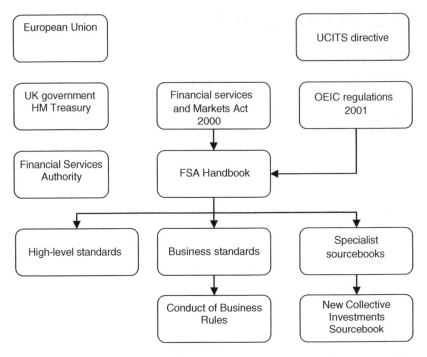

Figure 11.1 Overview of collective investment schemes regulations

Economic Area (EEA). This applies for UK schemes wanting to market their funds in Europe and vice versa.

As far as the UK is concerned, the key pieces of legislation are the Financial Services and Markets Act 2000 which sets out the regulations that authorised unit trusts operate under and the OEIC Regulations 2001 which does the same for OEICs.

The FSA then turns these into specific principles and rules that operators of collective investment schemes have to follow. Apart from the high-level standards that apply to all regulated firms, there is a specialist sourcebook relating to collective investment schemes. A new sourcebook was introduced with effect from February 2007 and is referred to as COLL.

Authorised funds

FSA rules are designed to provide the greatest levels of investor protection to those who need it the most, namely retail investors. The regulation of investment funds reflects this by differentiating between authorised and unauthorised funds.

The only investment funds that can be marketed in the UK are authorised funds or investment funds that are established in other EEA states under the UCITS directive.

For authorised funds, the COLL rules also differentiate between investment funds that can be marketed to retail investors and ones that can only be marketed to institutions and professional investors. Ones that can be promoted are known as retail funds and ones that can only be marketed to institutions and professional investors are termed qualified investor schemes.

Retail funds are required to comply with the full range of FSA rules so that adequate protection can be afforded to private investors. As qualified investor schemes can only be marketed to experienced investors, the FSA does not consider that the full set of rules need apply and instead there is a more limited framework to allow more flexibility in their operation.

11.3 TYPES OF UK FUNDS

Introduction

Collective investment schemes have existed in the UK for many years and naturally have developed over that time. As a result, there are a variety of schemes including investment trusts, unit trusts, OEICs and exchange traded funds.

They all share the same common characteristic that they pool together the funds of individual investors to meet a range of investment objectives. Their main differences arise from the way that they are legally constructed and how roles and responsibilities are distributed within each type of investment fund.

Unit trusts

Unit trusts have been used to pool investors' funds as long ago as the 1800s, but the first modern unit trust was launched by M & G in 1931.

A unit trust is a form of collective investment scheme that is legally constituted using a trust deed. The parties to the deed are the authorised fund manager and the trustee.

The role of the authorised fund manager is to manage the day-to-day operations of the unit trust, so it will be responsible for marketing the fund to the general public and investor dealing. It will usually appoint a separate investment manager who may or may not be part of the same group

The trustee is the legal owner of the trust's assets and may undertake the safekeeping of the assets themselves or appoint a custodian.

The trustee is obliged by the deed to deal with the assets in accordance with the manager's instructions and to ensure that the capital and income of the trust are applied for the benefit of the beneficial owners, the unit holders. The trustee will therefore undertake oversight of the manager to ensure that the rights of the investors are protected.

A unit trust consists of a pool of investments and the investors into the trust hold a number of units depending upon how much they have contributed.

The portfolio is valued daily and the price of the units is based on the net asset value of the underlying investments and is published daily by the managers of the trust. A unit trust is dual priced which means that it quotes separate buying and selling prices.

When an investor wishes to deal in a unit trust, he will place his order with the manager who will either create new units or cancel existing units in response to demand. Any deals are settled direct with the manager who will also maintains the share register.

OEICs

The term OEIC stands for an open-ended investment company. An OEIC is a collective investment vehicle that is structured as a company, with the investors holding shares. The OEIC invests shareholders' money in a diversified pool of investments and has the ability to issue more shares or redeem shares as demanded by investors.

OEICs were introduced in the UK in 1997 in response to the UK unit trust industry losing considerable market share in open-ended investment funds to continental and offshore fund management centres. Overseas investors, who had become familiar with the OEIC structure, didn't feel comfortable with an investment fund that was subject to UK trust law and was dual priced. OEICs typically have what is called an umbrella structure, within which the individual investment funds are known as sub-funds. These sub-funds can issue different classes of share, each with their own unique charging structure, and in a range of currencies. Also, rather than being dual priced, OEIC shares are single priced.

An OEIC is run by an authorised corporate director (ACD), whose responsibilities are broadly similar to that of a unit trust manager, whilst a depository, rather than a trustee, oversees the running and administration of the OEIC. A separate custodian will often be appointed to safeguard the assets.

Dealings and settlement in the shares of the OEIC are undertaken through the ACD and the ACD will either maintain the share register or delegate the function to a third party.

Investment trusts

Investment trusts have been in existence since the late 1800s when investment companies were set up to pool the assets of individual investors. They are structured as a limited company and are managed by a board of directors and have shareholders as with any other company. They can have different types of share capital and can issue debt securities.

They will be set up to meet a specific investment objective and the board will usually appoint an investment manager to manage the funds and then maintain oversight on achievement of investment performance. Safekeeping of the assets will usually be entrusted to a custodian.

Their shares are quoted on the stock exchange and so when an investor buys shares in an investment trust, they are buying them on the secondary market from another investor. The price that an investor will pay or receive will therefore be determined by the demand and supply for the shares.

The company will calculate the net asset value of its portfolio of investments and publish this from time to time. The price at which the shares trade will have a relationship to the net asset value but it can trade at either a premium or discount to it depending upon supply and demand for the shares.

The dealing and settlement arrangements are the same as for equities. Investment trust shares are dealt on the London Stock Exchange and settlement takes place at T+3 through Crest.

A new form of investment trust was made available from January 2007, namely a real estate investment trust or REITs. This is a normal investment trust that pools investors' funds to invest in commercial and possibly residential property.

One of the main features of REITs is they will provide access to property returns without the previous disadvantage of double taxation. Until recently, where an investor held property company shares, not only would the company pay corporation tax but also the investor would be liable to income tax on any dividends and capital gains tax on any growth. Under the new rules for REITs, no corporation tax will be payable providing that at least 90% of profits are distributed to shareholders.

REITs will be able to be held in both ISAs and SIPPs.

Exchange traded funds

An exchange traded fund (ETF) is an investment fund that is designed to track a particular index. In this regard, it is similar to a unit trust tracker fund.

An ETF is structured as an open-ended company but is quoted and traded on the London Stock Exchange. An investor buys shares in an ETF through their broker as with any other share but because are 'open-ended funds' further shares can be issue to meet demand or cancelled if sales outweigh purchases.

Like other shares, settlement takes place through Crest at T+3 but no stamp duty is payable on the purchase.

The ETF share price reflects just the value of the investments in the fund; they do not trade at a premium or discount to the underlying investments as investment trusts do. The investor's return is in the form of dividends paid by the ETF, and the possibility of a capital gain (or loss) on sale.

11.4 FUND ADMINISTRATION

Where investment trusts and exchange traded funds are held in a client's portfolio, the investment administration associated with them is identical to any other shares that are held.

With unit trusts and OEICs, which represent the majority of investment funds in the UK, the administration that is required is different. This is essentially because the firm will need to deal direct with the manager of the fund and this requires different processes.

A fund management group would typically have two main investment administration functions: fund accounting and a transfer agency.

The role of the fund accounting area is to keep detailed records of the investment portfolio, value this daily and produce prices that the fund will be dealt at.

A transfer agency will undertake a number of activities including taking dealing instructions from investors, maintaining the share register, paying dividends and investor reporting.

The latter are the main areas where an investment firm will become involved with the fund administration area of a unit trust or an OEIC and the following sections consider what takes place.

11.5 PRICING

Both unit trusts and OEICs are usually priced daily but there is a difference and it is important to understand the difference between the two.

As mentioned earlier, each unit or share represents a proportional part of the underlying investment fund. The price of each unit or share is arrived at by valuing net assets and dividing by the number of units or shares in existence. This is important because it removes the effect of supply and demand.

There are two pricing methods available, known as dual pricing and single pricing. Whichever one is used must be disclosed in the prospectus which provides all the details an investor might need to know about the fund.

Dual pricing is the traditional method used for unit trusts. This involves valuing the underlying portfolio using the closing bid and offer prices for each holding:

- Bid price – reflects the price that would be obtained on realisation of assets.
- Offer price – reflects more accurately the cost of acquiring the underlying portfolio.

The pricing used needs to also take into account other factors such as cash, income receivable, fees, broking charge and initial charges.

Two prices are then produced for dealing in the unit trust, a bid price at which investors can buy units and an offer price at which they can sell back their holding.

This can be understood by looking at an example. Figure 11.2 shows an imaginary portfolio for a unit trust.

This shows the closing bid and offer prices for the underlying investments, includes available cash and divides the total value by the number of units in issue. This then provides a bid and offer price for investors in the unit trust to deal at.

ABC Unit Trust	Bid		Offer	
Portfolio	Price per share (£)	Value (£)	Price per share (£)	Value (£)
1,000,000 BP ords	6.95	6,950,000	6.97	6,970,000
1,000,000 BT ords	2.11	2,110,000	2.13	2,130,000
1,000,000 HSBC ords	9.58	9,580,000	9.60	9,600,000
1,000,000 Marks & Spencer ords	5.85	5,850,000	5.87	5,870,000
1,000,000 Vodafone ord shs	1.27	1,270,000	1.29	1,290,000
Total Portfolio value		25,760,000		25,860,000
Cash		75,000		75,000
Total Capital Assets		25,835,000		25,935,000
Income for distribution		23,000		23,000
Total Asset Value		25,858,000		25,958,000
Unit Price				
1,000,000 No of Units in Issue		25.858		25.958

Figure 11.2   Calculating bid and offer prices (1)

This shows that there is a small difference between the two prices since the spreads for the underlying shares are not wide. This model, however, does not take account of the costs of dealing. These can now be factored in as shown in Figure 11.3.

For this example, an estimate of what the average broking charges might be has been made. They will obviously vary from fund to fund but what the example does incorporate is the higher costs of buying shares as a result of stamp duty.

The bid and offer prices are now wider and more accurately reflect what it might cost to buy a proportionate part of the underlying portfolio in the market and what might be received on a sale.

ABC Unit Trust		Bid		Offer	
Portfolio		Price per share (£)	Value (£)	Price per share (£)	Value (£)
1,000,000	BP ords	6.95	6,950,000	6.97	6,970,000
1,000,000	BT ords	2.11	2,110,000	2.13	2,130,000
1,000,000	HSBC ords	9.58	9,580,000	9.60	9,600,000
1,000,000	Marks & Spencer ords	5.85	5,850,000	5.87	5,870,000
1,000,000	Vodafone ord shs	1.27	1,270,000	1.29	1,290,000
Total Portfolio value			25,760,000		25,860,000
Notional Broking Charges		0.20%	−51,519	0.70%	181,020
Cash			75,000		75,000
Total Capital Assets			25,783,481		26,116,020
Income for distribution			23,000		23,000
Total Asset Value			25,806,481		26,139,020
Unit Price					
1,000,000	No of Units in Issue		25.806		26.139

Figure 11.3 Calculating bid and offer prices (2)

It now only remains to add in the cost of the initial charge which would only apply to purchases of units as shown in Figure 11.4.

The difference between the buying and selling prices can now be seen to be quite different and more properly reflect the costs of buying and selling.

Dual pricing produces a result that is fair to both buyers and sellers but as can be seen from the example above is both complex and time consuming to undertake.

The alternative method is single pricing which simply uses mid-market prices and ignores brokerage charges and underlying spread. This is a far simpler method and the rationale behind it is that administrative efficiency can be improved without detriment to investors provided

ABC Unit Trust		Bid		Offer	
Portfolio		Price per share (£)	Value (£)	Price per share (£)	Value (£)
1,000,000	BP ords	6.95	6,950,000	6.97	6,970,000
1,000,000	BT ords	2.11	2,110,000	2.13	2,130,000
1,000,000	HSBC ords	9.58	9,580,000	9.60	9,600,000
1,000,000	Marks & Spencer ords	5.85	5,850,000	5.87	5,870,000
1,000,000	Vodafone ord shs	1.27	1,270,000	1.29	1,290,000
Total Portfolio value			25,760,000		25,860,000
Notional Broking Charges		0.20%	−51,519	0.70%	181,020
Cash			75,000		75,000
Total Capital Assets			25,783,481		26,116,020
Income for distribution			23,000		23,000
Total Asset Value			25,806,481		26,139,020
Initial Charge				3.75%	980,213
Scheme Value			25,806,481		27,119,233
Unit Price					
1,000,000	No of Units in Issue		25.806		27.119

Figure 11.4   Calculating bid and offer prices (3)

that the:

- number of units traded is not material; and
- bid/offer spreads are narrow.

Single pricing is the method favoured throughout Europe. In the UK, it is only prescribed for OEICs and is optional for unit trusts.

The problem with single pricing is that large movements into or out of the fund can result in a diluting effect on the value of existing investors' holdings.

Single-priced funds get over this problem by making a separate charge when that occurs. It is known as dilution levy and it effectively makes an adjustment for large trades to offset effect of brokerage charges.

As an alternative, single-priced funds can adjust the price so that they use the mid-market price for normal transactions but switch to dual pricing for large trades. This is known as swinging single prices.

11.6 DEALING AND SETTLEMENT

Having looked at how the prices at which deals in unit trusts and OEICs are arrived, we can now consider how dealing and settlement take place.

Dealing and settlement arrangements differ completely from what takes place in the bond or equity markets. This is because there is no market infrastructure such as London Stock Exchange and Crest in which dealing and settlement takes place. Instead the trades are dealt directly with the unit trust manager or the ACD of the OEIC.

When a trade is placed with a fund group, it may be done by telephone which simply involves providing details of the order and it will then be dealt at the next valuation point, which is the next occasion at which the unit trust or OEIC is priced and dealt. Most unit trusts and OEICS are valued daily and many price their funds at 12 noon. All orders that have been received by that time are dealt at the price fixed at that point.

The order may also be placed electronically which is likely to be the case if the order is being placed by an investment firm which regularly deals in unit trusts. Many investment firms use a system called EMX which allows orders to be entered, aggregated together and then placed electronically with fund groups. Each order is then acknowledged and a further message is sent once the order is dealt confirming the details.

Contract notes will be issued for the deals and how they settle will depend upon whether it is a purchase or sale and whether a coverall agreement has been entered into.

If the order is a purchase, monies will normally be required at the time of purchase and no later than when settlement is due at T+4. On settlement, the investor's name will be entered on the share or unit register. At a later stage, a share certificate or confirmation of the holding will be issued.

For a sale, a renunciation form needs to be completed and sent. The certificate has a form of renunciation printed on the reverse so that it can be used for this purpose. If the holding is uncertificated then a separate renunciation form will need to be completed and submitted. Settlement for sales is also due at T+4 but, importantly, this is four days after the fund group has received the necessary documentation.

Investment firms who deal in unit trusts and OEICs regularly will enter into a coverall agreement in order to overcome the settlement delays that can otherwise take place. These are individual agreements between the firm and each fund group that it deals with which allow the completion of renunciation forms and associated paperwork to be dispensed with.

Undertaking dealing and settlement in unit trusts and OEICs is significantly more time consuming and people intensive than with equity dealing. This is due to the lack of a single market infrastructure.

Developments are underway, however, that may change this picture. At the of 2006, Euroclear announced that it had acquired EMX Co. and that it intended to develop, in conjunction with Crest, an automated straight-through processing system for the dealing and settlement of investment funds.

11.7 SHARE REGISTER

Both unit trusts and OEICs clearly need to maintain registers of their unit holders and shareholders. This is usually undertaken by the transfer agency. The rules surrounding share registers for both types of funds are similar to what is required for company share registers

The share or unit register is required to contain details of:

- name and address of the unit holder;
- number of units of each class held by the unit holder;
- the date the units were registered;
- the number of units of each class that are currently in issue.

As with a normal share register, up to four names can be registered and registration is limited to legally recognised persons. The main difference to a normal share register is that it must be available for inspection by holders but not to the public generally.

Certificates need not be issued, provided this is spelt out in the prospectus.

Both unit trusts and OEICS can also maintain 'plan registers', such as where investors subscribe to a regular savings plan. The plan register will record details of each of the underlying investors and the total holding will be recorded on the register in the name of the plan manager or nominee.

11.8 DIVIDEND AND INTEREST DISTRIBUTIONS

Unit trusts and OEICs can pay either interest or dividends.

Under FSA rules, an investment fund is required to pay the income it has received to its unit holders or shareholders no later than four months after end of accounting period. The amount of income that is to be distributed is calculated as shown in Figure 11.5.

There are two notable differences between these and what would normally be received on a holding of a shares or a bond. They are the circumstances in which a fund

Gross Income
+/– Equalisation
– Expenses
– Taxation
– Any income to be carried forward
= The amount available for distribution

Figure 11.5   Income distribution

can make an interest distribution and the treatment of equalisation.

An authorised unit trust or an OEIC can make an interest distribution when the market value of the interest bearing assets it holds has exceeded 60% for the entire distribution period. If that test is satisfied, the fund can choose to treat the distribution as an interest distribution and pay it subject to deduction of the lower rate of tax of 20%. The fact that part of the underlying income may consist of equity dividends is ignored. In the investor's hands, the interest distribution is treated exactly the same way as any other interest payment.

Equalisation payments are seen in many but not all investment funds.

When units in a fund are purchased, the price paid may include an amount of income that has accrued up to the date of purchase. This accrued income is referred to as equalisation.

Units that are purchased part way through a distribution period are referred to as group 2 units. When the next distribution is made, the payment made to investors is made up of income since the date of purchase and this accrued income.

So, when a dividend distribution is made, the supporting voucher will show a payment for both group 1 units and group 2 units. The equalisation part of the payment is a return of capital and is not taxable. It should instead be posted to the client's capital account and deducted from the cost of purchase for capital gains tax purposes.

Immediately after the distribution, the group 2 units will be automatically merged into group 1 units.

11.9 INVESTOR REPORTING

Investment funds are required to report to investors on the performance of their fund.

As with companies, both interim and annual reports are to be prepared. The reports have to comply with policies that are set for the accounting standards that have to be followed and for the presentation of the information contained in the reports. The standards are set by the Investment Management Association.

The FSA also sets rules about the timeliness with which reports have to be issued. An authorised fund manager is required to provide reports to investors in the following timescales:

- Annual reports – within four months of the end of the accounting period.
- Interim reports – within two months after the interim accounting date.

The different timescales recognise that the annual report is required to be audited and therefore more time is allowed.

The annual report is required to contain the following information:

- details of the fund;
- names and addresses of the ACD, investment manager, depositary, registrar and auditor;
- statements about the responsibilities of the ACD and depositary;
- depositary's report;
- auditor's report.

The report is also required to provide details of the investment fund so that investors are informed of its latest composition and how it has performed.

The reports can be lengthy and are not straightforward to understand. As a result, the FSA also requires a short version to be produced. It is this short report that must go to all investors, with the long reports being available on request

Chapter

12

....

TRUSTS

12.1 INTRODUCTION

Trusts are a fundamental part of the financial services landscape and an understanding of them is needed in investment administration.

They are widely used in estate and tax planning for high net worth individuals and are seen throughout retail investment firms from execution-only stockbrokers to private banks. They are also the underlying structure for many major investment vehicles, such as pension funds, charities and unit trusts.

All trusts contain financial assets of some kind and many contain extensive investment portfolios requiring the same full range of investment administration activities as any other portfolio.

In this chapter we will therefore consider how they have developed, the fundamentals underlying trusts and the special considerations that need to be applied when undertaking the investment administration of them.

12.2 DEVELOPMENT OF TRUSTS

Trusts have been a feature of the English legal system for over 1000 years; in fact, there are recorded instances of trusts being used from before the Norman Conquest.

To understand why they developed and why they became so widespread requires a brief review of their history, starting with a brief explanation of what a trust is.

Trusts were originally known as a 'use'. The term aptly describes their purpose – land was given to one person for the 'use' of another. The reason why that was done lies in the political and economic environment of the time.

In the Middle Ages, ownership of land carried with it economic, political and military power and as a result, the king would exercise control over who it went to on death.

Trusts were utilised to allow landowners to circumvent the king's control whereby they would deed their property to their church, in exchange for the promise that the church would grant the land back to their heirs when the landowner died.

This simple but at first ingenious device was therefore used to get around unpopular rules of law such as, the restrictions on leaving freehold land by will, or for a man to settle land on his wife or even to give land to various charities. Each of these rules could be avoided by using a trust and, in addition, were the mediaeval equivalent of a tax avoidance scheme as they could save tax.

Their use developed considerably and inevitably ended up with legal disputes. Eventually, the chancellor began intervening to enforce the terms of the trust, recognising that although the trustees were the legal owners, it was not acceptable that they abuse their position. The chancellor's court would issue directions to trustees to follow the terms of the trust and respect the rights of the beneficial owners and if they failed to do so, find them in contempt of court and liable to imprisonment.

This established the fundamental concept of duality of ownership in English law, in other words, that there can be separate legal and beneficial rights to property. This principle is now firmly embedded in the financial services industry and underlies, for example, the basis of how a custodian undertakes its activities.

Trusts continued to develop and became so popular that by 1500, it was said that the greater part of land in England and Wales was held in 'use'. The king, however, was losing too much tax revenue and passed a law in 1535, the Statute of Uses, to ban their use and trustees were required to hand the property to the beneficiaries.

Some trusts were still permitted and they continued until middle of the seventeenth century. The loss of tax revenue was no longer an issue and the chancellor began to enforce trusts again and restored duality of ownership. It was at this stage they became more commonly known as trusts.

Over the centuries a massive body of legal decisions and enactments came into being to govern the activities of all concerned with trusts.

This historic background to trusts and the body of legal decisions that have built up also explains why the management and administration of trusts is sometimes not caught by today's compliance rules. Whenever there is a conflict between trust law and compliance rules, trust law prevails.

In administering the investments of a trust, it is essential therefore to understand what they are and the different rules that can apply.

12.3 FUNDAMENTALS OF TRUSTS

Introduction

As trusts have been around for hundreds of years they have unsurprisingly developed their own specialist terms.

An understanding of some of the terminology used is needed to get a clearer picture of a trust and understand where they are used and the considerations that need to be borne in mind when administering the investments they hold.

What is a trust?

A trust is the legal means by which one person gives property to another person to look after on behalf of yet another individual or a set of individuals.

Starting with the individuals involved, the person who creates the trust is known as the 'settlor'. The person he gives the property to, to look after on behalf of others, is called the 'trustee' and the individuals for whom it is intended are known as the 'beneficiaries'. Their respective roles and responsibilities will be considered in more detail in the next section.

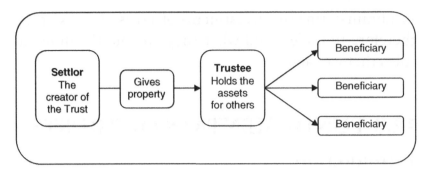

Figure 12.1   What is a trust?

Diagrammatically, this can be shown as in Figure 12.1.

A trust is therefore a means of giving property to others without giving them full immediate control over it. A simple example can show why someone would want to do this.

Let's say that grandparents want to make financial provision to ensure that their young grandchildren have the best start in life but do not want them to have the money until they are 21 years old, as they do not think they will be financially responsible enough before then. They could create a trust and pass assets to the trustee who would hold them and, following their wishes, pass the funds to the grandchildren only when they attained 21 years of age.

It should also be noted that the settlor may choose to be involved in the affairs of the trust so that he or she can continue to exercise control and guidance over what they have given by being the trustee or one of the trustees. For example, a wealthy individual might choose to create a trust to benefit their favourite charitable causes and want to be a trustee so that they are able to guide which causes benefit most and by how much.

At this stage the main term to note is 'settlement', which is simply another term that can be used for a trust and in practice, both terms are used interchangeably.

Ownership of assets

By creating a trust and placing assets into it, the settlor is giving away ownership of the assets and creating a set of rights and obligations.

The assets will be transferred into the names of the trustees who will have legal ownership of the assets, but they will not be free to do what they will with the assets. They are bound to follow the terms of the trust and to hold the assets for the beneficiaries who are the ultimate beneficial owners. Figure 12.2 describes this.

This is the concept of a division of ownership between legal and beneficial ownership which trust law brings about and which is seen throughout the investment industry, not just in private trusts.

The use of trusts

A trust can be created over any type of property including cash type assets, stocks and shares, residential and

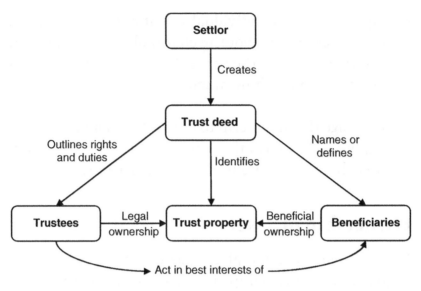

Figure 12.2 Creating a trust

commercial properties and other financial products such as life assurance policies.

The following are some of the most common reasons for the use of trusts:

- To provide funds for a specific purpose such as the maintenance of children.
- To protect capital from being dissipated and so that it can be passed to future generations.
- To set aside funds for disabled or incapacitated children in order to protect and provide for their financial maintenance.
- To protect capital from creditors as they will normally have no access to assets placed in trust sufficiently early as legally the settlor no longer owns them.

- To reduce future inheritance tax liabilities by transferring assets into a trust and so out of the settlor's ownership.
- To separate out rights to income and capital, so that for example the spouse of a second marriage receives the income during their life and the capital passes on that person's death to the settlor's children.

In summary, it is reasonable to say that trusts have two principal uses. The first is to ensure that assets pass to selected beneficiaries and the second is to save tax. The use of trusts in this way is known as estate planning.

Trusts may also be used by those, such as politicians, business people, stockbrokers, corporate financiers and financial journalists, who need to avoid the appearance of a conflict of interest.

Such trusts are called blind trusts and are a simple arrangement whereby the individuals remain the beneficial owners of the trust property, but they have no say in the management of the assets.

Parties to a trust

As we saw earlier, there are three parties involved in the creation and existence of a trust:

- the settlor;
- the trustees;
- the beneficiaries.

There is a fourth role that can also be created, that of a trust protector; each of these are reviewed below.

Settlor

The settlor is the person who creates the trust, in other words, the person who executes the legal document that creates the trust and then transfers the property into the trust.

More than one person can be a settlor, such as a couple jointly creating a trust for their children. A settlor can also be a company, such as when a pension scheme or unit trust is established.

Trustees

The trustees are the persons who hold the property for the benefit of the beneficiaries. They are the legal owners of the trust property but are bound to hold or use it for the benefit of the beneficiaries and only in accordance with the terms of the trust deed.

The trustees are usually appointed in the trust document itself and it will usually contain the power to appoint further trustees as and when required. Anyone over 18 years of age can be a trustee provided they are of sound mind and not bankrupt.

The trust deed will provide powers to allow the trustees to administer the trust fund and to invest the assets and these will direct and limit what actions they can take. Over and above that, they have an overriding responsibility to perform the trusts honestly and in good faith for the benefit of the beneficiaries.

Equally importantly they must exercise actual control of the assets and are not allowed to blindly follow the wishes of the settlor or the beneficiaries, but must exercise their duties even if that puts them at odds with some or all of the other parties.

If the trustees fail to carry out their duties or act in accordance with the terms of the trust then they are in breach of trust which can lay them open to legal action for damages.

Beneficiaries

The beneficiaries are the persons who are intended to benefit from the trust, either immediately or at some future date.

Whilst the legal title to the assets is vested in the trustees, the beneficiaries have the beneficial ownership. Their eventual right to the assets, however, does not allow them to direct how the trustees exercise day-to-day control of the trust or how they exercise their discretion.

Should the beneficiaries discover that a breach of trust has been committed they can bring a court action against the trustees personally.

There is a wider range of terms used in referring to beneficiaries, including:

- Life tenant – an individual who receives the income from a trust for their life or other period.
- Remaindermen – the beneficiaries who will receive the capital once the rights of the life tenant to receive income has finished.

Trust protector

A settlor may want to exercise additional control over the trustees and would normally achieve this by including provisions in the trust that will allow him the power to exercise certain control over the trustees during his life.

There may be occasions, however, where for tax reasons the settlor is unable to do this, such as with an offshore trust as it may generate unwanted tax problems. In such cases, the settlor could appoint a trust protector to protect the interests of the beneficiaries.

There is no specific law covering the duties or powers of the protector and his rights or powers will always depend on the terms of the trust document. The role has, however, been confirmed in case law as being a fiduciary one, which implies that any exercise of the powers has to be in good faith and for the benefit of the beneficiaries.

The types of powers given to the protector would include requiring his consent before certain transactions can be carried out or to enable him to direct the trustees in certain matters, including the power to dismiss the trustees and appoint new ones.

Types of trusts

There is a wide variety of trusts and it is necessary to understand what these are, because each has differing characteristics and tax treatments that will drive different investment administration requirements.

Trusts can be looked at either by their tax treatment or by their title, purpose and characteristics.

The most commonly used categorisation is how they are treated for tax purposes and four main types are recognised as shown in Figure 12.3.

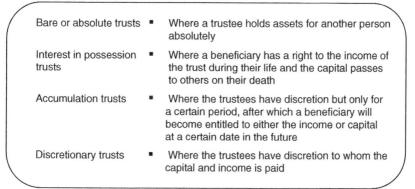

Bare or absolute trusts	▪ Where a trustee holds assets for another person absolutely
Interest in possession trusts	▪ Where a beneficiary has a right to the income of the trust during their life and the capital passes to others on their death
Accumulation trusts	▪ Where the trustees have discretion but only for a certain period, after which a beneficiary will become entitled to either the income or capital at a certain date in the future
Discretionary trusts	▪ Where the trustees have discretion to whom the capital and income is paid

Figure 12.3 Types of trust

Each of these is considered below, along with two further types of trust that have slightly different tax treatment and which are known as disabled trusts and trusts for the vulnerable.

Bare trusts

Under a bare trust both capital and income are held by the trustee for the absolute benefit of the beneficiary.

A simple example is where grandparents give money to their grandchildren but it is held by their parents in trust until they are adult. In such cases, the trustee can often be referred to as a nominee.

A different example could be where a client signs up to a discretionary investment management agreement. They will transfer the legal title to their investments to the firm managing their portfolio, who will hold them as nominee for the client. In essence, this is a bare trust.

Sometimes such trusts are also created by operation of the law. A legacy may be left in a will to a minor child but, under English law, a child cannot give a valid receipt until they are 18 years old and so the legacy will often be paid to the parents who will hold it as a bare trustee for the child.

Interest in possession trust

The term 'interest in possession trust' is used for trusts where one beneficiary has an immediate entitlement to any income produced by the trust either for life or a predetermined period and a different set of beneficiaries are entitled to the capital following that event.

These types of trust are most commonly created in wills where it is desired to give a guaranteed right to income during the lifetime of a beneficiary, for example, to the surviving spouse, but with no outright access to capital. This is known as a life tenancy and the person receiving the income is known as the life tenant.

They are often used in the wills of married couples who wish to ensure that the assets of the first to die pass intact to the next generation but the surviving spouse has the right to income.

For example, it might be used in a second marriage situation, where a spouse wants to ensure that a certain part of his or her assets passes to the children of the first marriage. They could create a trust whereby their partner is able to enjoy the income arising from the capital for the rest of their life and provide that on their death the capital passes to the children of the first marriage.

There are many potential variations on this theme. The right to income may be only until remarriage, it might be for a stated period of years only or the trust might provide for yet a further life interest to another person before it eventually passes to the final beneficiaries.

The advantage of such trusts is that the capital passes eventually to the intended beneficiaries but they have a potential disadvantage in that the surviving spouse or partner's financial circumstances might change and they may end up having a desperate need for capital. It is usual, therefore, for the trustees to be given the power to appoint the right to the trust capital to protect against such eventualities.

Discretionary trusts

As the name suggests, a discretionary trust gives the trustees total discretion as to the use of capital and the distribution of income.

The potential beneficiaries, known as the class of beneficiaries, will be described in the trust document but the final decision as to the frequency and amount of any payments is left to the trustees. This means that no beneficiary has the right to any income or capital until a distribution is made and any income that is not distributed is accumulated and becomes capital.

Some of the key features of a discretionary trust are as follows:

- The settlor can provide guidance to the trustees on how they should exercise their discretion in a letter of wishes, although it will not be binding on the trustees.
- The settlor or the trustees will normally be given the power to add to the class and even remove a discretionary beneficiary.
- The discretion of the trustees over income and capital can extend over the whole term of the trust, which can be up to 80 years.

- The trustees will normally also be able to accumulate trust income within the normal accumulation limits.
- Rather than simply paying the capital to the beneficiaries, the trustees can appoint capital to any of the discretionary beneficiaries and thus create new trusts with completely different terms.

These advantages give discretionary trusts a great degree of flexibility, hence their attraction and widespread use.

Discretionary trusts are commonly used in wills in order to minimise inheritance tax.

For example, a married couple might want to leave an amount equal to the nil-rate band to their children but are concerned whether the surviving spouse will have sufficient money at the time to afford it. An option open to them, is to leave all of their estate subject to a discretionary trust with the surviving spouse as one of the beneficiaries. This gives the flexibility to defer making a decision until the death of the first spouse. Provided that the distribution out of the trust is made within two years of death, no inheritance tax will be charged on that distribution. Instead the estate will be taxed as if the will had provided for it.

Accumulation and maintenance trust

Accumulation and maintenance trusts are usually referred to as A&M trusts. They are a type of discretionary trust and are usually used created by wills. The beneficiaries will normally be children or grandchildren and the trust deed will usually state the age at which they can benefit from the trust income, which has to be no later than by the time they attain the age of 25. The right to capital can be delayed until they are aged 40 or even later or left subject to a power of appointment being exercised by the trustees.

During the accumulation period it is possible to advance capital to or for the benefit of the beneficiaries or pay or apply income for their benefit without giving any rights to income until the specified age.

There are a number of issues surrounding A&M trusts which can cause difficulties with their administration. Under English law, it is not permissible to accumulate income within the trust for more than 21 years. This can place it at odds with a settlor's wish that a beneficiary only becomes entitled to the income at 25.

If an intervening period arises, then the beneficiaries do not acquire a vested right to the income; instead, the trustees have an obligation to distribute any income that arises. Once the beneficiary reaches the specified age, the income will belong to him automatically and the trustees will have no discretion as to whether to distribute or not.

Disabled trusts

Trusts established for disabled persons will normally be discretionary trusts but they benefit from different treatment for inheritance tax and capital gains tax.

In this context, disabled persons are individuals who are incapable of managing their affairs due to a mental disorder or individuals who are in receipt of an attendance allowance or a disability living allowance. A trust like this might be created where a person wants to make provision for a disabled child or relative and wants to ensure that there is a trustee appointed who can ensure that any surplus funds are used for their benefit.

Trusts for the vulnerable

A new tax regime for trusts for the most vulnerable was introduced in 2004. 'The most vulnerable' in this context are either individuals who have a disability or minor children following the death of a parent. Trusts for either of these categories of beneficiary are treated as trusts for the most vulnerable.

The definition of disabled is the same as for trusts for the disabled but is extended to include individuals who may not qualify under the above test but who have been moved into care for medical reasons.

Trusts for minors qualify where the trust is set up either under the intestacy rules or under the terms of the parent's will.

Under these new rules, an irrevocable election can be made whereby the trust will be taxed on the basis of the vulnerable beneficiary's individual circumstances for both income tax and capital gains tax. This, in effect, means that the trust is treated as a bare trust for the vulnerable beneficiary.

Creation of a trust

Drafting a trust deed

Drafting a trust deed requires extensive knowledge of trust law and the administration of trusts and, as a result, there are limitations on who can prepare a trust deed.

Essentially, this is limited to solicitors and in fact, it is an offence for anyone else to do so. Many life companies offer draft trust documents to use with the purchase of their products but as no fee is charged, they are not in breach of the law.

Requirements for a valid trust

To be valid, a trust must be able to meet certain conditions known as the three certainties. They are:

- Certainty of intention – the words used to create the trust must be clear, unambiguous and show the clear intention of the settlor to impose a binding fiduciary obligation on the trustees.
- Certainty of object – beneficiaries must be named or capable of identification with certainty.
- Certainty of subject – the assets of the trust must also be clear and unambiguous.

To be effective, these three certainties must be satisfied and the trust assets must be properly vested in the hands of the trustees. If any is missing, the trust will fail.

Appointment and removal of trustees

As mentioned earlier, anyone over 18 years of age and not bankrupt can be a trustee.

The settlor or other family members may be the trustees but it may also be professionals, such as accountants, solicitors or a trust corporation. The latter is a company whose articles of association allow it to carry out the duties of a trustee, for example, where banks act as trustee of private family trusts or pension funds.

The initial trustees are appointed by the trust deed, but there is no rule as to how many trustees are required. The exception is trusts of land, where there can be no more than four trustees.

New trustees may be appointed either using a power in the trust deed or relying on trust law. The latter allows the continuing trustees to appoint new ones where a trustee is dead, remains out of the UK for more than 12 months, desires to be discharged, refuses or is unfit to act or is incapable of acting or is an infant.

Having accepted the duties of being a trustee, it is possible for that person to execute a deed and retire provided that there remains either a trust corporation or two individual trustees.

It is also possible for trustees to be removed from office. There may be a special power in the trust deed that enables this which might be used in cases where a trustee refuses to cooperate but does not wish to retire voluntarily. If not, it may be possible to do so under legislation that was introduced recently, the Trusts of Land and Appointment of Trustees Act 1996 and as a last resort, the court always has the power to remove a trustee.

Death of the last trustee

When the sole or last remaining trustee of a trust dies, his executors or administrators are required to take over the role of trustees.

This is to ensure that there is continuing management of the trust and they gain both their power to act and their obligation to do so, once they obtain a grant of probate or a grant of letters of administration. They can continue to act as trustees or they can appoint new trustees and retire themselves.

The position in Scotland is different as the executors must obtain a separate authority to act and can only do so as an interim measure, until they appoint new trustees.

Rights and duties of trustees

Under the trust, the trustee owes particular personal obligations to the beneficiaries, such as:

- Duty to keep the trust accounts, i.e., proper records of his dealings with the trust.

- Duty to deal with and distribute the assets according to the trust terms.
- Duty to invest the trust funds.

Breaches of trust

If the trustee breaches any of his duties he will be personally liable for breach of trust, and the beneficiaries can sue him for breach of trust so long as the trustee lives or against his estate if he has died.

If the trustee becomes bankrupt they also have the right to claim their equitable ownership of the trust assets against the trustee in bankruptcy.

Whilst the right to sue the trustee provides some protection for the beneficiaries, its value is limited to the assets that the trustee has. There will be occasions, therefore, where the trustee transfers assets in breach of trust and the beneficiaries will need to attempt to recover them.

As the legal title to assets is held by the trustees, the rights of the beneficiaries are known as equitable ones. To explain how they are able to enforce their rights, we need to look firstly at what would happen if someone stole something from you, so that we can compare it to what would happen if a beneficiary needed to enforce their equitable rights.

Private individuals can enforce their title to their assets against anyone who comes to possess it without their agreement. This is even against an innocent person who paid good money to buy it from someone who stole it from you. Though both you and that buyer of the asset are innocent, the law says that the thief could not acquire good title from you by stealing the asset, and so he had no right to the asset to sell. The innocent buyer therefore bought nothing.

The rule is different for the beneficiaries' equitable title to trust assets. This right cannot be exercised against an innocent purchaser for value of the trust assets from the trustee – that person takes the asset free and clear of the trust. It can be enforced, however, against what is known as a volunteer, which is any person to whom the trustee gives the trust assets in breach of trust without taking any payment in return.

12.4 INVESTMENT ADMINISTRATION

New business

Transfer of assets to a trust

A trust deed by itself does not constitute an effective trust unless the trust property is transferred to the trustees, or their nominees.

The process involved in transferring assets is similar to any other type of business, as can be seen below:

- Cash assets: the transfer of cash assets would normally involve the trustees opening a new account and the settlor paying the funds to the trustees for deposit in that account.

- Quoted assets: transfer of quoted assets will follow the standard method of a stock transfer form which when lodged will move the holding into the names of the trustees on the company register. The name on the company register could, of course, be from or into a nominee account.
- Private companies: although transfer is also by stock transfer form, it will be necessary to check the articles and memorandum of association for any restrictions or consents that may be needed.
- Land: to transfer land to the trustees requires execution of a land registry form and an entry in the Land Registry. If the land is unregistered, then transfer will be by a conveyance and an application to register the land in the Land Registry.
- Life assurance policy a transfer is accomplished through execution of a deed of assignment and notice being lodged with the life office.
- Chattels: a deed of assignment is needed to transfer assets, chattels or equitable interests under a trust, such as a right to income or a reversionary interest.

The transfer of ownership may be into either the names of the trustees or into a nominee account that can be identified back to the underlying trust. If the asset is held directly, then it should be registered in the name of the trustees and with reference to the trust, such as 'John Smith as trustee of Jane Smith Trust'. It is not possible to register the trust itself as a holder of assets.

Money laundering

Although the transfer of assets to the trustees is straightforward, undertaking money laundering checks is less so.

Basically, the provisions and requirements of money laundering legislation apply to trusts. This is because it is necessary to identify both the source and the destination of the funds.

JMLSG guidance

Detailed guidance on how to comply with money laundering requirements is provided by the guidance notes issued by the Joint Money Laundering Steering Group (JMLSG). This requires confirming the identity of the settlor, trustees and beneficiaries as well as the source of funds.

Importantly, it needs to be noted that the FSA views compliance with the guidance as a key factor in assessing compliance with the money laundering regulations.

Money laundering issues with trusts

With trusts, the major issue is ascertaining the beneficiaries who need to be identified.

If the trust is an interest in possession one, then it is quite possible that all of the beneficiaries are known, but if the residuary or eventual beneficiaries are say the children of the life tenant who are alive when they die, then it is somewhat more difficult.

If it is a discretionary trust where there are a class of beneficiaries who may possibly benefit or who may not, then how far do the identification requirements extend.

The practical difficulties of this are recognised including the fact that this could be both onerous and at times, impossible.

Current practice is to take a practical and risk-based approach that takes account of the type of customer, business relationship or transaction. In low-risk cases, verification of beneficiaries should be permitted after having established the business relationship but, in any event, before a distribution of assets to the beneficiaries.

General guidance

The first part of the JMLSG guidance notes provides some general guidance on the approach to be adopted for trusts. Some of the key points that emerge are as follows:

- Firms should take account of the different money laundering or terrorist financing risks that trusts of different sizes and areas of activity present when developing their money laundering processes.
- The obligation to identify the customer attaches to the trustees, rather than to the trust itself.
- The firm should verify the identities of the trustees who have authority to operate an account or to give the firm instructions concerning the use or transfer of funds or assets.

In respect of trusts, the firm should obtain the following information:

- full name of the trust;
- nature and purpose of the trust, e.g. discretionary, testamentary, bare;
- country of establishment;
- names of all trustees;
- name and address of any protector or controller;
- where the trustee is a regulated firm, a publicly quoted company or other type of entity the standard identification procedures should be adopted;
- for trusts presenting a lower money laundering or terrorist financing risk, the standard evidence will be sufficient;
- where a trust is assessed as carrying a higher risk of money laundering or terrorist financing, the firm should carry out a higher level of verification.

Detailed guidance for different sectors of the financial services industry is contained in Part 2 of the JMLSG guidance notes.

Summary

The latest guidance issued by JMLSG moves the approach that firms should adopt from a prescriptive one to a more risk-based approach, meaning that greater discretion and responsibility is given to firms' management. This recognises the fact that, like the vast majority of customers, trusts present a low risk.

In summary, therefore, when an investment is made by the trustees of an existing trust an adviser will need to take account of the following.

Clearly all the trustees need to be identified. Equally given that the adviser will be required to consider the needs of the beneficiaries, all the relevant details surrounding the trust, including who the settlor is or was, who are the beneficiaries, what are their objectives and so on will be clearly required before any advice can be given on the investment of the trust funds.

The guidance reduces the requirements for beneficiary identification and verification and makes them more practical so as to reflect the realities of any money laundering risk. In many cases, especially with flexible or discretionary or A&M trusts, beneficiaries will be defined merely by their relationship to the settlor.

Trading

There are no special considerations to be aware of when undertaking trading for a trust other than for ensuring that the correct type of units are purchased when investing in a unit trust or OEIC.

When investing trust funds, trustees have a general duty to maintain a balance between the potentially conflicting interests of beneficiaries, such as the life tenant and the remainderman. This can present problems with the choice of units and shares in unit trusts and OEICs.

Many collective investment schemes offer accumulation units where the income is not distributed to the investor but reinvested within the fund and the investor stills pays income tax on the income as if it had been distributed.

The life tenant is entitled to the income that arises in the trust and such an investment would mean that the life tenant is being disadvantaged. As a result, if accumulation units are purchased then any additional units that are acquired as a result of the reinvestment of income belong to the life tenant absolutely.

Other funds are now structured on the basis that dividends are not actually distributed but are reinvested in the fund and so, rather than buying additional shares, it is reflected in the share price. As such it is not possible to keep track of the future value of such reinvested distributions.

From a suitability and administrative viewpoint, both types of fund are best avoided.

Settlement

As we have seen above, a trust is effectively a legal wrapper containing a portfolio of assets which will commonly include quoted bonds and equities.

The settlement of a trade of a quoted stock held in a trust is no different from any other trade with the exception of how the trust can be registered.

In the UK, section 360 of the Companies Act 1985 expressly forbids the registration of a trust on a share register. Any attempt to register a trust will be rejected by the company registrar.

The reason for this can be traced back to the duality of ownership which trusts bring about – the trustees have legal title to the asset and the beneficiaries have the beneficial title. The trustees can therefore be entered on the share register but not the trust itself.

Where a trust acquires a shareholding, therefore, a method of designating the holding as a trust is needed to differentiate the trust's asset from any personal assets of the trustees.

Crest requirements for this are set out in the manual titled 'Input of Investor Details in Crest'. The manual sets standards for input of items such as title, name, address and designations. It also explicitly deals with how trusts are to be recorded. The manual provides the details shown in Figure 12.4 of how a trust may be registered.

The only exception to this rule is for companies incorporated in Scotland where trusts are recognised and can be entered in the share register.

Corporate actions

As with settlement, the treatment of corporate actions generally follows exactly the same process as for any other quoted holding but with some differences.

Example:

- Investor - Third Duke of Northumberland Discretionary Trust
- Trustee - David Brown Esq

	Commences at Character	
Investor type indicator		I
Investor designation		DND
Investor name details		
Prefix	1	
Forename(s)	21	DAVID
Surname	91	BROWN
Suffix	131	ESQ

The points to note are:
1. These details contain no reference to a trust.
2. To enable David Brown to identify that this is a trust and not his own personal holding, a suitable investor designation has been used.

Figure 12.4   Registering a trust in Crest *Source*: Crest

Introduction

A corporate action on a trust holding will carry the same entitlements as for any other holding but differences arise in how they are processed where there are separate beneficiaries entitled to capital and income.

Earlier in this chapter, we looked at a type of trust known as an interest in possession trust. Typically, this type of trust would have a life tenant who would be entitled to the income during their life and following that person's death, the capital would pass to other beneficiaries known as remaindermen.

These differing rights to income and capital can give rise to issues regarding who is entitled to the benefit arising under some corporate events. The two main areas where differences arise are for accrued income on bonds and the treatment of capital reorganisations, both of which are considered below.

Accrued income

To understand the issue with accrued income, consider a straightforward sale of a government bond. When the holding is sold, the sale proceeds will include the consideration for the bond and accrued interest to the date of sale. Is the element of accrued interest capital or income?

For a normal investor, if a bond was sold the consideration and any accrued interest would not be differentiated and the whole proceeds would be posted to the capital of a portfolio and be available for investment. If the holding was a trust asset, the differing rights to capital and income do not allow this process to be followed.

If the holding had not been sold, then the interest would have been eventually received and be due to the life tenant. If the accrued interest is treated as capital, then the life tenant loses the income to which they are due and the remaindermen gain by having cash added to the capital of the fund that they will eventually receive to which they are not entitled.

A similar situation arises with purchases of bonds where accrued interest is added to the consideration. If the life tenant were to receive the whole of the next interest payment, they would be receiving more than they were entitled to and the remaindermen would suffer.

Processing accrued income in the same way as for a private investor would therefore be a breach of trust and leave the trustee liable to recompense the trust.

As a result of this, it is necessary for additional entries to be posted to trust accounts to ensure that the accrued interest is held in the correct part of the fund.

For sales of bonds, it will be necessary to debit the capital of the fund with an amount equal to the accrued interest and post this to the income account and vice versa for purchases.

Capital reorganisations

The issues surrounding capital reorganisations arise from the complex way in which trust law classifies what is income and what is capital.

The courts have established a set of rules to determine what is income or capital and in doing so the courts often draw on the metaphor of a tree and its fruit. Property which can be characterised as the 'tree' is usually treated as capital whereas the 'fruit' which it produces is classified as income. So for example, rents received from property or interest on a loan is clearly income.

In most cases the rules simply reflect common sense except when it comes to classifying receipts from companies where the rules are complicated and sometimes result in unfairness.

Some of the issues that arise can be seen in the following example of a corporate action involving a demerger.

Let's say that company A wants to demerge part of it business. This would be put into effect by the company transferring the appropriate parts of its business to a new subsidiary company, Company B, and then declaring a dividend to its shareholders. The dividend is then satisfied by the company issuing to its shareholders the entire share capital of Company B.

Whilst for a private investor that would be regarded simply as a distribution of shares in a new company, the position is not the same for trusts. In fact, court cases have settled that these shares are received by shareholders as income.

The complex nature of the rules surrounding how trust law classifies income means that each corporate action needs to be examined carefully to determine how it should be treated and processed.

The following points should be considered for each corporate action:

- Where there has been a judicial decision on how it should be treated, then clearly that ruling needs to be followed.
- The prospectus detailing the issue should be examined as it will often provide guidance on the correct treatment.

- The structure of the corporate action should be established as a company can only return capital to its shareholders by an authorised reduction of capital.
- Any other payment made by a company can only be made out of profits and should be treated *prima facie* as income.

The Law Commission has undertaken a consultation on this area of trust law and is looking to introduce legislation that will bring about a simplified structure to replace the current complex one.

Chapter

13

. . . .

CHARITIES

13.1 INTRODUCTION

There are nearly 170,000 charities in the UK and the number is growing rapidly, having risen by 40% since 1995. They range from small community-based charities to the international charities that are household names.

Most charities will have funds that they invest to generate income which they can spend on charitable objectives. Charities are required to obtain professional advice on the investment of the funds that they control and so, investment firms will have regular dealings with them whether when giving advice or acting as their investment managers.

Staff working in investment administration will, therefore, regularly come into contact with charity investment accounts and an understanding of the rules surrounding them is needed so that the differences in how they are managed and administered can be appreciated.

13.2 WHAT IS A CHARITY?

Broadly, a charity can be set up for any of the following purposes:

- the relief of poverty
- the advancement of education
- the advancement of religion; and
- other purposes beneficial to the community.

They can be established as an unincorporated association, a limited company or a trust.

Charitable trusts are probably the most common form of charity. Where the charity is set up under a trust, the governing document will be the trust deed or the will creating the trust.

In the case of an unincorporated association, the governing document will be its constitution or rules and if it is set up as a company, its governing document will be the memorandum and articles of association.

Each charity has someone appointed who will be in charge of running the charity. They may be called trustees, managing trustees, committee members, governors or directors, or may be referred to by some other title.

The trustees are responsible for holding, managing and applying charity money and property for the benefit of others and are not allowed to benefit from their position as trustees.

Apart from their obvious responsibilities – raising funds and using them in accordance with the aims of the charity – they have some specific responsibilities that relate to investment which include:

- managing the funds that the charity has;
- making sure that the charity funds are invested wisely;
- making sure that proper books and accounts are kept

Charities are supervised by the Charity Commission. It maintains a public Register of Charities and agrees the charitable status of a charity. All charities in England and Wales must be registered with the Charity Commissioners which is where the term 'registered charity' comes from.

13.3 LEGAL BACKGROUND TO INVESTMENT BY CHARITIES

The main legislation governing the operation of charities is the Trustee Act 2000 and the Charities Act 1992 and 1993.

From an investment point of view, the investment powers of a charity will be set out in the trust deed or other governing documentation. This will set out the investment powers of the trustees but if the deed does not contain any powers, then trustees can rely on the powers contained in the Trustee Act 2000.

The exception is where the trustees are managing common investment funds and common deposit schemes that have been expressly set up under the Charities Act 1993. The background to these schemes is considered later in this chapter.

The legislation mentioned above relates to charities in England and Wales. The legislation is different in Scotland and Northern Ireland, although as far as the investment of charitable trusts is concerned they are generally the same.

Despite the relatively recent dates for the legislation, some of the rules surrounding charities date back over 400 years. An overhaul of the rules is to take place and the legislation that will enable it is the Charities Act 2006 which received the Royal Assent in November 2006.

The changes being brought about by the Act are to be introduced in stages. The first set of changes came into force in February 2007 and dates for the remainder will be announced later. In the first set of changes, there is only one amendment affecting the investment of charitable funds which is to allow charities in Northern Ireland and Scotland to invest in common funds

In the following sections, consideration is given to the rules contained in the Charities Act and Trustee Act that affect the investment of charitable funds.

Investments and Charities Act 1992 and 1993

Trustees have always had an obligation to ensure that the funds within a charity are appropriately invested. These duties have, however, been reinforced and strengthened over time to define more clearly what is expected of a trustee when exercising their fiduciary responsibility to the trust.

The first legislation that attempted to specifically address the duties of a trustee when investing funds was the Trustee Investments Act 1961. Although it was generally described at the time as one of the most poorly drafted pieces of legislation ever, it did require trustees to have regard to the need for diversification of a trust's investment portfolio and to obtain qualified advice on the continuing suitability of the investments they held.

The duties relating to trustees of charities were considerably strengthened by the Charities Act 1992 and 1993 which imposed more onerous responsibilities on charity trustees.

The 1992 Act relaxed some of the more onerous restrictions that were placed on trustee investments but at the same time, imposed a duty on the trustees to manage the property of the charity prudently. This required that trustees have a wider knowledge of what they are dealing with and to ensure any decision was appropriate for the charity after proper research had been undertaken.

Following the passing of the Charities Acts, the Charity Commissioners issued guidelines for trustees on investment policy which included the following key requirements:

- The trustees of every charity should draw up an investment policy for the charity.

- Trustees with sums to invest in excess of £100,000 should appoint an investment manager to advise them in drawing up their investment policy and in the selection of appropriate investments.
- The investment manager appointed must be a regulated person.
- Charities too small to appoint an investment manager should obtain impartial investment advice.

In addition, their advice contained further guidelines about diversification, speculation, monitoring of investment performance and ethical investments.

Many of the provisions with regard to charities that are constituted as trusts have now been superseded by the provisions of the Trustee Act 2000.

It is important to recognise, however, that not all charities are constituted as trusts. These guidelines remain valid for those charities that are set up as companies or are not governed by the Trustee Act 2000.

Charity investments and the Trustee Act 2000

The Trustee Act 2000 brought about a long overdue overhaul of the duties and responsibilities of trustees in general. Its provisions apply equally to those charities that were constituted as a trust.

The relevant provisions of the Trustee Act that apply to charities are:

- The statutory duty of care applies to charitable trusts unless it is excluded in the trust deed.
- The general wide investment power applies to charitable trusts in the same way as it applies to other trusts, unless it is excluded in the trust deed.
- The requirements to take proper advice and to have regard to the standard investment criteria apply.
- The powers to employ agents and to delegate functions are available.

The latter power to delegate investment management is of particular importance for many charities that do not have that power expressly included in their trust document.

13.4 TRUSTEE INVESTMENT POWERS AND DUTIES

The powers of investment contained in Trustee Act 2000 essentially allow trustees to invest in any kind of investment, excluding land, in which they could invest if they were the absolute owner of those funds.

Anyone used to examining an investment clause in a will or trust deed will recognise the terminology used in the act, as it has been standard practice to include wide powers of investment in wills and trust deeds for the last 25 or 30 years.

The point to note, however, is that this is the automatic power that trustees will have where there is no provision in the charity's governing document which restricts or excludes the power. This needs to be considered against the background that trustees who cause loss to a charity by speculating may find themselves liable to personally make good the loss.

The Charity Commission therefore issued new guidelines on the investment of charitable funds, which have since been updated in 2005.

Details of some of the key points are considered in the following sections.

Power of investment

The basic principle expressed in the guidance is that when exercising their powers to make investment decisions, the trustees must take a prudent approach.

In order to discharge the duty to adopt a prudent approach to the investment of the charity's funds, the Charity Commission require that trustees must:

- know their investment powers;
- discharge their duties properly when they take decisions about investments;
- have proper arrangements in place for holding investments on behalf of the charity;
- follow certain legal requirements if they are going to appoint someone to manage the charity's investments on their behalf;

- understand what is acceptable practice if they apply an ethical approach to the charity's investments.

They must also ensure that they maintain a balance between the short-term and long-term objectives of the charity, namely:

- providing an income to help the charity carry out its purposes in the short term; and
- maintaining and, if possible, enhancing the value of the invested funds, so as to enable the charity to carry out its purposes in the longer term.

Duties of trustees

There are other duties contained in the Trustee Act relating to the investment of funds which are held on trust.

There is a general duty to exercise care and skill in their dealings with the trust investments and specific duties including:

- Ensuring the suitability of any proposed investments and that there is appropriate diversification of investments.
- Reviewing the investments held at regular intervals and determining whether they should be retained or varied.
- Obtaining advice on whether the investments should be retained or varied.

When assessing the suitability of any proposed investments, the trustees are also required to consider the asset allocation of the portfolio and the risk profile of the portfolio and individual stocks. They are also required to ensure their decisions maintain a balance between the short- and long-term objectives of the charity.

Total return

As mentioned previously, trustees have a duty to ensure that their investment decisions balance the short and longer term interests of the charity.

Until the Trustee Act, many charities were normally only permitted to spend the income from their investments and this led to trustees weighting their investment policy towards maximising the type of return they wanted, sometimes at the expense of getting the best overall return on their investment.

Following the Trustee Act, the Charity Commissioners decided to allow charities to adopt a total return approach. Charities can now apply for an order from the Charity Commission that would allow them to spend some of the capital growth of the portfolio.

By not labelling the return received from investments as either income or capital allows the trustees to allocate the total return between the present and future beneficiaries in the way they consider best in the circumstances.

Permitted investments

The guidance from the Charity Commission also clarified what were acceptable forms of investment in the light of the Trustee Act 2000. Broadly, charities can essentially now invest in any asset which is consistent with the proper discharge of the trustees' duties.

Acceptable investments include shares, bonds, collective investment schemes and land. It does not include, however, land purchased and developed with a view to sale or works of art or commodities such as gold or vintage wine, acquired with a view to resale in the future at a profit. This is because the purchase and sale of such items will usually be viewed as trading.

Derivatives may be used provided that their use is to manage risk or transaction costs within the investment process. If the related investment proposal is changed or abandoned, the derivative transaction should be closed out as soon as it is economically sensible to do so.

Underwriting new share issues is within the ambit of the general power of investment, but is unlikely to be appropriate. If the charity acquires any shares it is likely to be at a price which exceeds that at which the shares could be purchased in the market and if the purpose is simply speculative it would not be regarded as a proper discharge of the trustees' duties.

Stock lending may also not be appropriate as the risk of non-repayment and the tax position of stock-lending fees may be incompatible with the investment duties of the trustees.

The guidelines also deal with hedge funds and private equity. As a type of collective investment scheme, charities can invest in hedge funds and private equity, however, the issue for charities to consider is whether it is the right sort of investment for them. It is likely that they would not be suitable for most charities and where they are, the investment would only ever form a small part of a well-diversified investment portfolio.

In determining appropriate investments, trustees are also required to pay due consideration to their tax treatment. Some investments are treated as non-qualifying investments by HMRC, and investment by the charity can lead to a restriction of the charity's tax reliefs. The type of investments involved, however, are likely to be unsuitable for charities anyway.

13.5 INVESTMENT POLICY

The Charity Commission strongly recommends that trustees decide on an investment policy for their charity, record it in writing and keep it under regular review.

The investment policy should address the following considerations:

- the need for enough resources for the charity to carry out its present and future activities effectively;

- the level of acceptable risk and how to manage it; and
- the charity's stance on ethical investment, if any.

Trustees must prepare a policy statement before an investment manager is authorised to act as their agent. If the trustees have appointed an investment manager, this should be done in consultation with them. If they have not appointed an investment manager, this must be done in consultation with a suitability qualified and experienced professional.

When an investment manager is appointed, the policy statement is intended to give guidance to the manager to whom investment management has been delegated. It provides a written framework for a charity's investment strategy and should contain the principles that will govern the detail of the investment decisions taken by the investment manager.

The document recording the investment policy should record:

- the investment objectives of the charity taking account of the needs of present and future beneficiaries and how the charity will meet these needs;
- the balance to be maintained between capital growth and income generation;
- the acceptable levels of risk the charity is willing to take;
- the degree of liquidity required and the nature and timing of any cash requirements in the future;

- any special preferences for investing in particular sectors of the market or any relevant ethical considerations;
- when and how often the investment policy will be reviewed;
- any constraints on how the investment manager is to exercise the discretion given to manage the portfolio.

Many trustees of charities will consider it best practice to place the management of the investments in the hands of a specialist.

There are two main ways of doing this which are considered in the following sections:

- investing in one or more collective investment schemes, such as unit trusts, open-ended investment companies or common investment funds for charities; or
- delegating their investment decisions by appointing an investment manager.

13.6 APPOINTING AN INVESTMENT MANAGER

The advantage of using an investment manager is that the manager can pursue an investment strategy that is tailor-made to the needs of the particular charity.

The Trustee Act 2000 allows trustees to delegate the investment management of the fund. This and the Charity

Commission guidelines require that:

- the agreement to delegate must be in or evidenced in writing;
- the investment manager must be regulated under the Financial Services and Markets Act (FSMA) 2000;
- the trustees must be satisfied that the manager is a proper and competent person to carry out the management of the investments;
- the trustees must inform the manager in writing of the extent of their investment powers and have his written acknowledgement;
- the trustees must give the manager a copy of their investment policy statement and keep him informed of any changes.

The legal agreement appointing the investment manager to act must include a clause to the effect that the investment manager will comply with the investment policy statement.

The effect of this requirement is that the investment manager is contractually bound to follow the instructions in the policy statement unless there is good reason not to do so.

The trustees must also ensure that they have adequate internal controls and procedures, which will ensure that any delegated power is being exercised properly and prudently.

There must also be proper arrangements for the manager to report regularly to the trustees on the performance of the investments and the trustees must agree with the manager the criteria by which his performance will be judged.

13.7 COMMON INVESTMENT FUNDS

Many smaller charities have insufficient funds to warrant the appointment of an investment manager and one option for smaller funds would be to invest in common investment funds.

Common investment funds are particularly relevant for smaller charities that may not have the facilities or the expertise necessary to undertake the management of a portfolio of investments.

The creation of common investment funds was authorised by the Charities Act 1960. Each common investment fund has an independent board of trustees who set the investment strategy and monitor the investment and administration performance of each fund. Day-to-day management is entrusted to full-time investment managers.

Every common investment fund is a registered charity in its own right and as such trades free of stamp duty and pays all dividends gross of tax. Common investment funds are available for investment in equities as well as fixed interest investments and deposits.

The Charity Commission maintains a list of common investment funds currently registered in England and Wales, which are open to any charities to invest in.

13.8 USE OF NOMINEES AND CUSTODIANS

The Trustee Act 2000 has brought about changes to when a charity can use a nominee or custodian.

As explained in Chapter 6, a custodian is a firm that safeguards the assets of the trust. It will usually have a subsidiary company who is the nominee and in whose name the investments of the charity will be entered on the share register.

The Trustee Act 2000 enables the trustees of a trust, including a charitable trust, to appoint a custodian or nominee. This power is in addition to any power in the trust deed or other governing document but does not apply to common investment funds or charitable trusts where there is a custodian trustee.

The Charity Commission requirements when appointing a nominee or custodian are:

- The arrangements must be such that allow the trustees, if necessary, to prove legally their beneficial ownership of the assets.

- Unless the custodian is controlled by the charity, then it must be a firm who is engaged in the business of providing nominee and custodian services.
- They should be independent from anyone that the firm has delegated investment management.
- Appropriate reporting arrangements should be put in place so that they can review the performance of the custodian.

In practice, the discretionary investment manager will select the custodian to be used. The guidance therefore also applies to them.

Chapter
14

....

SELF-INVESTED PERSONAL PENSIONS

14.1 INTRODUCTION

A self-invested personal pension or SIPP is a personal pension that allows an investor to manage his/her own investments.

Within a SIPP the investor can hold a range of investments including shares, bonds, unit trusts and OEICs, foreign shares and property. A SIPP also gives the investor flexibility over how the investments are managed. The investor can choose to manage the investments himself or can choose one or even several investment managers if the fund is large.

Under a SIPP, the management of the investment portfolio is separated from the pension administration which can make self-management of a pension a realistic option.

Estimates suggest that 130,000 individuals have self-invested personal pension plans and that total is expected to grow significantly over the next few years as investors take advantage of the new pension rules that came in April 2006. Under the new rules, it is possible to hold a SIPP in addition to belonging to a company pension scheme.

Although a SIPP is a pension scheme, the fact that the investment portfolio can be managed separately means that it is now a common feature in investment firms and for the staff who undertake investment administration.

14.2 DEVELOPMENT OF SIPPS

Self-invested personal pension plans were introduced in 1989 to give individuals greater control of their pension investments and more flexibility.

For many years, governments have allowed contributions to personal pension schemes to enjoy tax advantages. Despite this they have suffered from two major drawbacks, namely a lack of choice over how the contributions could be invested and the need to buy an annuity at retirement in order to draw pension benefits at whatever the prevailing annuity rate is at the time.

Insurance companies have traditionally offered individual pension schemes on the basis that any contributions are invested in one of their pooled investment funds including their unit-linked managed fund or with-profits fund.

This meant that the investor could not direct how his contributions were invested beyond picking from a small range of available sub-funds that may or may not have matched his investment objectives and risk profile. This problem was then compounded by the poor investment returns achieved by many of the funds on offer.

The requirement to purchase an annuity also presented problems. Pension rules required the investment fund that had been built up to be used to purchase an annuity at retirement in order to be able to pay retirement benefits.

An annuity is a product offered by an insurance company whereby in exchange for investing a lump sum, the insurance company agrees to pay a regular income to you for the rest of your life. The amount that is paid from an annuity is dependent on the rate of interest at the time it is purchased.

This left the investor open to the vagaries of interest rates at the time they retired. If interest rates were high, they could potentially secure a good long-term income but if rates were low then they were locking into that rate for the rest of their life. There was no option for the investor to purchase the annuity earlier or later so as to pick the optimum time when the best rates could be secured.

SIPPs were introduced in 1989 to overcome some of these issues. The respective parts of the pension scheme are broken down into their component parts, namely the investment management, the investment administration and the pension administration. Each of these can be arranged with a separate provider which can result in reduced overall fees.

They also offer the investor the choice as to how they manage the investments, either themselves or by choosing which investment manager to appoint. Not only can they choose the investment manager, they can replace him if the investment performance is poor.

The issue surrounding annuities was addressed by giving the flexibility to take pension benefits at any time from the age of 50 to 75 irrespective of whether they continued working. The benefits do not need to be taken all at the same time so that by constructing the pension as a series of individual policies, the SIPP can adapt to the changing income needs of an individual.

14.3 WHAT IS A SIPP?

So, a SIPP is a personal pension that allows an investor to manage his/her own investments.

Not only does a SIPP offer investment flexibility, but the flexibility to choose who delivers which part of the overall service.

Figure 14.1 shows the components that make up a SIPP. The advantage that this structure brings is that the investor can not only choose who to deal with but also can deal with pensions specialists for pension advice and administration and investment specialists for investment management and investment administration.

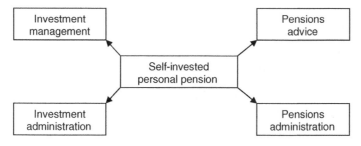

Figure 14.1 Components of a SIPP

Investment firms who offer SIPPs recognise that this type of choice is important to their customers. They will structure their products in such a way that they offer their normal investment services and contract out the pension administration to a specialist company.

This allows the respective firms to focus on their core business and to offer the product with a competitive pricing structure. There will typically be a set-up charge, an annual management charge and transaction charges when you buy and sell investments.

As a result of these charges, it has generally been considered that you need to build up an investment fund of £100,000 to make a SIPP practical. The growing use of SIPPs, however, is allowing firms to build up economies of scale and offer more competitive pricing. Some firms now make no initial charge to set up the fund and are reducing the annual charges and transaction charges. This is making SIPPs a practical option for a greater range of investors.

The overall benefits of SIPPs can be summarised as follows:

- They have the same tax advantages as other pension arrangements.
- There is an open market option which means that the most appropriate type of annuity can be purchased when taking benefits.
- There is flexibility over when benefits can be taken.

- The investor can choose how the funds are invested and match them to their investment policy objectives and attitude to risk.
- There are no hidden charges and the investor can use different providers for the different components of the pension plan.

14.4 SETTING UP A SIPP

The rules surrounding the setting up of a SIPP, how much can be contributed and the benefits that can be taken are broadly the same as for personal pensions. The key differences are around the underlying investments that the SIPP can invest in. The rules are devised by HM Revenue & Customs.

A SIPP can only be established by an authorised pension provider and it must be set up under an irrevocable trust to allow the freedom of investment permitted. The authorised pension provider will be appointed as a trustee and will undertake the pension administration. The investor can be appointed as a co-trustee if they plan to play an active role in investment decisions or alternatively an investment firm can be appointed to do the same.

To establish a SIPP under an irrevocable trust requires a straightforward trust deed that covers its establishment, the trustees' powers, and the HMRC rules. HMRC publishes a set of model rules and if these are included without amendment, then it should ensure the SIPP is approved for tax purposes.

14.5 ELIGIBILITY AND CONTRIBUTIONS

As with all pension schemes there are rules surrounding who can contribute to a SIPP and the amounts that can be contributed.

Most people under the age of 75 are eligible to invest in a SIPP provided that they are resident and ordinarily resident in the UK and have relevant earnings.

Everyone who meets the eligibility requirements can pay in at least £3600 gross per tax year. But many people will be able to pay in more. From April 2006, unlimited contributions are allowed but tax relief is only given on the first £3600 or an amount up to 100% of earnings where this is a personal contribution.

If the contributions exceed the annual allowance, which for the tax year 2007/8 is £225,000, then the surplus is taxed at 40%. There is also a lifetime limit on how much can be contributed which for 2007/8 is £1.6 million but which will increase in stages to £1.8 million by 2010. If the investor saves more than the lifetime limit, the surplus may be taxed at up to 55%.

14.6 PERMITTED INVESTMENTS

HMRC sets restrictions on the types of investment that a SIPP may invest in to ensure that schemes are used for the sole purpose of retirement provision.

The investments that are eligible for inclusion are detailed in the HMRC rules and in summary include:

- stocks and shares listed or dealt on a recognised stock exchange including equities, depositary interests, government and corporate bonds, convertible bonds and warrants;
- authorised unit trusts and OEICs, unauthorised unit trusts that do not hold residential property and investment trusts;
- futures and options traded on a recognised futures exchange;
- hedge funds provided that they meet certain conditions;
- commercial property.

There is also a list of prohibited investments that a SIP cannot invest in which includes investments such as:

- unlisted shares;
- gold bullion;
- premium bonds;
- residential property;
- personal chattels such as antiques.

As with ISAs, checks need to be made when investments are being purchased, assets transferred in or when a new holding is received as part of a corporate action that it qualifies for inclusion under the HMRC rules.

In doing so, it needs to be borne in mind that the rules are different and so what is eligible for an SIPP may not be eligible for an ISA and vice versa.

14.7 BENEFITS

It is not necessary to retire to take the benefits from a SIPP. Instead, the pension benefits can be taken at any time between the ages of 50 and 75.

When the pension benefits are taken, the investor can take up to 25% of the investment fund as tax-free cash. The rest must be used to provide a taxable income.

The investor has a choice about how he takes an income. He can either use the remaining fund to buy an annuity which will pay him an income for the rest of his life, or draw an income directly from the SIPP up to the age of 75 years. This practice is known as income drawdown.

There are two main types of annuity. There are conventional annuities where the income is fixed, inflation-linked, or set to increase by a fixed percentage each year. The other type is investment-linked, where the income rises or falls depending on the performance of the underlying funds.

Income drawdown allows the investor to continue with the SIPP investment portfolio and draw an income each year from the fund. Income drawdown allows the investor to keep the investment portfolio and defer buying an annuity. Once the investor reaches the age of 75 years, they then have to buy an annuity.

With income drawdown, the funds are still invested and therefore subject to stock-market movements. The income withdrawals and charges will be a drain on the fund and so income drawdown is usually recommended only for those with large funds of over £100,000 or other sources of income.

The other difference between income drawdown and an annuity is that if the investor dies while taking income drawdown, the remaining money can be used to provide an income for their dependants or can be paid, less a tax charge, to their heirs.

There is no requirement to convert the pension fund into an annuity or income drawdown in one go, instead it is possible to phase when to take the retirement benefits.

The pension scheme can be can split into segments which can be converted gradually over a period of time, so that the investor receives a series of tax-free cash payments and an increasing income, until the fund is fully converted which has to take place no later than age 75.

Chapter

15

....

DERIVATIVE PRODUCTS

15.1 INTRODUCTION

A derivative is a financial instrument that is based on another asset, such as commodities, shares in an individual company, an index or any other financial asset.

Derivatives are constructed and used to solve a wide range of specific needs. In their original form, they were developed so that a farmer growing crops could secure the price he was to obtain in advance rather than being open to the vagaries of what the price might be when he could harvest his crop and get it to market.

Derivatives have had a controversial history because of their ability to generate huge losses and have been at the core of some major business failures such as the collapse of Barings Bank, the bankruptcy of Orange County in the United States and more recently, the failure of the hedge fund, Long Term Capital Management.

They are often portrayed in the news as being the cause of a problem that has arisen. Invariably, however, it is not the derivative itself that is a problem but its inappropriate use, lack of control or lack of knowledge that allows problems to arise. What it does highlight is the risk attached to the use of these instruments.

Derivatives have traditionally not been included in the portfolios of private clients. This is now changing and there is a range of derivative products appearing that are opening this asset class up to the retail investor. This can be seen in the range of derivative products that are now listed on the London Stock Exchange and which can be traded and held and settled in Crest like any other quoted investment.

15.2 TYPES OF DERIVATIVES

A derivative is an instrument whose value is based on the price of an underlying asset, such as individual shares, an index, interest rates, currency or commodities.

The asset that the derivative is based on, for example shares in a company, is referred to as the underlying. The market in which the underlying is traded, shares in this example, is referred to as the cash market in order to differentiate it from the futures market.

Most derivatives take the form of forwards, futures, options or swaps.

Forwards

A forward contract is a legally binding obligation between two parties for one to buy and the other to sell a prespecified amount of an asset at a prespecified price on a prespecified date.

They originated in the farming industry where, as mentioned previously, there was a need for farmers to be able to secure the price at which their crop would be sold once harvested. It was not just the farmers who needed this certainty but also food manufacturers who needed to ensure firstly a continued supply of goods and then to guard against price fluctuations.

Forward contracts are usually individually negotiated and tailored to meet the needs of each party. As a result, they are not usually traded on exchanges which require contracts to be standardised in order for them to be traded. Instead, they are dealt off-exchange and are a type of over-the-counter (OTC) derivative.

Futures

Futures are similar to forward contracts but are standardised contracts that can be traded on an exchange.

They were a development on forward contracts that occurred in the nineteenth century. Forward contracts were very popular in the Mid-West grain markets in the United States and as their use grew, there developed a need for standardised contracts that could be traded on an exchange.

This led to the opening of the first derivatives exchange, the Chicago Board of Trade (CBOT), which soon developed standardised futures contracts that specified the quality and quantity of the agricultural product. Unlike forward contracts, a futures contract could itself be traded and so the obligation to make or take delivery could be transferred to a third party.

In the mid-1970s, the market developed further with the introduction of the first financial futures contracts. This was the start of the amazing growth of both exchanges and financial derivatives that has been seen since.

The main difference between forwards and futures is that futures are exchange traded and have standardised contract features. Trading takes place on derivatives exchanges with a central counterparty guaranteeing each trade.

Another major difference between the two is that not all futures contracts require the eventual physical delivery of the underlying asset and instead, the gain or loss is settled in cash. Indeed very few financial futures contracts run to the delivery date and instead are closed out by entering into an equal and opposite transaction so as to offset the original contract.

Options

An option is a contract that gives the right to one party to the trade to either buy or sell an asset at a predetermined price at a predetermined future date in exchange for the payment of a premium.

The major difference between options and futures is that the contract confers a right rather than an obligation for delivery of the underlying asset and that this is done in exchange for payment of a premium.

Options have been around for hundreds of years but their use in financial markets did not really take off until the development of the famous Black–Scholes option-pricing model in 1973. The two US academics who developed it won the Noble Prize for economics in recognition of the fact that until then, options contracts could not be easily priced, which restricted how they could be traded.

The two parties to an options contract are known as the holder and the writer. The writer is the party that confers the right on the holder to buy or sell an asset at an agreed price and date and who receives a premium for doing so.

There are two types of option, a call option and a put option. Where the contract confers the right to buy the asset it is known as a call option, in other words the holder can call on the writer to deliver the underlying asset. Where the contract confers the right to sell the asset it is known as a put option, in other words the holder can put the asset back to the writer.

The holder of the option has the right to either buy or sell but does not have to exercise this right if the transaction is not worthwhile. Instead, the holder can simply abandon the option and the loss is limited to the premium they have paid. The writer, however, is obliged to satisfy this right if the holder chooses to exercise it.

Most options can be exercised on or before the expiry date and are known as American-style options. Ones that can only be exercised on the expiry date are known as European-style options. In practice, most options are cash settled rather than physically settled.

Swaps

A swap is a derivative contract where two counterparties exchange one stream of cash flows for another. The cash flows are referred to as the legs of the swap and are calculated based on a notional principal amount.

The most common type of swap is an interest rate swap. For example, a firm may want to borrow money to fund the cost of buying new plant and equipment and would typically have to pay variable interest rates. This leaves it exposed to interest rate increases which might affect the viability of its investment plans. It could therefore enter into an interest rate swap where it exchanged the variable rate of interest for a fixed rate.

As part of this swap, the firm would make periodic interest payments based on a fixed rate of, say, 5% to a bank. In return, the bank would pay to the firm periodic interest payments based on a variable rate of interest. The variable rate of interest will usually be based on the London inter bank offered rate (LIBOR) plus a margin and so might be LIBOR plus 50 basis points or 5.25%.

The rate of interest that the firm paid would be set for the duration of the contract. The variable rate would be reset at agreed periods, say half yearly, at the LIBOR rate plus the margin. In this way, the firm secures fixed-rate financing for its investment and the bank takes the risk that interest rates do not move in such a way as to change its margin from being a profit into a loss.

There are a whole range of other types of swaps including total return swaps, equity swaps and credit default swaps. What they all have in common is that they are OTC derivatives, that is individually negotiated contracts and so are not traded on an exchange.

15.3 USES OF DERIVATES

As we saw above, derivatives started life as contracts that could be used to eliminate the price risk associated with the farming industry.

Since then, they have developed to become a major tool in the management of risk. Companies, financial institutions and other organisations have increasingly used derivatives as a key mechanism for managing price risk.

The global derivatives industry has grown at a rapid pace throughout the past 20 years and financial institutions such as hedge funds, mutual funds, insurance companies and smaller banks have become much bigger users of derivatives.

Within investment management, derivatives are seen as having four main uses:

- hedging;
- anticipating future cash flows;
- asset allocation;
- arbitrage.

Hedging refers to the technique used to reduce the impact of adverse price movements on the investments held within a portfolio. For example, an investment manager might use a FTSE 100 Index future to hedge against a market fall and depending upon which way the market goes, he could subsequently close out the future for a gain or a loss. Alternatively, the investment manager could use options on either the FTSE or on individual stocks and in exchange for paying the premium he would have the right to sell instead.

Another use is to hedge against a potential rise in prices when a large inflow of cash is expected. If an investment manager anticipated that prices would rise before the funds were available, then he could buy a FTSE 100 Index future. If the market rose as anticipated, the underlying shares would still have to be bought at a higher price but some of that difference would be offset by the gain on the futures contract. Again, the alternative would be to use options which have the advantage that if the market were to instead fall, then it would only be the premium that would be lost.

Derivatives can also be used when changes to the asset allocation of a portfolio are planned. Asset allocation is a term used to describe the breakdown of a portfolio between cash, fixed income and equities and between different markets. Changes to this asset mix can take time to implement and futures contracts can be used to establish the new position quickly and protect the portfolio from adverse price movements whilst the switch is taking place.

The other main use for derivatives is arbitrage. Differences can arise between the prices of an investment in one market to another or between the cash market and the futures market. Arbitrage refers to the fact that it is possible to profit from this by simultaneously buying and selling the same asset in the two different markets.

Apart from their use as an investment tool, derivatives can also be used purely for speculation. Because of their nature, derivatives provide an ideal means by which to speculate on both rising and falling prices.

15.4 DERIVATIVES MARKETS

To be able to trade a derivative on an exchange requires that it has standardised features. As we have seen previously, however, not all derivative contracts are standardised and instead, forwards and swaps are contracts that are separately negotiated between the parties to the trade. As a result, trading regularly takes place both on exchange and off exchange.

Derivatives exchanges

Euronext.liffe is the financial derivatives exchange in the UK, with metals, energy futures and other commodities being traded on the London Metal Exchange and the Intercontinental Exchange (ICE).

Only members of Euronext.liffe are permitted to trade on the exchange and depending upon their status may trade only for themselves or for anyone else. Non-members have to enter into an agreement with an exchange member in order to execute trades.

Like any other derivatives exchange, trading derivatives on Euronext.liffe involves there being a series of standard features in each of the contracts that are traded.

The typical items that would be specified in a contract include:

- Quality – specifies exactly what is to be delivered and where it can be quantified a clear description in order to avoid any confusion or disagreements.
- Quantity – specifies the size of the contract or the amount of the underlying asset on which the contract is based, such as one long gilt future equals £100,000 nominal of gilts.
- Price – specifies the method that is used to quote the price of a contract such as the price per £100,000 nominal of gilts for the long gilt future or the price per tonne for a commodity. It will also specify the tick size and tick value, which are the minimum price movement and value of the contract–
- Delivery – specifies when delivery will take place and in what form it will take place, that is physical or cash.
- Trading – specifies at what time during the day that a contract may be traded, the last trading day in the delivery month that the exchange permits trading in the derivative and the price that the exchange will use to settle a futures contract that is held until delivery.

The contracts traded on Euronext.liffe include the FTSE 100 Index Future, long gilt futures, short-term interest rate futures (STIR) and universal stock futures.

All trades on Euronext.liffe are settled through a clearing house, LCH.Clearnet.

A clearing house is essential to the effective operation of a derivatives exchange and involves the clearing house interposing itself between buyer and seller to become the single counterparty for every trade. In this way, it minimises the risk of the other party to a trade defaulting. It also requires collateral or margin to be deposited when a position is initially taken and then throughout the term of the contract on any losses accumulated whilst the position is open.

OTC derivatives

Over-the-counter (OTC) derivatives, by contrast, are ones that are not traded on an exchange and which do not have standardised features.

The deals are not conducted through a formal exchange but directly between the parties with screen display providing an indication of terms and prices. There is no central counterparty so the credit-worthiness of each party is a fundamental concern and it is not always possible to subsequently trade them.

They do, however, represent a product that can be designed to meet the individual needs of market

participants. As a result, the value of outstanding contracts is measured in the hundreds of trillions of US dollars and the value of contracts negotiated daily is more
than one and a half billion dollars.

The UK is the major centre for OTC derivatives trading and the largest type of contracts traded are interest
rate swaps. There is substantial trading in other types of
OTC derivatives, especially in credit derivatives which
has been one of the major growth areas of recent years.

Stock exchange traded derivatives

As mentioned earlier, derivatives have not usually featured in the portfolios of private investors. The market
for derivatives has been geared towards professional investors and the amounts required to be invested along
with the associated risks made it unattractive.

This is now changing with the development of standardised derivatives that can be traded on the London Stock
Exchange. These include structured products, covered
warrants, exchange traded commodities and contracts for
difference.

Each of these is becoming available not just for the portfolios of wealthy individuals but also for those investors
using the services of internet stockbrokers.

Although they carry significantly higher risks and require
a higher degree of knowledge to utilise them correctly

and safely within a portfolio, the fact that they are traded and settled on the London Stock Exchange makes them simple to use.

In the following sections, we will consider the features of these new products.

15.5 STRUCTURED PRODUCTS

Structured products is a term that is used to describe a series of investment products that are more commonly known as guaranteed growth bonds, FTSE capital protected bonds and a whole variety of other marketing names.

These types of structured product have been around for some time and their features and terms differ markedly from product to product. There are ones designed for the mass retail investment market, ones that target the high net worth market only, ones that are for the customers of a single private bank and even ones designed around individuals for the ultra wealthy.

What are structured products?

Structured products are packaged products based on derivatives which generally feature protection of capital if held to maturity but with a degree of participation in the return from a higher performing, but riskier, underlying asset.

They are created to meet the specific needs of high net worth individuals and general retail investors that cannot be met from standardised financial instruments that are available in the markets.

These products are created by combining underlyings such as shares, bonds, indices, currencies and commodities with derivatives. This combination can create structures that have significant risk/return and cost-saving advantages compared to what might otherwise be obtainable in the market.

The benefits of structured products can include:

- protection of initial capital investment;
- tax-efficient access to fully taxable investments;
- enhanced returns;
- reduced risk.

Interest in these investments has been growing in recent years and high net worth investors now use structured products as a way of achieving portfolio diversification. Structured products are also available at the mass retail level, particularly in Europe, where national post offices, and even supermarkets, sell investments on to their customers.

Development of structured products

Structured products have their base in the guaranteed bonds marketed by life offices from the 1970s onwards.

In recent years, the providers of these products have explored ever more innovative combinations of underlying asset mixes which have enabled them to offer a wider range of terms and guarantees.

Structured products have offered a range of benefits to investors and generally have been used either to provide access to stock market growth with capital protection or exposure to an asset, such as gold or currencies, that would not otherwise be achievable from direct investment.

Their major disadvantage has been the fact that they have had to be held to maturity to secure any gains. The gain that an investor would make on, say a FTSE100 linked bond, would only be determined at maturity and few bonds offered the option of securing profits earlier.

This need for greater flexibility led to the development of listed structured products and in May 2005, the London Stock Exchange created a new market segment to accommodate both primary and secondary markets in them.

Types of listed structured products

There is a wide range of listed structured products and the terms of each are open to the discretion of the issuing bank. They are known by a variety of names including certificates and investment notes.

Despite being traded on the London Stock Exchange, they are not standardised exchange products and the specification will change from issuer to issuer. One key feature they do have is that they are listed, held and settled in Crest.

They do, however, fall into some broad categories that are considered below.

Trackers

As the name suggests, trackers replicate the performance of an underlying asset or index. They are usually long-dated instruments or even undated so that they have an indefinite lifespan.

As a tracker replicates the performance of the underlying asset, its price will move in proportion to it. No dividends are paid on the tracker and instead, any income stream is built into the capital value of the tracker over its lifetime.

Where the underlying asset is say, an index on an overseas market such as the Standard & Poors 500, an investor may be exposed to currency movements. Some trackers will therefore incorporate features that ensure the tracker is constantly fully hedged for currency risk.

An investor can achieve the same performance as a tracker by buying other instruments such as an exchange traded fund or a unit trust tracker fund. Where they come into their own is their ability to be used to track other assets such as commodities and currencies or an index representing the same.

Accelerated trackers

With an accelerated tracker, the investor will participate in the growth of the underlying index or asset provided that when it matures its value is greater than the initial value.

If the asset or index is valued at less than its initial value, then the investor will lose the same amount.

For example, an accelerated tracker might provide for the investor to participate in 200% of the growth of an index. If an investor buys £1000 of an instrument and the index it is based on grows by 10%, then they will receive back their initial investment of £1000 plus 200% of the growth which amounts to £200 – that is, £100 growth × 200% = £200.

If the final value of the underlying asset is say 10% less than the issue price, then the investor will receive back the initial price of £1000 less the change in the underlying asset – 10% or £100 – which amounts to £900.

The investor will usually surrender any right to the underlying income stream form the asset in exchange for the right to participate in any performance.

Reverse trackers

A reverse tracker is similar to a standard tracker except that should the underlying asset fall, then the value of the tracker will rise. These trackers are also referred to as bear certificates.

Capital protected trackers

Capital protected trackers, as the name suggests, allow investors to gain some exposure to the growth of an underlying asset or index whilst providing protection for the capital invested.

The amount of participation in any growth and the protection over the capital invested will vary from product to product and is obtained by surrendering any right to income from the underlying asset.

For example, an instrument might be issued to track the performance of the FTSE 100 and provide participation of 140% of any growth but with 100% capital protection. If the FTSE 100 index is at a higher level at maturity, then the investor will receive back the initial price plus 140% of the growth over that period. If the index is lower than at the start, then the capital protection kicks in and the investor will receive back the initial price.

Trading and settlement

Listed structured products will usually be structured as an instrument such as a zero coupon bond and will be firstly offered in the primary market where they are made available to investors.

They are treated as derivatives for the purpose of conduct of business rules. A firm distributing these products must give a two-way risk warning, in the form of a generic warrants/derivatives warning notice and either a tailored risk warning or a copy of the listing particulars.

Once the investment date has passed, they can be traded in the secondary market. The issuers of the products are obliged to maintain continuous prices throughout the lifetime of the product and to adhere to the standard market-maker obligations of minimum size and maximum spread.

On any subsequent dealing in the secondary market, a contract note is issued as normal which will specify the name of the investment, the nominal amount purchased, the price at which it has been dealt and any commission charged.

Purchases of listed structured products are exempt from stamp duty, as with all securitised derivatives. They are a qualifying investment for self-select ISAs, PEPs and SIPPs provided that the outstanding term of the instrument is not less than five years.

The instruments are issued in uncertificated form and are held in Crest. Settlement takes place as normal at T+3.

At the end of the term, the investor will usually sell the investment on the last valuation day but if it is not traded, then the instrument representing the structured product will be redeemed using Crest functionality.

15.6 COVERED WARRANTS

Covered warrants are well established in many international markets but were only introduced into the UK in 2002.

They are a securitised derivative and provide investors with the ability to leverage their investment and take positions in a range of stocks and indices.

What are covered warrants?

A covered warrant is an instrument that resembles an option but is traded on the London Stock Exchange.

As with an option, a covered warrant gives the holder the right to buy or sell an underlying asset at a specified price, on or before a predetermined date. Again as with an option, it does not carry an obligation to buy or sell, so that an investor's maximum loss is restricted to their initial investment.

Covered warrants are issued by financial institutions and they get their name from the fact that when the issuer sells a warrant, they will often 'cover' or hedge their exposure by buying the underlying stock in the market.

Types and uses of covered warrants

As with options, there are two basic types of covered warrants, namely calls and puts.

A call covered warrant gives the buyer the right to buy the underlying asset from the issuer and a put covered warrant gives the buyer the right to sell to the issuer.

In both cases, the buyer has the right to buy or sell on or before an expiry day and at a predetermined price known as the exercise or strike price.

Covered warrants can be issued on a variety of underlying assets including individual stocks, a basket of shares, an index, commodities and currencies:

- Stock warrants – these are single stock warrants where the underlying asset is a blue chip share and which account for the majority of covered warrants in issue.
- Baskets – the underlying assets for these warrants are a number of stocks representing a particular sector or theme that are grouped together into a 'basket'.
- Index – these warrants give exposure to stock market indices, such as the FTSE 100 and to other indices such as the Halifax house price index.
- Commodities – the underlying asset for these warrants are commodities such as gold, silver and oil.
- Currencies – covered warrants are available on a range of exchange rates including sterling/dollar, sterling/euro and yen/dollar.

Covered warrants have a range of uses within an investor's portfolio including hedging, speculation and the ability to include currency and commodity exposure.

Covered warrants are not eligible for inclusion within an ISA but can be held within a SIPP.

Features and terminology

Although a covered warrant is defined as the right to either buy or sell to the issuer an underlying asset, it is in practice a cash-settled instrument.

This means that the holder is under no obligation to make or take delivery of the asset should the holder decide it is not in their interest to do so.

If it is not profitable, the covered warrant can be abandoned or sold prior to expiry and the maximum loss on the position is limited to the premium paid for the covered warrant.

Equally, if it is profitable the investor does not necessarily have to 'buy' the underlying but can either sell the warrants in the market or they can have any profit automatically transferred to them at expiry.

Although covered warrants are similar to options, they do have a number of features that differentiate them from options and other derivatives.

Some of their key differences are:

- They typically have longer maturities than options and on average have a life of 6 to 12 months.

- They are issued over a wider range of assets, including individual shares, indices, baskets and currencies.
- The terms are more varied and can be structured to meet market demand, for example by removing any gearing to provide a lower risk exposure.
- There are no margin calls.

Some of the main terminology used in association with covered warrants is as follows:

- Calls – a call warrant gives the holder the right, but not the obligation, to buy the underlying asset and usually rises in value when the price of the underlying asset rises.
- Puts – a put warrant gives the holder the right, but not the obligation, to sell the underlying asset and usually rises in value when the underlying asset falls in value.
- Exercise date – warrants will usually have a predetermined ate at which they will mature and the expiry date is the last date that the covered warrant can be exercised.
- Strike price – the strike or exercise price represents the price at which the investor has the right to buy or sell the underlying asset.
- Premium – the premium is the price an investor will pay to buy the covered warrant in the market.
- Conversion ratio – the conversion ratio is the number of covered warrants that must be exercised to buy or sell one share in the underlying asset.

- Exercise style – covered warrants can be either European or American style but this distinction is of little relevance as selling the instrument will almost always be more profitable than an early exercise.

Trading and settlement

Covered warrants are traded on the London Stock Exchange as with any other stock and can be bought and sold at any time during their life.

Four major financial institutions design and issue covered warrants and make a secondary market in them. These are:

- Dresdner Kleinwort Benson;
- Goldman Sachs;
- Société Général
- UBM (Trading Lab).

Trade instructions are placed with a broker as with any other trade and the broker will place the deal with one of the issuing institutions.

The costs of dealing are usually the same as for any other trade and unlike equities, warrants are not subject to stamp duty.

The pricing of covered warrants is carried out by the financial institution that issued the warrant and is based on the price of the underlying asset. Each issuer is required to quote two-way prices with a maximum percentage spread and a minimum dealing size throughout each trading day.

As covered warrants are a leveraged investment, firms are required to issue to investors a risk warning that highlights the warrant's volatility and the risk of losing all of the initial investment. Brokers who offer an online dealing facility will also require investors to complete a suitability assessment.

Covered warrants are not only traded like equities, they are also issued, held and settled in the same way through Crest.

An issue of covered warrants follows the same process as an initial public offering (IPO). The issuer will need to appoint a registrar who will credit the issuer's Crest account with the number of warrants to be issued. The warrant issuer will use a standard delivery transaction to transfer the warrants to the 'placees' against the simultaneous movement of cash. The register will then be updated to reflect the transfer of the assets from the issuer to the holder.

Once the warrants have been issued, they can be settled as with any other security with settlement taking place at T+3 as usual.

The warrants will then continue to be traded and settled as normal until expiry.

It should be noted that at expiry the holder does not receive or deliver any physical stock. Covered warrants are a cash-settled instrument which means that at expiry, the issuer will pay a cash amount for the intrinsic value of the warrant which is equivalent to the difference between the strike price and the value of the underlying asset at expiry.

Where the warrant issuer is due to pay the warrant holder cash, Crest will set up a redemption type of corporate action and the issuer or the registrar will input unmatched stock event transactions into Crest to deliver cash to the holder.

The warrant will then be removed from Crest using the standard security expiry functionality.

15.7 EXCHANGE TRADED COMMODITIES

Commodities have always had a place in the portfolios of private clients, especially where they are managed by discretionary investment managers.

Within the asset allocation of a portfolio, a percentage would usually be allocated to commodity exposure. This exposure has usually been obtained by holding the shares of companies involved in one aspect or another of the commodities world. For example, an investment manager might determine that he wants to achieve exposure to gold or other minerals and he would therefore include the shares of companies quoted in the mining sector or an investment fund that specialised in the sector.

Achieving exposure to commodities in this way has never been an optimal solution, as the share price of the company would be influenced both by the prospects for the movement of the underlying commodity and by the prospects for the company itself. However, there was no realistic alternative until exchange traded commodities came along.

Exchange traded commodities (ETCs) are investment vehicles that track the performance of an underlying commodity index. There are two main types of exchange trade commodity, namely single commodity ETCs such as gold and oil and ones that track an index.

ETCs are open to all investors and can be used for a number of purposes where commodity exposure is needed, such as exposure to a single commodity such as gold or as part of an asset allocation strategy.

They are an open-ended collective investment vehicle and so, additional shares are created to meet demand. They are similar to exchange traded funds in that they are dealt on the London Stock Exchange in their own dedicated segment. They have market-maker support so that there is guaranteed liquidity during market opening hours and are held and settled through Crest in the same way as any other shares.

15.8 CONTRACTS FOR DIFFERENCE

A contract for difference (CFD) is an equity derivative that allows investors to speculate on the movement of a share price.

Traditional CFDs

A CFD is a contract between two parties, a buyer or investor and a seller or counterparty. A CFD contract will stipulate that the seller will pay to the buyer the difference between the current value of an asset and its value at contract time. If the difference is negative, then the buyer pays instead to the seller.

The contracts are settled for the cash differential between the price of the opening and closing trades.

CFDs are dealt on margin which means that the investor has to deposit a percentage of the full value of the CFD trade which can typically be between 5% and 15%. They are also required to maintain a certain amount of margin at all times, so if the market turns down then the investor will be subject to margin calls and be required to deposit further monies. The investor's maximum exposure is therefore not limited to their initial investment; instead, it is possible to lose more than they originally invested.

CFD trades attract commission charges that are normally 0.25% of the full value of the trade. For example, if an investor buys a CFD on a FTSE 100 stock that required 10% margin then they would pay £10,000 initial margin and commission of 0.25% on the full £100,000 value of the trade. They are also subject to daily financing charges.

CFDs are being increasingly used for hedging and are also being used by hedge funds to acquire shares in companies that are subject to takeover bids.

Listed CFDs

A listed CFD works in the same way as the unlisted versions and therefore provides a leveraged way of investing in the underlying shares. Listed CFDs are an eligible investment for a SIPP but not for an ISA.

Where they differ from unlisted CFDs is in the arrangements surrounding how they are bought and sold. Some of the major differences are:

- They are quoted in their own segment of the London Stock Exchange with guaranteed market-maker liquidity which means that they can be dealt at market prices throughout the trading day.
- They can be bought and sold through any UK stockbroker.
- Brokers' commission is charged only on the amount of margin that is paid, in other words the amount invested, and many online brokers will charge flat fees in the region of £10 to £25.

- The minimum trade size is just one contract for one share giving the flexibility to trade small positions as well as large ones.
- There are no margin calls.
- Financing charges and dividends are included in the CFD price.
- Listed CFDs also have a guaranteed stop loss built into the contract so that any loss is limited to the value of initial margin payment.

Main differences with listed CFDs

A listed CFD has three major differences in the way it operates to an unlisted one, namely:

- they have a standardised contract;
- there are no margin payments; and
- they have an in-built stop loss.

When an investor buys a listed CFD, they purchase an existing contract that has an entry level price, the theoretical price at which the CFD was originally created, which is less than the current market price of the underlying share. The difference between the two represents the current price of the CFD. When the investor subsequently sells the CFD, the difference between the price at which they sell and the price at which they bought represents the gain or loss on the transaction.

There are no margin payments on a CFD. The amount invested represents a payment of the initial margin and regardless of how markets subsequently move, there are no further margin calls.

All listed CFDs have an in-built stop loss to provide protection against adverse market movements. The amount invested is limited to the initial payment and there are no further margin calls. The effect of this is that the investor can never lose more than the initial investment. In addition to this, each listed CFD has a further stop loss which is generally about 3% away from the entry level price. If the price drops below this level, then the position is automatically closed out and the remaining value paid out to the investor.

GLOSSARY

· ·

A glossary is provided below that provides an explanation of many of the terms used in this book along with a number of others that may be needed for reference purposes.

Accumulation trusts Where the trustees have discretion but only for a certain period, after which a beneficiary will become entitled to either the income or capital at a certain date in the future.

Across principal closing The settlement of two transactions in the same security entered into by the same agent with a selling principal and a buying principal.

Active risk The risk that arises from holding securities in an actively managed portfolio in different proportions to their weighting in a benchmark index. Also known as **tracking error**.

Administrator A person appointed by the courts to administer the estate of a deceased person.

Agency cross A transaction by which a member firm acting as an agent matches the buy and sell orders of two or more non-members at the same price and on the same terms.

AIM security A security which the exchange has admitted to trading on AIM and is traded on SETSmm, SEAQ or SEATS Plus.

American form A form of transfer endorsed on a stock certificate, execution of which enables the holder to pass title to another.

Annual equivalent rate (AER) *See* Effective rate.

Annual general meeting (AGM) The annual meeting of directors and ordinary shareholders of a company. All companies are obliged to hold an AGM at which the shareholders receive the company's report and accounts and have the opportunity to vote on the appointment of the company's directors and auditors and the payment of a final dividend recommended by the directors.

Annuity   An investment that provides a series of prespecified periodic payments over a specific term or until the occurrence of a prespecified event, e.g. death.

Approved persons   Employees in controlled functions must be approved by the FSA.

Articles of association   The legal document which sets out the internal constitution of a company. Included within the articles will be details of shareholder voting rights and company borrowing powers.

Asset allocation   The process of investing an international portfolio's assets geographically and between asset classes before deciding upon sector and stock selection.

At best order   An unpriced order with a specified size which may execute, either in part or in full, against eligible orders with any unexecuted portion being rejected.

Authorisation   Required status under FSMA 2000 for firms that want to provide financial services.

Authorised corporate director (ACD)   Fund manager for an OEIC.

Authorised unit trust (AUT)   Unit trust which is freely marketable. Authorised by the FSA.

Automated input facility   Any electronic trading system which fully automates the decision to submit orders to an order book and submits at least 20 simultaneous orders.

Balance of payments   A summary of all the transactions between a country and the rest of the world. The difference between a country's imports and exports.

Bank of England   The UK's central bank. Implements economic policy decided by the Treasury and determines interest rates.

Bare trust   Also called absolute trusts, where a trustee holds assets for another person absolutely.

Basket   A contract or other instrument for the purchase or sale of a predefined group of international equity market securities, where the component securities are individually delivered upon settlement in proportion to their weighting.

Bearer securities Those whose ownership is evidenced by the mere possession of a certificate. Ownership can, therefore, pass from hand to hand without any formalities.

Beneficiaries The beneficial owners of trust property.

Bid price Price at which dealers buy stock.

Block trade A transaction for which the block trade facility is used, which is at least a certain number of times the normal market size.

Bond *See* Fixed interest security.

Bonds Interest-bearing securities which entitle holders to annual interest and repayment at maturity. Commonly issued by both companies and governments.

Bonus issue The free issue of new ordinary shares to a company's ordinary shareholders in proportion to their existing shareholdings through the conversion, or capitalisation, of the company's reserves. By proportionately reducing the market value of each existing share, a bonus issue makes the shares more marketable. Also known as a **capitalisation issue** or **scrip issue**.

Broker dealer A London Stock Exchange (LSE) member firm that can act in a dual capacity both as a broker acting on behalf of clients and as a dealer dealing in securities on its own account.

Bull market A rising securities market. The duration of the market move is immaterial.

Buying-in notice A notice issued by the exchange at the instigation of the buyer to a seller who has failed to deliver a security in settlement of an on-exchange transaction.

Call option An option that confers a right on the holder to buy a specified amount of an asset at a prespecified price on or sometimes before a prespecified date.

Capital gains tax (CGT) Tax payable by individuals on profit made on the disposal of certain assets.

Central bank Those public institutions that operate at the heart of a nation's financial system. Central banks typically have responsibility for setting a nation's or a region's short-term interest rate, controlling the money supply, acting as banker and lender of last resort to the banking system and managing the national debt. They increasingly implement their policies independently of government control. The Bank of England is the UK's central bank.

Central bank money   Settlement is described as being central bank money if payment moves directly and irrevocably between accounts on the books of the central bank.

Central counterparty (CCP)   Legal entity that acts as an intermediary to the parties to a securities trade.

Central securities depository (CSD)   An institution that performs, as a mere agent, the whole range of post-trade functions.

Certificated   Ownership designated by certificate.

Certificates of deposit (CDs)   Certificates issued by a bank as evidence that interest-bearing funds have been deposited with it. CDs are traded within the money market.

Clearing member   A member of a clearing house. A direct clearing member is able to settle only its own obligations. A general clearing member is able to settle its own obligations as well of those of its customers.

Clearing/Clearance   The process of transmitting, reconciling, and in some cases, confirming payment orders or security transfer instructions prior to settlement, possibly including the netting of instructions and the establishment of final position for settlement.

Clearstream   The German central securities depository based in Luxembourg.

Closing out   The process of terminating an open position in a derivatives contract by entering into an equal and opposite transaction to that originally undertaken.

Collateral   Financial or tangible asset pledged by a borrower to secure an obligation. If the borrower defaults, the collateral is used to repay the obligation.

Commission   Charges for acting as agent or broker.

Confirmation   Agreement of the terms of a trade.

Controlled functions   Job roles which require the employee to be approved by the FSA.

Corporate actions   Actions by the issuer of a security that affect that security. Some examples are stock splits (existing shares are split into several new ones to increase liquidity), rights issues (the issuer raises new capital) dividends, as well as other events affecting the security such as takeovers.

Corporate governance   The mechanism that seeks to ensure that companies are run in the best long-term interests of their shareholders.

Court of Protection Responsible for assisting people who are unable to manage their own financial affairs.

Covered warrant A domestic market security that is a warrant issued by a party other than the issuer or originator of the underlying asset.

Covered warrant order book An order-driven trading service with committed principals for trading covered warrants.

Credit creation Expansion of loans which increases the money supply.

Credit risk The risk that the counterparty does not settle an obligation for the full value.

Crest Electronic settlement system used to settle transactions for UK shares.

Custodian An entity, often a bank, that performs custody services for its customers.

Custody Safekeeping and administration of securities and financial instruments on behalf of others.

Debenture A corporate bond issued in the domestic bond market and secured on the issuing company's assets by way of a fixed or a floating charge.

Delivery versus payment (DVP) A link between a securities-transfer system and a funds-transfer system that ensures delivery of securities occurs only with the delivery of cash.

Dematerialised (form) System where securities are held electronically without certificates.

Derivative An instrument whose value is based on the price of an underlying asset. Derivatives can be based on both financial and commodity assets.

Disabled trusts Trusts established for a disabled person will normally be a discretionary trust but they benefit from different treatment for inheritance tax and capital gains tax.

Discretionary trusts Where the trustees have discretion to whom the capital and income is paid to.

Diversification Investment strategy of spreading risk by investing in a range of investments.

Dividend The distribution of a proportion of a company's distributable profit to its shareholders. Dividends are usually paid twice a year and are expressed in pence per share.

Dividend yield   Most recent dividend as a percentage of current share price.

Dow Jones index   Major share index in the USA, based on the prices of 30 company shares.

Dual pricing   System in which a unit trust manager quotes two prices at which investors can sell and buy.

Economic and Monetary Union (EMU)   System adopted by most members of the European Union where their individual currencies were abolished and replaced by the euro.

Economic cycle   The course an economy conventionally takes as economic growth fluctuates over time. Also known as the **business cycle**.

Economic growth   The growth of GDP or GNP expressed in real terms usually over the course of a calendar year. Often used as a barometer of an economy's health.

Effective rate   The annualised compound rate of interest applied to a cash deposit. Also known as the **annual equivalent rate** (AER).

Enduring power of attorney (EPA)   A legal document that gives a person (the attorney) the right to manage another person's financial affairs.

Equity   That which confers a direct stake in a company's fortunes. Also known as a company's ordinary share capital.

Eurobond   International bond issues denominated in a currency different from that of the financial centre(s) in which they are issued. Most eurobonds are issued in bearer form through bank syndicates.

Euroclear   A Brussels based international central securities depository. Euroclear also acts as the central securities depository for Belgium, Dutch, French, Irish and UK securities.

Euronext   European stock exchange network formed by the merger of the Paris, Brussels and Amsterdam exchanges.

euronext.Liffe   UK derivatives exchange for financial products. Owned by Euronext.

European Monetary Union (EMU)   The creation of a single European currency, the euro, and the European Central Bank (ECB), which sets monetary policy across the eurozone. Currently, 12 of the EU's 15 members participate in EMU.

Exchange   Market place for trading investments.

Exchange rate   Rate at which one currency can be exchanged for another.

Ex-dividend (XD) The period during which the purchase of shares or bonds (on which a dividend or coupon payment has been declared) does not entitle the new holder to this next dividend or interest payment.

Execute and eliminate order An order with a specified size and limit price which may execute, either in part or in full, against eligible orders with any unexecuted portion being rejected.

Executor An individual named in a will who is given the authority to administer a deceased's estate.

Exercise an option Take up the right to buy or sell the underlying asset in an option.

Ex-rights (XR) The period during which the purchase of a company's shares does not entitle the new shareholder to participate in a rights issue announced by the issuing company. Shares are usually traded ex-rights on or within a few days of the company making the rights issue announcement.

Fill or kill order An order with a specified size and, optionally, a specified limit price which either executes in full against eligible orders at the price of those orders or is rejected in full.

Financial Reporting Action Group (FRAG) A committee that has set standards on a wide range of accounting issues for the Institute of Chartered Accountants.

Financial Services Authority (FSA) The UK regulator for financial services created by FSMA 2000.

First General Order A document issued by the Court of Protection, setting out the role and powers that have been granted to a receiver.

Fiscal policy The use of government spending, taxation and borrowing policies to either boost or restrain domestic demand in the economy so as to maintain full employment and price stability. Also known as **stabilisation policy**.

Fit and proper FSMA 2000 requires that every firm conducting financial services business must be 'fit and proper'.

Fixed interest market maker A member firm which is registered as such with the stock exchange and which is obliged to quote on an enquiry to trade fixed-interest securities in a marketable quantity.

Fixed interest security A tradeable negotiable instrument, issued by a borrower for a fixed term, during which a regular and predetermined fixed rate of interest based upon a nominal value is paid to the holder until it is redeemed and the principal is repaid.

Fixed rate borrowing Borrowing where a set interest rate is paid.

Flat rate The annual simple rate of interest applied to a cash deposit.

Forex Abbreviation for foreign exchange trading.

Forward A derivative contract between two parties to buy or sell a prespecified amount of an asset at an agreed price on an agreed future date.

FTSE 100 Main UK share index of 100 leading shares ('Footsie').

FTSE 250 UK share index based on the 250 shares immediately below the top 100.

FTSE 350 Index combining the FTSE 100 and FTSE 250 indices.

FTSE all share index Index comprising around 98% of UK listed shares by value.

Fund manager Firm that invests money on behalf of customers.

Future A derivatives contract that creates a legally binding obligation between two parties for one to buy and the other to sell a prespecified amount of an asset at a prespecified price on a prespecified future date. Futures contracts differ from forward contracts in that their contract specification is standardised so that they may be traded on a derivatives exchange.

Future value The accumulated value of a sum of money invested today at a known rate of interest over a specific term.

Gilt inter dealer broker A stock exchange member firm who intermediates as a riskless principal between gilt-edged market makers only, who subscribe to its service.

Gilt strip A tradeable security constituting an individual coupon or principal cash flow of a gilt-edged security and appearing on a list maintained by the UK Debt Management Office.

Gilt-edged and fixed interest market The market provided by the stock exchange for transactions in gilt-edged securities and fixed interest securities.

Gilt-edged market maker A stock exchange member firm which has been accepted as a gilt-edged market maker by the UK Debt Management Office.

Gilt-edged security UK government bond.

Gilts UK government securities issued primarily to finance government borrowing. *See also* Public sector net cash requirement (PSNCR).

Global custodian A custodian that provides a customer with custody services in respect of securities traded not only in the country where the custodian is situated but also in a number of other countries throughout the word.

Grant of probate A court document that confirms the appointment of an executor or administrator who has the authority to deal with a deceased's estate.

Gross redemption yield (GRY) The annual compound return from holding a bond to maturity taking into account both interest payments and any capital gain or loss at maturity. Also known as the **yield to maturity** (YTM).

Hedging Refers to the technique used to reduce the impact of adverse price movements.

Hit order An order to execute automatically against a firm exposure order.

Hybrid trading service A trading service with features of both an order-driven trading service and a quote-driven trading service.

Iceberg order An order with a specified price and size with only the peak of the order displayed.

ICSD An organisation that settles trades in international securities, such as Euroclear and Clearstream.

Immobilisation Placement of physical certificates for securities and financial instruments in a central vault to facilitate book entry transfers.

Independent financial adviser (IFA) A financial adviser who is not tied to the products of any one product provider and is duty bound to give clients best advice. IFAs must establish the financial planning needs of their clients through a personal fact find and satisfy these needs with the most appropriate products offered in the market place.

Index An index whose components are securities traded on an exchange market.

Index linked gilts Gilts whose principal and interest payments are linked to the retail price index (RPI) with an eight-month time lag.

Inflation The rate of change in the general price level or the erosion in the purchasing power of money.

Inflation risk premium The additional return demanded by bond investors based on the volatility of inflation in the recent past.

Inheritance tax (IHT)   Tax on the value of an estate when a person dies.

Initial public offering (IPO)   *See* New issue.

Insider dealing   Criminal offence by people with unpublished price-sensitive information who deal, advise others to deal or pass the information on.

Integration   Third stage of money laundering.

Interest in possession trust   Where the beneficiary has a right to the income of the trust during their life and the capital passes onto others on their death.

International bulletin board   An order-driven trading service for international equity market securities.

International equity market   The market provided by the stock exchange for transactions in international equity market securities.

International order book   An order-driven trading service for trading international equity market securities.

International retail service   A quote-driven trading service for trading international equity market securities.

Investment bank   Business that specialises in raising debt and equity for companies.

Investment trust (company)   A company, not a trust, which invests in diversified range of investments.

Irredeemable gilt   A gilt with no redemption date. Investors receive interest in perpetuity.

Irredeemable security   A security issued without a prespecified redemption, or maturity, date.

Individual savings account (ISA)   An investment account carrying tax advantages.

ISIN   The international security identification number.

Issuing house   An institution that facilitates the issue of securities.

Joint Money Laundering Steering Group (JMLSG)   A committee which issues guidance on how firms should implement anti-money laundering procedures.

Layering   Second stage in money laundering.

Life tenant   Individual who receives income from a trust for their life or other period.

Liffe Connecttm   Order-driven trading system on LIFFE.

Limit order   An order with a specified size and price which is either held on the exchange trading system or executes, either in part or in full, against eligible orders with any remaining unexecuted portion being added to the relevant order book.

Liquidity The ease with which a security can be converted into cash. Liquidity is determined by the amount of two-way trade conducted in a security. Liquidity also describes that amount of an investor's financial resources held in cash.

Liquidity risk The risk that shares may be difficult to sell at a reasonable price.

Listing Companies whose securities are listed on the London Stock Exchange and available to be traded.

Loan stock A corporate bond issued in the domestic bond market without any underlying collateral, or security.

Local agent A custodian that provides custodial services for securities that are traded and settled in the country which it is located to counterparties and settlement intermediaries located in other countries.

London Clearing House (LCH) The institution that clears and acts as central counterparty to all trades executed on member exchanges.

London interbank offered rate (LIBOR) A benchmark money market interest rate.

London International Financial Futures & Options Exchange (euronext.Liffe) The UK's principal derivatives exchange for trading financial and soft commodity derivatives products. Since it was purchased by Euronext, LIFFE is commonly referred to as euronext.liffe.

London Metal Exchange (LME) Market for trading in derivatives of certain metals, such as copper, zinc and aluminium.

London Stock Exchange (LSE) The UK market for listing and trading domestic and international securities.

Market All exchanges are markets – electronic or physical meeting place where assets are bought or sold.

Market capitalisation The total market value of a company's shares or other securities in issue. Market capitalisation is calculated by multiplying the number of shares or other securities a company has in issue by the market price of those shares or securities.

Market maker An LSE member firm which quotes prices and trade stocks during the mandatory quote period. Relevant for medium-sized companies trading on SEAQ or SETSmm.

Market order An unpriced order with a specified size which may execute against eligible orders, either in part or in full.

Maturity Date when the capital on a bond is repaid.

Memorandum of association The legal document that principally defines a company's powers, or objects, and its relationship with the outside world. The memorandum also details the number and nominal value of shares the company is authorised to issue and has issued.

MiFID Markets in Financial Instruments Directive that is intended to bring about a single conduct of business rulebook across Europe.

NASDAQ The second-largest stock exchange in the US. NASDAQ lists certain US and international stocks and provides a screen-based quote driven secondary market that links buyers and sellers worldwide. NASDAQ also operates a stock exchange in Europe (NASDAQ Europe).

NASDAQ composite NASDAQ stock index.

National debt A government's total outstanding borrowing resulting from financing successive budget deficits, mainly through the issue of government-backed securities.

Negotiable security A security whose ownership can pass freely from one party to another. Negotiable securities are, therefore, tradeable.

Netting An agreed offset of positions or obligations by trading partners or participants. If two parties agree to net this is called bilateral netting. If three or more parties positions are netted this is called multilateral netting.

New issue A new issue of ordinary shares whether made by an offer for sale, an offer for subscription or a placing. Also known as an initial public offering (IPO).

Nikkei 225 Main Japanese share index.

Nominal value The face or par value of a security. The nominal value is the price at which a bond is issued and usually redeemed and the price below which a company's ordinary shares cannot be issued.

Normal market size The minimum quantity of securities for which a market maker in quote-driven securities, other than a reduced size market maker, is obliged to quote a firm a two-way price on the exchange trading system.

Offer price Price at which dealers sell stock.

Office of Fair Trading (OFT) Government agency that refers proposed takeovers to the Competition Commission.

Officially listed Admitted to the official list of the UK Listing Authority and admitted to trading by the exchange under the exchange's Admission and Disclosure Standards.

Open Initiate a transaction, e.g., an opening purchase or sale of a future. Normally reversed by a closing transaction.

Open economy Country with no restrictions on trading with other countries.

Open ended Type of investment such as OEICs or unit trusts which can expand without limit.

Open ended investment company (OEIC) Collective investment vehicle similar to unit trusts. Alternatively described as an ICVC (investment company with variable capital).

Opening Undertaking a transaction which creates a long or short position.

Operational risk The risk that deficiencies in information systems or internal controls, human error, or management failure will result in unexpected losses.

Options A type of derivative that gives the right to either buy or sell an asset at a predetermined price at a predetermined future date in exchange for payment of a premium.

Ordinary shares *See* Equity.

Over-the-counter (OTC) derivatives Derivatives that are not traded on an exchange

Par value See Nominal Value.

Participant code An identification code notified to the stock exchange and used by a member firm when submitting transaction reports.

PEPs & ISAs Managers Association (PIMA) A trade association that represents the interests of PEP and ISA managers.

Perpetuities An investment that provides an indefinite stream of equal prespecified periodic payments.

Personal allowance Amount of income that each person can earn each year tax free.

Personal equity plan (PEP) A tax-exempt investment account that has now been replaced by the ISA.

Placement First stage of money laundering.

Pre-emption rights The rights accorded to ordinary shareholders under company law to subscribe for new ordinary shares issued by the company, in which they have the shareholding, for cash before the shares are offered to outside investors.

Preference shares Those shares issued by a company that rank ahead of ordinary shares for the payment of dividends and for capital repayment in the event of the company going into liquidation.

Primary market The function of a stock exchange in bringing securities to the market and raising funds.

Provisional allotment letter That which is sent to those shareholders who are entitled to participate in a rights issue. The letter details the shareholders' existing shareholding, their rights over the new shares allotted and the date(s) by which they must act.

Proxy Appointee who votes on a shareholder's behalf at company meetings.

PTM levy The levy set by and payable to the Panel on Takeovers and Mergers (PTM).

Quote-driven trading service A trading service subject to the quote-driven trading service rules.

Recognised BIC A bank identification code (BIC) which identifies a member firm within the exchange trading system.

Redeemable security A security issued with a known maturity, or redemption, date.

Redemption The repayment of principal to the holder of a redeemable security.

Registrar An official of a company who maintains the share register.

Remaindermen Beneficiaries in a trust who will receive the capital once the rights of the life tenant to receive income has finished.

Retail price index (RPI) An expenditure weighted measure of UK inflation based on a representative basket of goods and services purchased by an average UK household.

Rights issue The issue of new ordinary shares to a company's shareholders in proportion to each shareholder's existing shareholding, usually at a price deeply discounted to that prevailing in the market. *See also* Pre-emption rights.

RNS The company news service of the London Stock Exchange.

Running yield The return from a bond calculated by expressing the coupon as a percentage of the clean price. Also known as the **flat yield** or **interest yield**.

Safekeeping Storage of physically evidenced securities in a vault.

Scrip issue *See* Bonus issue.

SEAQ The Stock Exchange Automated Quotation system, a quote-driven trading service.

SEATS Plus The Stock Exchange Alternative Trading Service, a hybrid trading SEATS security as a security which is traded on SEATS Plus.

Secondary market Market place for trading in existing securities.

Securities Bonds and equities.

SETS The Stock Exchange Electronic Trading Service, an order-driven trading service.

SETS participant A partnership, corporation, legal entity or sole practitioner approved by the exchange whose only on on-exchange activity is to trade on SETS.

SETSmm An order-driven trading service.

Settlement The payment of cash for securities or the delivery of securities against cash.

Settlement agent A person providing settlement services and who may also submit transaction reports.

Settlor The creator of a trust.

Shape The split for delivery purposes of part or all of a transaction.

Share buyback The redemption and cancellation by a company of a proportion of its irredeemable ordinary shares subject to the permission of the High Court and agreement from the Inland Revenue.

Share capital The nominal value of a company's equity or ordinary shares. A company's authorised share capital is the nominal value of equity the company may issue whilst issued share capital is that which the company has issued. The term share capital is often extended to include a company's preference shares.

Share split A method by which a company can reduce the market price of its shares to make them more marketable without capitalising its reserves. A share split simply entails the company reducing the nominal value of each of its shares in issue whilst maintaining the overall nominal value of its share capital. A share split should have the same impact on a company's share price as a bonus issue.

Self-invested personal pension (SIPP) A personal pension plan where the investments can be managed by the individual.

Special resolution Proposal put to shareholders requiring 75% of the votes cast.

Spot rate A compound annual fixed rate of interest that applies to an investment over a specific time period. *See also* Forward rate.

Spread Difference between a buying (bid) and selling (ask or offer) price.

Stamp duty Tax on purchase of certain assets.

Stamp Duty Reserve Tax (SDRT) Stamp duty levied on purchase of dematerialised equities.

Standard settlement The normal settlement arrangement applicable to a security as specified by the exchange.

Stock exchange An organised market place for issuing and trading securities by members of that exchange.

Stock Exchange Alternative Trading Service (SEATS Plus) The London Stock Exchange's electronic order driven bulletin board for trading less liquid securities, notably those fully listed or AIM shares with less than two registered market makers.

Straight-through processing The fully automated completion of the clearing and settlement processes based on trade data that is only entered once, manually into the system.

Structured products Packaged products based on derivatives.

Sub-custodian A custodian who provides custodial services for another custodian.

Subordinated loan stock Loan stock issued by a company that ranks above its preference shares but below its unsecured creditors in the event of the company's liquidation.

Swaps A derivatives contract where two counterparties exchange one stream of cash flow for another.

Swift Society for Worldwide Interbank Financial Telecommunications: a cooperative organisation created and owned by banks that operates a networking facility that allows the exchange of payments and other financial messages between financial institutions throughout the world.

T+3 The three-day rolling settlement period over which all deals executed on the London Stock Exchange's SETS are settled.

Takeover When one company buys more than 50% of the shares of another.

TARGET Trans European Automated Real Time Gross Settlement Express Transfer: a payment system composed of one RTGS system in each of the EMU member states. The domestic RTGS systems and European Central Bank payments mechanism are interconnected according to common procedures to allow cross-border transfers.

Trade matching The issue and capture of details of a trade and the matching of these to the original instructions.

Traditional option A right, but not obligation, to buy or sell a given quantity of shares for an agreed price and in accordance with the calendar published by the exchange.

Transaction report A confirmation report of the details of a transaction effected on-exchange, consisting of one market-side report and as many client-side reports as are required.

TRAX A reporting system operated by the International Securities Market Association uncertificated securities held in, or capable of being held in (as the context admits), uncertificated form pursuant to the Uncertificated Securities Regulations 2001 or in the case of Irish securities, the Companies Act 1990 (Uncertificated Securities) Regulations 1996.

Treasury bills Short-term government-backed securities issued at a discount to par via a weekly Bank of England auction. Treasury bills do not pay coupons but are redeemed at par.

Trust protector A person appointed to protect the interest of the beneficiaries in a trust.

Trustees The legal owners of trust property who owe a duty of skill and care to the trust's beneficiaries.

Trusts A legal means whereby one person gives property to another party to look after on behalf of yet another individual or set of individuals.

Trusts for the vulnerable Trusts set up for individuals who have a disability or minor children following the death of a parent.

Undertakings for Collective Investments in Transferable Securities (UCITS) Directive An EU directive originally introduced in 1985 but since revised to enable collective investment schemes (CISs) authorised in one EU member state to be freely marketed throughout the EU, subject to the marketing rules of the host state(s) and certain fund structure rules being complied with.

Unit trust   A system whereby money from investors is pooled together and invested collectively on their behalf into an open-ended trust.

Warrant   An instrument which gives the holder the right to acquire or dispose of securities at a stipulated price.

Worked principal agreement   An agreement to effect, at some future time, as principal, a transaction in certain types of stock within agreed price and size parameters.

Writer   Party selling an option. The writers receive premiums in exchange for taking the risk of being exercised against.

XETRA DAX   German shares index, comprising 30 shares.

Yellow strip   Section on each SEAQ display, showing the most favourable prices.

Yield   Income from an investment as a percentage of the current price.

BIBLIOGRAPHY

Bank for International Settlements, *Outsourcing in Financial Services*, February 2005.

Charity Commission, *Investment of Charitable Funds, Detailed Guidance*, February 2003.

Charity Commission, *CC42 Appointing Nominees and Custodians: Guidance under s.19(4) of the Trustee Act 2000*, February 2001.

Crest, *Input of Investor Details in Crest*, July 1996.

Depositary Trust and Clearing Corporation and OXERA, *Corporate Action Processing: What are the Risks? A Joint Study*, May 2004.

European Central Securities Depositaries Associations, *Cross Border Corporate Action and Events Processing*, November 2002.

European Central Securities Depositaries Associations, *Cross Border Settlement*, February 2002.

Financial Services Authority, *Conduct of Business Sourcebook*.

Financial Services Authority, *Client Assets Sourcebook*.

Financial Services Authority, *New Collective Investment Sourcebook*.

Financial Services Authority, *Senior Management Arrangements, Systems and Controls*, Chapter 3A, Operational Risk: Systems and Controls, 3A.9 Outsourcing.

Group of Thirty, *Global Clearing and Settlement Plan of Action*, January 2003.

HM Revenue and Customs, *PEPs and ISAs, Guidance Notes for PEP and ISA Managers*, April 2006.

HM Revenue and Customs, *Personal Pension Schemes Guidance Notes*, IR76, 2000.

HM Revenue and Customs, *Residents and Non-resident, Liability to Tax in the United Kingdom*, International SeriesIR20, October 1999.

International Organisation of Securities Commissions (IOSCO), *Principles on Outsourcing of Financial Services for Market Intermediaries*, February 2005.

Joint Money Laundering Steering Group (JMLSG), *Prevention of Money Laundering/Combating the Financing of Terrorism, Part 1 – Guidance for the Financial Sector and Part 2 – Sectoral Guidance*, March 2005.

Markets in Financial Instruments Directive (MiFID) 2004/39/EC.

READING MATERIAL

....

WEALTH MANAGEMENT

International Financial Services London, *Fund Management*, August 2006.
International Financial Services London, *International Private Wealth Management*, December 2006.
Price Waterhouse Coopers, *Global Private Banking/ Wealth Management Survey*, 2005.

NEW AND CLOSING BUSINESS

Bank for International Settlements, *Customer Due Diligence for Banks*, October 2001.
Bank for International Settlements, *Consolidate KYC Risk Management*, October 2004.
Law Society, *Your Guide to Probate*, 2005.

TRADING

City of London, *European Government Bond Markets: Transparency, Liquidity, Efficiency*, May 2006.

City of London, *European Corporate Bond Markets: Transparency, Liquidity, Efficiency*, May 2006.

Debt Management Office, *UK Government Securities: A Guide to Gilts*, June 2006.

Debt Management Office, *A Private Investor's Guide to Gilts*, December 2004.

Debt Management Office, *Gilts: An Investor's Guide*, October 2003.

Euronext, *Economics of Cash Trading: An Overview*, May 2005.

European Commission, *Securities Trading, Clearing, Central Counterparties and Settlement in EU 25, An Overview of Current Arrangements*, June 2005.

International Financial Services London, *Securities Dealing*, July 2005.

London Stock Exchange, *Overview of Markets and Data*, 2005.

London Stock Exchange, *Rules of the London Stock Exchange*, December 2005.

World Federation of Exchanges, *Annual Report and Statistics*, 2005.

SETTLEMENT

Bank for International Settlements, *Cross Border Securities Settlement*, March 1995.

Crest, *Crest Reference Manual*, December 2005.

Crest, *Crest Rules*, January 2005.

Crest, *Communicating with Crest*, February 2005.

Crest, *Joining Crest*, November 2005.

Crest, *Market Practice for Residual Deliveries*, February 1997.

Deutsche Börse, *European Post-Trade Market: An Introduction*, December 2006.

European Central Bank, *Target 2 Securities, Economic Feasibility Study*, January 2007.

European Central Securities Depositaries Association, *Cross Border Clearing and Settlement through CSD Links*, October 2006.

CORPORATE ACTIONS

Crest, *Blue Book: Corporate Actions Standardisation*, November 2004.

Crest, *Blue Book: Dividends and Interest Distributions in Crest*, July 2004.

Crest, *Crest CCSS Operations Manual*, June 2003.

Crest, *Takeover Procedures in Crest*, July 2001.

Department of Trade and Industry, *Pre-Emption Rights*, February 2005.

European Central Securities Depositaries Association, *Response to Giovannini Report Barrier 3, Corporate Actions*, June 2005.

TAX

HM Revenue and Customs, *Capital Gains Tax: An Introduction*, CGT1, April 2007.

POWERS OF ATTORNEY

Court of Protection, *Pubic Guardianship Office Guide to Enduring Power of Attorney*, November 2003.
Court of Protection, *Public Guardianship Office Receivers Handbook*, January 2006.

COLLECTIVE INVESTMENTS

Euroclear, *Mutual Fund Processing in Europe*, December 2006.
FSA Guide to Collective Investment Schemes.
HM Revenue and Customs, *Authorised Unit Trusts and Open Ended Investment Companies, Guidance Notes Relating to Payment of Interest Distributions*, September 2003.

INDEX